AFRICAN TRADITIONAL ARCHITECTURE

AFRICAN TRADITIONAL ARCHITECTURE

An Historical and Geographical Perspective

SUSAN DENYER

Line Drawings by Susan Denyer
Maps by Peter McClure

AFRICANA PUBLISHING COMPANY
NEW YORK

A division of Holmes & Meier Publishers, Inc.

First published in the United States of America 1978
by Africana Publishing Company
a Division of Holmes & Meier Publishers, Inc.
101 Fifth Avenue
New York NY 10003

Library of Congress Cataloging in Publication Data

Denyer, Susan
  African Traditional Architecture

  Bibliography, P.
  includes Index.
1. Architecture, Primitive-Africa, Sub-Saharan.
2. Architecture, Anonymous-Africa, Sub-Saharan.
I. Title
GN 645.D444 1978   720'.967   77-16428
ISBN 0-8419-0287-9 (hard-cover)
ISBN 0-8419-0336-0 (paperback)

Printed in Great Britain

Contents

Acknowledgements

I would like to express my thanks to my publishers; to Dr David McMaster, Reader in the University of Edinburgh Centre of African Studies for kindly reading an earlier version of the text and providing many valuable comments; and to my husband for his invaluable help and encouragement throughout the project. Any shortcomings remain, however, my own responsibility.

The Library and photographic staff of the following institutions have been most helpful: Ahmadu Bello University, University of Sussex, School of Oriental and African Studies, University of London, University of Manchester, Kaduna Library, National Museum of Tanzania. Also I would like to thank the following people who helped in a variety of ways: David Buxton, Francis Uher, Robert Hobson, Alhaji Abdul Malik Mani. My debt to the often unnamed late nineteenth and early twentieth century photographers (and those who carried their equipment) will be obvious.

Finally, and perhaps most important of all, I must acknowledge the hospitality accorded to me in many countries of Africa by countless people, both friends and strangers alike, who showed me their homes, towns and villages. It is to them and their children that this book is dedicated.

The author and publishers would like to thank the following copyright holders who have kindly allowed illustrations to be reproduced.

Abuja, Emir of, **299, 330**
Aerofilms Ltd., **138, 215**
American Geographical Society, **225**
Bierman, Professor, B., **173, 175, 177**
British Institute in Eastern Africa, **313, 314, 321**
British Museum, **128**
Buxton, David, **31, 32, 104, 212, 325–9**
Cameroon, Ministry of Information, **29, 75–6, 80, 84**
Collins and Harvill Press (in Adamson, J., *The Peoples of Kenya*, London, 1967), **253**
Cornell University Press (in Rigby, P., *Cattle and Kinship among the Gogo*, London, 1969), **98**
Documentation Française, **24, 150, 213, 262, 264, 267–9, 304** and (in Beguin, J. et al, *L'habitat au Cameroun*, Paris, 1952), **26, 74, 77–8, 210–1**
East African Publishing House (in Richards, A., *The Changing Structure of a Ganda Village*, Nairobi, 1966), **198**
Fagg, Bernard, **293**
Garlake, P. S., **45**
Gebremedhin, N., **162–4**

NOTES

The numbers in bold type set against the text throughout refer to the relevant illustrations.

The dates given in the captions in the Illustration Sections which follow show when the photographs were taken or the original drawings were made and not when the buildings were erected.

Maps

Key to Maps nos. 1 and 2

1	Acholi	54	Haya	107	Matakam	160	Songhai
2	Alawa	55	Hehe	108	Masai	161	Sonjo
3	Ambo	56	Heiban	109	Massa	162	Sotho
4	Amhara	57	Herero	110	Maure	163	Ssola
5	Angas	58	Hidkala	111	Mbala	164	Suku
6	Ankole	59	Holo	112	Mbugwe	165	Sukuma
7	Asante	60	Hottentots	113	Mende	166	Susu
8	Bamileke	61	Hutu	114	Mesakin	167	Swahili
9	Bamoun	62	Ibibio	115	Moro	168	Swazi
10	Bangadji	63	Ibo	116	Moroa	169	Tallensi
11	Bangi	64	Igala	117	Mousgoum	170	Tambernu
12	Bari	65	Ijo	118	Mumoye	171	Tangale/Waja
13	Bariba	66	Ikulu	119	Nabdam	172	Taturu
14	Baya-Kaka	67	Ila	120	Nalya	173	Taung
15	Bemba	68	Iraqw	121	Nandi	174	Teda
16	Bena	69	Jaba	122	Nankanse	175	Temne
17	Bira	70	Jukun	123	Ngala	176	Teso
18	Birom	71	Kamba	124	Ngelima	177	Thembu
19	Bobo	72	Kanuri	125	Ngongo	178	Tigre
20	Bondei	73	Kaonde	126	Ngoni	179	Tikar
21	Bunda	74	Katab	127	Ningi	180	Tindiga
22	Burungi	75	Khassonke	128	Nounouma	181	Tira
23	Bushmen	76	Kikuyu	129	Nuer	182	Tiv
24	Bussa	77	Kinga	130	Nupe	183	Toma
25	Calabari	78	Kipsigis	131	Nyakusa	184	Tonga
26	Chagga	79	Kisi	132	Nyamwezi	185	Toupouri
27	Chamba	80	Koalib	133	Nyasa	186	Tswana
28	Chewa	81	Kofyar	134	Nyika	187	Tuareg
29	Cuabo	82	Kongo	135	Nyoro	188	Tubu
30	Dagomba	83	Konjo	136	Panga	189	Tullishi
31	Dinka	84	Konkomba	137	Papeis	190	Tusi
32	Diola	85	Korongo	138	Pare	191	Tutsi
33	Dogon	86	Kru	139	Pende	192	Twa
34	Dorze	87	Kuba	140	Pondo	193	Venda
35	Dourou	88	Lango	141	Poto	194	Vinza
36	Edo	89	Lafofo	142	Pygmies	195	Wagenia
37	Ekoi	90	Laro	143	Rangi	196	Wanda
38	Fipa	91	Lele	144	Roka	197	Wanji
39	Fulani	92	Limba	145	Ron	198	Wela
40	Fur	93	Lobi	146	Sabei	199	Xhosa
41	Gagu	94	Loko	147	Safwa	200	Yako
42	Galla	95	Lomotwa	148	Saho	201	Yalunka
43	Gamergu	96	Lozi	149	Sambaa	202	Yaonde
44	Ganda	97	Luba	150	Samo	203	Yoruba
45	Ghoya	98	Luguru	151	Sangi	204	Zande
46	Gogo	99	Lunda	152	Sango	205	Zulu
47	Gorowa	100	Luo	153	Shilluk		
48	Grebo	101	Lutoko	154	Shona		
49	Gurage	102	Luyia	155	Shuwa Arabs		
50	Guro	103	Mamprussi	156	Sidamo		
51	Gwari	104	Mandinka	157	Soga		
52	Gweno	105	Mangbettu	158	Somali		
53	Hausa	106	Manjak	159	Somolo		

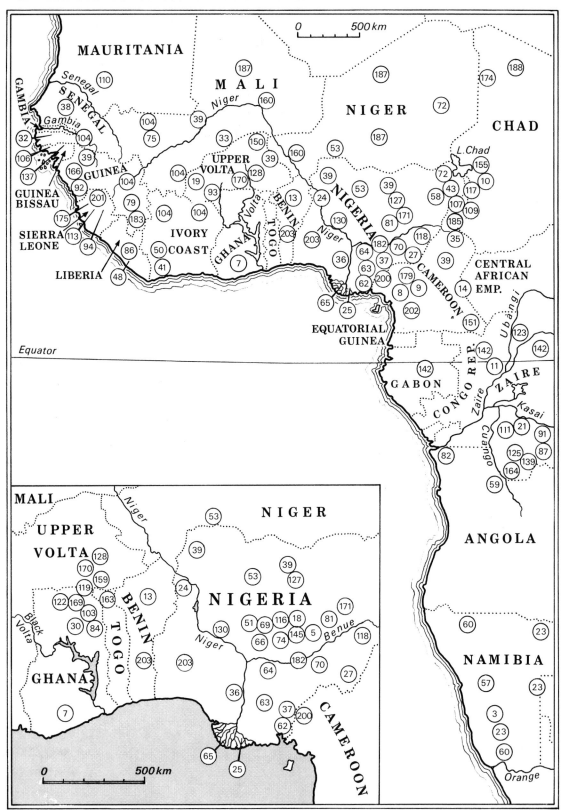

Map 1 Location of Peoples

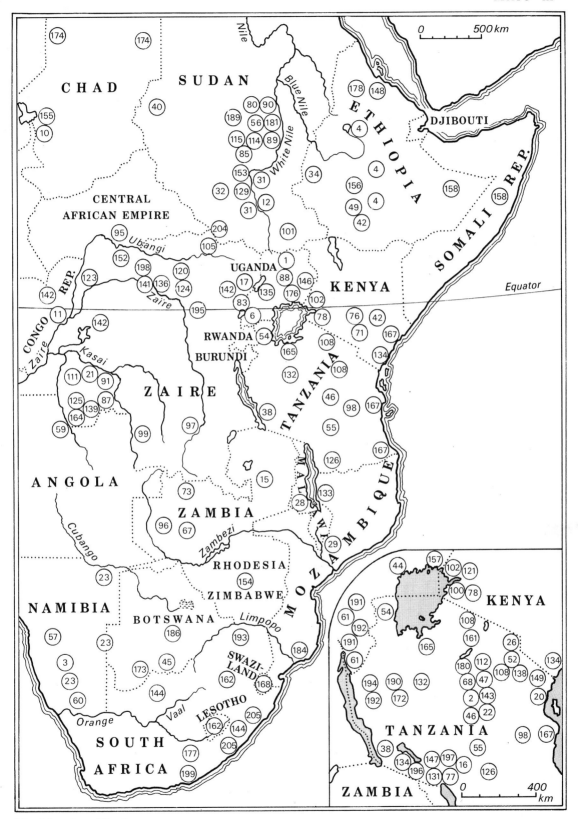

Map 2 Location of Peoples

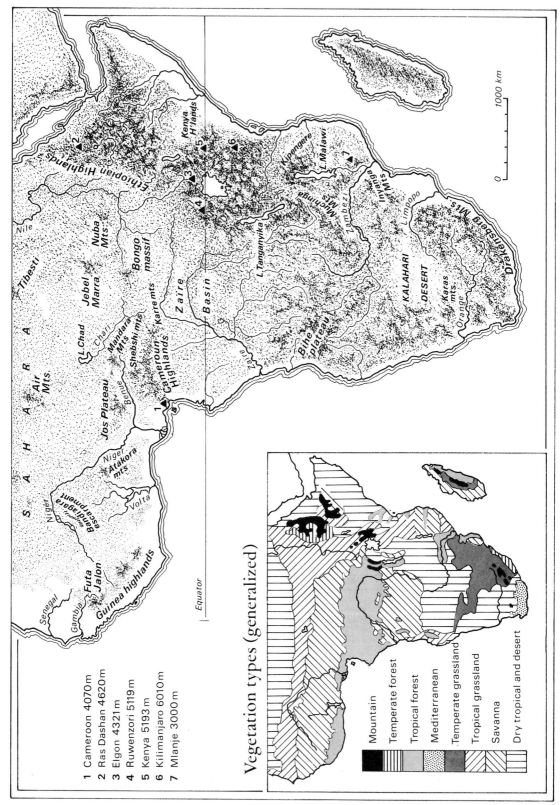

Map 3 Comparative Relief and Natural Vegetation

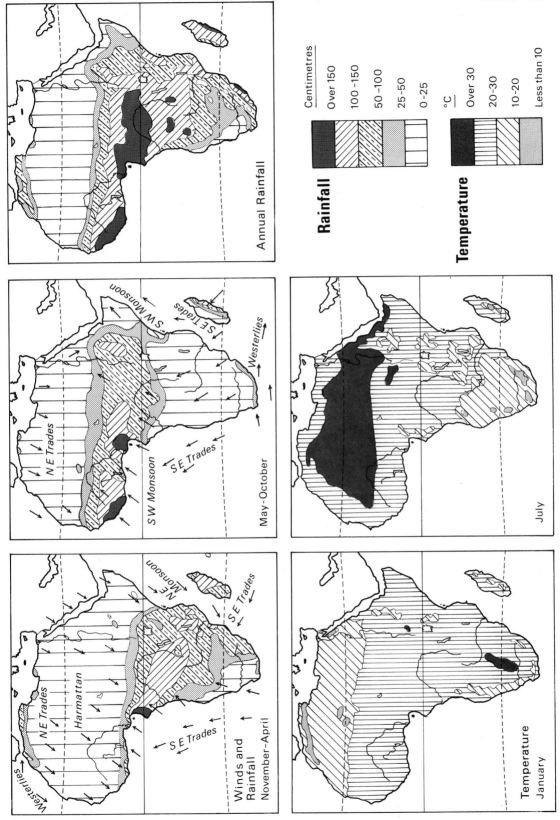

Map 4 Rainfall and Temperature

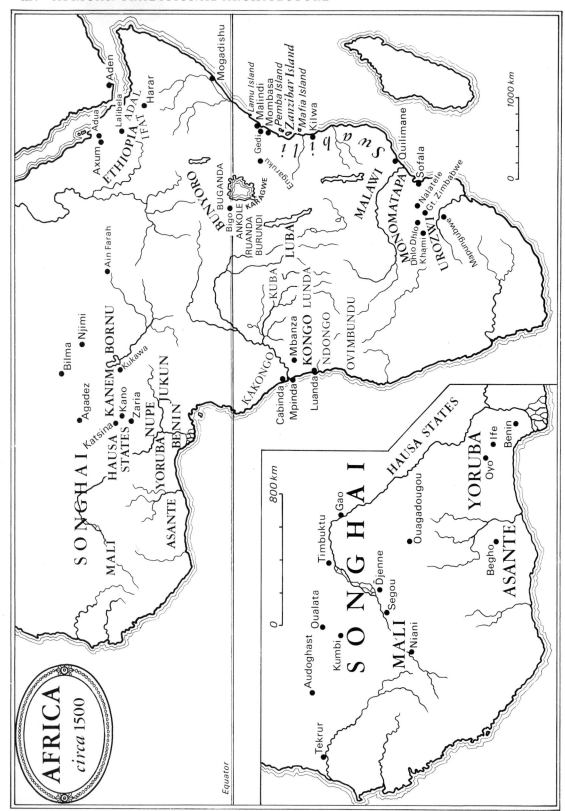

Map 5 States and Towns about AD 1500

1 Introduction

The myth of darkest Africa is persistent and there are still many people who find it difficult to accept that the traditional buildings of the continent merit more than passing consideration. One only has to consider for a moment the vocabulary used to refer to them (including such basic words as 'mud' and 'hut', which in English have such derogatory overtones) to realize that even for those who know and respect other aspects of African culture it is hard to avoid being drawn into a web of selective and distorted perception. The modern shanty buildings which so often line the roads to airports and urban centres merely serve to confirm ideas about temporary makeshift 'shelters'; and even people who venture out into the countryside find rough buildings along motor roads and railways which themselves tend to attract the more rootless sections of populations. Apparently traditional villages close to roads are often of fairly recent origin, and the larger ones also attract to their centres immigrant traders whose requirements and obligations are quite different from those of the indigenous communities. Sensational modern accounts of 'underdevelopment' can also paradoxically serve to reinforce earlier stereotypes of darkest Africa and its 'primitive' material culture.

Some early foreign visitors to the continent saw things in quite a different light and their accounts are of very considerable historical interest. To Joseph Thomson travelling in the savannah lands of East Africa in the last century 'it seemed a perfect Arcadia', not just the fertile and pleasant countryside but the whole landscape of well planned neat farms interspersed with immense shady trees and the 'charmingly neat circular huts with conical roofs and walls hanging out all round with the clay worked prettily into rounded bricks and daubed symmetrically with spots'.[1] This picture of prosperity and planned neatness was not at all confined to this one area. In the west, the elegant walled towns of Hausaland were the foci of park-like farmland, shaded with mature cotton trees. The countryside was landscaped and planned around the towns and gave an air of studied permanence, commending itself to many visitors. Of the Transvaal in 1829 Moffat[2] wrote: 'the walls [were] ... so well polished that they had the appearance of being varnished. The walls and doorways were neatly ornamented with architraves and cornices; the pillars supporting the roof in the form of pillasters projecting from the walls and fluted showing much taste.'

One must not of course allow oneself to be carried away by sentimentalism—which may with justification be criticized almost as much as ill-founded disparagement—and it is only fair to add to these accounts that in Africa, as elsewhere, there were wars, enslavements and food shortages which brought about suffering and hardship. They did not, however, by any means stifle feelings of dignity, order and destiny or serve to breed feelings of permanent insecurity. On the contrary there was probably more feeling of permanence in many African societies than in, say, medieval Europe. Such feelings were strengthened through religion and social order, through such ideas as that people were ancestors in the making and that the aged had authority, in order to counter the hazards impinging on society. Death was for people no gateway to escape into a better world from the rigours of this one; this world was for living in and it was up to every family and community to make the best of it.

It would be quite wrong, therefore, to see the temporary nature of many of the buildings as epitomizing an unstable, unsure society. Houses were built using local materials. Permanent houses would have been an embarrassment for many people, for instance the hunters and gatherers such as pygmies and bushmen, the migrant pastoralists such as the Fulani and the Masai, or the peoples who practised land rotation agriculture and moved on every four or five years. Amongst the Hausa divorce was frequent and the adoption of children common, and so families changed often in size and composition and the houses changed to suit the new needs. When one Tiv chief died and another was appointed, houses were gradually reorientated as they were rebuilt to face the house of the new chief; houses were built to reflect the social arrangement and people did not move to fit in with the arrangement of the houses.

The study of vernacular architecture demands an interdisciplinary approach. This makes it exciting, but one of its inherent drawbacks is that it is inevitable that things will be said with which specialists in individual disciplines will take issue. Moreover, since this particular work also covers over fifteen hundred different groups or 'tribes', those with special knowledge of some of these will also inevitably find generalizations which they consider imprecise or even totally misleading. A further problem has been the patchiness of the information. This is partly a reflection of official policies of colonial governments; partly of the degree of interest and precision shown by research workers; and partly of the imbalance of population (almost a quarter of the people of tropical Africa at the present time being Nigerians, for example). A final—but certainly not insignificant—impediment has been the inaccessibility of many of the original sources on which the survey of the literature is primarily based. Very little of the published material is specifically on architectural topics: most of it comes in general anthropological or anecdotal accounts.

In places archaeological evidence has been referred to. The boundary between archaeology and other disciplines has often been the site of friction, and perhaps undue weight has been given to a few oversimplified hypotheses relating archaeological finds to present-day life styles. Anyone discussing African architecture immediately wants to know the answers to the questions why, where and when: why this shape; when was it first used and where did it come from, if anywhere? Archaeology should be able to help find some of the answers. Recent research in Ethiopia, for example, has shown just how remarkably persistent some styles are. An excavated pottery model of a house in the Tigre area was found to be almost identical with modern Tigre farmers' houses.[3] It is hoped that a classification of contemporary building styles and techniques will be of use in interpreting archaeological finds.

This book aims to cover the whole of mainland Africa south of about 15°N. One of the main reasons for trying to cover such a large area was to try to avoid the temptation of explaining away the source of some style as being somewhere outside the particular area of Africa covered (see, for example, Haselberger[4] on the impluvium style). The aim is to describe and discuss not only the 'finished products', that is, the forms and groupings of buildings, but also the social, economic and environmental features associated with their production. Where possible details of materials and techniques of construction are also given.

Map 3   Sub-Saharan Africa covers the arid zones of West, South-West and North-East Africa which have a meagre 100 mm annual rainfall and the moist humid forest regions of the Zaïre Basin and the West Africa littoral with up to 4000 mm of rain annually. In between there is the large zone of tropical savannah land covering much of East, South-East and West Africa with grass and widely spaced trees. Arising out of this are the highland areas of, for example, North Cameroon, Ruanda, Burundi, Ethiopia, Kenya and parts of Rhodesia.

Map 4   In architectural terms, the annual amount of rainfall is not as significant as how it falls. In the humid forest regions the rain is often well distributed throughout the year, in a few areas falling every month. The desert and semi-desert, on the other hand, receive very little rainfall but what they do get comes in a few storms. This means that buildings in the high forest have to be resistant to persistent but relatively mild rain, while those in the Sahel have to withstand up to 200 mm of rain falling in a few hours.

In the forest areas there is little variation in temperature between day and night and the sun is often hazy. The semi-desert areas and highlands, on the other hand, are characterized by bright sunshine and extremes of temperature between day and night; frost is not unknown at certain times of the year. Here buildings and walls need to provide shade from the glaring midday sun as well as warmth at night; in some places mud beds are built with space underneath for a fire.

Map 3   What divides Africa into specific regions far more than its vegetation and climate, however, are its pronounced river basins. The six main ones are the Niger, Nile, Zaïre, Zambezi, Volta and Chad (which has no outlet to the sea). Despite cataracts and anastamosing swamps, all the main rivers have been used for short-distance water transport. It is interesting to note that each river basin has several distinctive building characteristics. The reasons for this are not at all clear and the statement is put forward here only as a tentative observation.

The illustrations and their captions are intended to be as important as the text. Photographs have been selected for their substantive content and not necessarily for their technical quality or composition. The rapid pace of social and economic change during the last hundred years has meant that many features and in some cases whole styles have disappeared. The only record of several styles may be one single photograph which has been reproduced here.

Traditional societies, whose total cultural heritage is handed down orally from one generation to the next, have shown themselves to be peculiarly vulnerable to the impact of the modern sector economy. Some features such as the name of the society and its location have remained unchanged, and these have naturally been referred to in the present tense. On the other hand many ethnographic details have often changed out of all recognition from those described in the primary sources and so for them the past tense has generally been used. Some loss of immediate clarity is therefore inevitable.

In all but a very few cases the architecture considered here was created without the aid of architects or even specialized builders. But as Equino wrote in the eighteenth century: 'Every man is a sufficient architect for the purpose. The whole neighbourhood afford their unanimous assistance in building . . . and in return receive and expect no other recompense than a feast.'[5] He wrote this about his Ibo homeland but it could equally well have been written about hundreds of other societies in tropical Africa then and now.

Their architecture was a personal adaptation of a group solution. The houses erected by a particular society were in a style which had been communally worked out over several generations and consequently were closely tailored to the needs of its people. Buildings were renewed every few years; but the fact that the originators cannot be named does not make them any less valid as architecture. They are a society's solution to its habitation problems.

One of the most frequent sources of error on questions of African architecture, even amongst some quite serious writers, is the tendency to generalize from a very narrow base of experience. Only recently an eminent scholar in another field has said, 'as a rule traditional African houses are round in shape . . . one can only speculate [on] the symbolic meaning of African villages which so remarkably resemble one another all over tropical Africa.'[6] In this book the illustrations alone will I hope show that such notions of a homogeneous material culture throughout the continent cannot be sustained. Indeed, it is arguable that on the particular question of house plans there were originally many more rectangular than circular ones.

Today more and more architects are turning to vernacular architecture for inspiration, not because they wish to repeat the structures they find—the social orders, materials and technology they have to deal with are quite different—but because it is recognized that these structures obviously satisfied their communities' psychological needs far better than most modern suburban settlements do. Up until now, studies of vernacular architecture have mainly been centred on Europe and the Mediterranean area, but it is hoped that this book will begin to extend the field to tropical Africa.

REFERENCES

1. Thomson, J., *To the Central African Lakes* vol. 1 (London, 1881)
2. Moffat, R., *Missionary Labours and Scenes in South Africa* (London, 1842)
3. Gebremedhin, N., 'House Types of Ethiopia', in Oliver, P. (ed.), *Shelter in Africa* (London, 1971)
4. Haselberger, H., *Bautraditionen der Westafrikanischen Negerkulturen* (Vienna, 1964)
5. Curtin, P. O. (ed.), *Africa Remembered, Narratives by West Africans from the Era of the Slave Trade* (London, 1967)
6. Mbiti, J. S., *African Religions and Philosophy* (London-Ibadan-Nairobi, 1969)

The references for all the illustration sections will be found at the end of Illustration Section X, p. 202

Illustration Section I

1 *Mumoye houses near Zinna, northern Nigeria, about 1950.* The Mumoye occupy an area of 2500 km² between the Jos Plateau and Mambila plateau. They practised a sophisticated system of land husbandry using a four field rotation; composting and manuring from livestock; and communal farmers' guilds.[1] In the hill farms stone terracing was used; but most people have now left the hills.

2 *Mumoye granaries near Zinna, northern Nigeria, about 1960*

3 *Tangale/Waja homesteads, Tuka, near Kaltungo, northern Nigeria, 1956.* Notice the building on the left with stone walls and the stone walls between buildings. The unthatched mud building was a granary and would have been thatched later.

4 *Tangale/Waja homesteads, Tuka, near Kaltungo, northern Nigeria, 1956.* Notice the woven finials on some roofs. The forked sticks in the foreground were used as ladders to stand on when filling and emptying granaries and thatching.

5 *Ron granaries, Bargesh, northern Nigeria, 1955.* The Ron are one of many peoples living on the high plateau area of northern Nigeria. On the western and southern sides the plateau is bounded by an escarpment some 600 m high and the granite hills rise to 1830 m. The terrain is extremely uneven with frequent rocky outcrops. The Ron number about 7000 people. In their villages, the spaces between the houses were often filled with stone walls and the entrance to each house was through a winding passage.

6

6 *Ron homestead, Bargesh, northern Nigeria, 1955.* These buildings were built of mud strengthened with layers of large stones. Each household had at least two double-storey buildings; the upper storey was used as a store or sleeping room and was entered by means of a ladder. The round doorways are very satisfactory shapes in a mud wall since rectangular openings tend to crack and crumble.

7 *Ron house, Bargesh, northern Nigeria, 1955.* The pillars on either side of the doorway were reinforced with stones. Round the doorway and on either side of the ventilation holes are incised patterns of wavy lines and dots, the latter made by rolling a maize husk along the wet plaster.

8 *Ron granaries, Bargesh, northern Nigeria, 1955.* Notice the model of a lizard on one of the granaries on the left.

9 *Stone bridge, Bokhos, northern Nigeria, 1960.* Several stone bridges like this one can be found in the Ron district. They were built of granite boulders, roughly shaped and laid in a bed of mud mortar. They were usually built concave to the flow of the stream and extended 7–10 m onto the banks on each side.

10 *Plan of Birom village, northern Nigeria, about 1950.* The Birom live on the Jos Plateau. The homesteads and much of the cultivated land (about 1200 ha) were within the defensive euphorbia hedge. The cultivated land was divided up into fields, also surrounded by euphorbia hedges, and was kept in continuous cultivation by the use of manure and crop rotation.

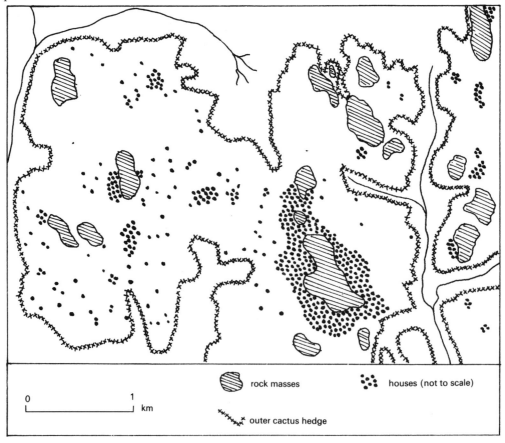

rock masses   houses (not to scale)

0   1 km

outer cactus hedge

11 *Plan of Birom homesteads, northern Nigeria, about 1949.* The walls of Birom buildings were of mud and straw often reinforced with stones. The roofs were thatched, but the sleeping houses often had a mud roof under the thatch. There was a high degree of building specialization, as many as twenty different types of building being constructed.[2] The first to be erected in a new homestead was always the beer hut. Homesteads and whole villages alike were usually surrounded by euphorbia hedges. This plan shows two homesteads connected together.

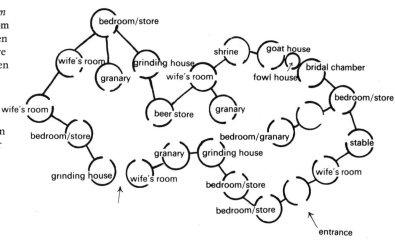

12 *Birom village, Bukuru, northern Nigeria, about 1920.* This euphorbia tunnel was part of a scheme of defence apparently designed to frustrate the Hausa horsemen of the plains. About 4·5 m high, it started over 1 km from the village and led to the only entrance gate. It was planned like a maze, with branches leading either to blind alleys or back to the main tunnel. In this way, it either ambushed horsemen or led the front sections of a hostile cavalry back face to face with the rear sections.[3] (Euphorbia's white latex sap is carcinogenic and will blind eyes and burn skin.)

13 *Gwari village, Kujama, northern Nigeria, 1965.* The Gwari used to be confined to rocky outcrops in Nupeland and southern Hausaland but they have recently been coerced into moving down to the plains. This photograph shows a new village viewed from the abandoned site of the old. There is a new Hausa village next to it and the rectangular buildings of the Gwari village show Hausa influence.

9

14 *Gwari homestead, Kujama, northern Nigeria, 1969.* Each homestead was built on a ring pattern and contained an entrance house, wives' houses, grain stores, a cooking house, graves and several shrines. The buildings were joined together by matting or thin slabs of stone. Kitchens had mud roofs under the thatch and a circular hole (about 30 cm across) in the apex as a chimney. This was covered by an umbrella of thatch supported on a stick which could be raised or lowered. Chimney arrangements were rare in African houses.

15 *Gwari granary, Kujama, northern Nigeria, 1969.* This granary had just been filled and sealed when the photograph was taken. The owner was an old man who had to have his fears about the evil eye quelled before he allowed the photograph to be taken. (Unfortunately, when the author returned to the village three weeks later the granary was in ruins, since an untimely shower of rain had come before it had been thatched; but the camera rather than the rain was being blamed.)

16 *Gwari grindstones, Kujama, northern Nigeria, 1969.* Gwari villages were divided into kinship units with one communal grinding house for each unit. This photograph shows the interior of one of these buildings. The nine grindstones were set into a raised mud bench. The floor was tessellated with small pottery sherds set into a very hard mud. It is interesting to note the similarities to the houses of the Jos Plateau 150 km away and the Nuba over 2400 km further east (see no. 19).

17 *Lafofa house, Nuba mountains, southern Sudan, about 1932.* The Nuba consist of a complex of peoples with a wide range of cultural attributes (including architectural styles). They live in the Nuba hills in southern Kordofan, an area of granite west of the White Nile. Nowadays many of their homesteads are scattered over the plains, but until the end of the last century their nucleated villages were mostly built in the hills. A ritual connection is still kept with the old sites which provide a long-distance focus for the new dispersed homesteads, which decrease in density away from the hills. They were mixed farmers and terraced the slopes of the hills, and sometimes irrigated small plots near wells or streams. Many of the homesteads were built on a ring pattern with individual buildings arranged in a circle and joined by a wall or fence. The house walls were of red, gravelly clay, often on a foundation of large stones. They were sometimes decorated inside as well as outside with geometric patterns in red, white and black. Sleeping houses sometimes had high raised floors as a protection against dampness.

18 *Lafofa house, interior, Nuba mountains, southern Sudan, about 1932.* The floors of Nuba houses and also the grindstone benches were often decorated with tessellations. The grindstones were usually within a daughter's sleeping house. Notice the similarities to Gwari grindstones (no. 16).

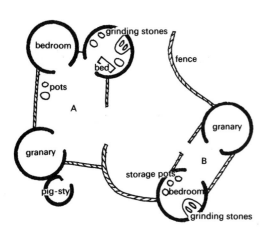

19 *Plan of Tira houses, Nuba Mountains, southern Sudan, about 1945*. This plan shows two adjoining houses, one belonging to a man, his wife and two children and the other to the first man's brother and his wife. Each Tira wife usually had her own homestead.

20 *Tira house, Nuba mountains, southern Sudan, about 1955*. Here the individual buildings are joined by a fence of grain stalks.

21 *Plan of Mesakin house, Nuba mountains, southern Sudan, about 1945*. Young unmarried girls or boys slept on a raised mud platform in one half of the pigsty. A small round circular hole halfway up the wall gave access to this sleeping platform.

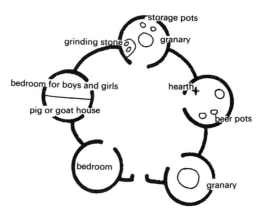

22 *Mesakin house, Nuba mountains, southern Sudan, about 1955*. The houses were built of layers of swish-puddled mud on a stone platform.

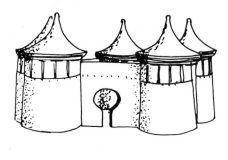

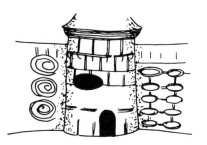

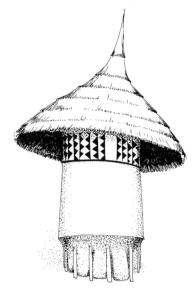

23 *Drawings of a Mesakin house, Nuba mountains, southern Sudan, about 1938.* The lower drawing shows the two doorways in the children's bedroom/pigsty.

24 *Drawing of a Heiban granary, Nuba mountains, southern Sudan, about 1945.* In Heiban when a granary was filled to the brim a special ceremony called 'orinyate' celebrated the occasion. The granary was painted in red and white and a feast was provided for guests.

25 *Matakam homesteads near Mora, Cameroon, about 1950.* The Matakam, who number only about 2000, live in the Mandara Mountains on the border between Nigeria and Cameroon. They are one of many small groups who live in these granite mountains (height 1400 m) and who practise an intensive and highly planned system of agriculture based on stone terracing, composting and manuring, crop rotation, tree planting and management, selective stock breeding and irrigation (see Chapter 9). Most of these communities lived in scattered homesteads which were often separated by several hundred vertical metres. Nine or ten homesteads formed a patrilineal clan. Matakam homesteads were often enclosed within stone walls which gave protection from the enormously strong winds and rain which lash this area.

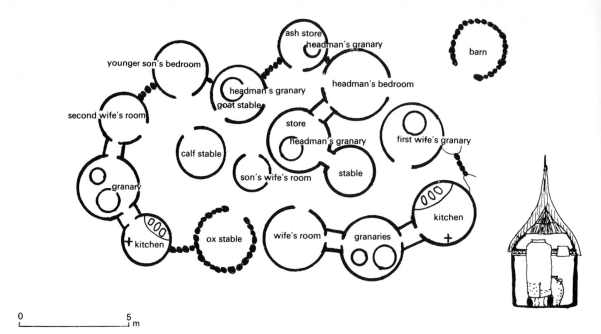

26 *Plan of Matakam homestead near Mora, Cameroon, about 1950.* Many of the buildings had stone walls. As can be seen, several were interlocking, for instance the wife's sleeping room, her granary and her kitchen, and the man's room, his stable and his granary. This homestead contained only two generations, but three generations were common. Most peoples in this area were monogamous (the connection between family structure and the economy is discussed in Chapter 2). A distinctive feature of this area was the high degree of building specialization. Buildings were constructed not only for sleeping and cooking quarters and as granaries, but also for horses, ashes and latrines, goats, sheep and cattle. These last three were all kept inside at night and during the whole of the rainy season when they were hand-fed and watered and the manure was cleared out each day.[4] The inset drawing shows the double thatched roof put on some of the buildings.

27 *Gamergu/Hidkala homsteads near Gwoza, north-eastern Nigeria, about 1955.* This view is of the edge of the Mandara Mountains. Many of the Hidkala have in this century moved away to the plains (see Chapter 10), where their homesteads are enclosed by thorn hedges. Compare the round entrance with no. 6.

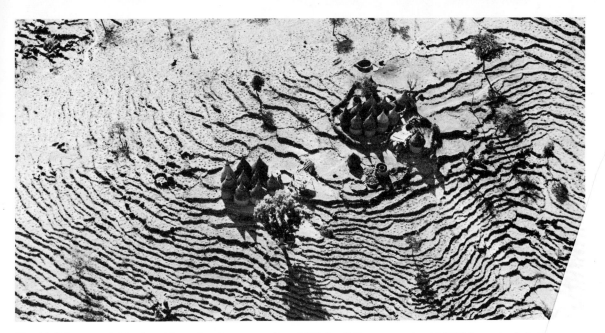

28 *Kirdi homestead, Mandara Mountains, Cameroon, about 1960.* In all there were about 10 000 homesteads in th
Mandara Mountains in 1939 giving a population density of about 75 people to the square kilometre. Stone terra
be seen all over the hill. The terrace walls varied in height from about 20 cm to 3 m, and their median dimensi
about 1·25 m high and 2·25 m deep. It has been estimated that in the whole area of the Mandara Mountains th
at least 30 000 km of terracing.[5]

29 *Baya-Kaka homestead near Batouri, Cameroon, about 1950.* The Baya-Kaka live both sides of the border between
Cameroon and the Central African Republic. Although not far from the tropical rain forest zone, the area is hilly with
relatively sparse vegetation. The house walls were built of mud and stone.

2 Rural Settlements

Social and Economic Background

In the past rural Africa was largely an amalgam of small-scale societies. Despite the more obvious differences there were certain strong economic similarities between them. Most families depended for their basic livelihood on their own farms or herds and there was little differentiation of productive labour. A subsistence economy like this was hazardous, especially in areas of infertile soil, arduous climate and a quite fearsome incidence of pestilence and disease, affecting not only humans but also animals and crops as well. So it was inevitable that many societies should direct much of their energy towards the task of mere self-preservation. For many societies, survival was dependent on preserving a delicate balance of forces and treading and retreading a path worked out empirically over many generations. Each new generation had to reassert the way and pass on the method to the next generation. Of the Dinka, Lienhardt[1] has written, 'there is nothing of importance in Dinka material culture which outlasts a single lifetime. The labours of one generation hence do not lighten or make a foundation for those of the next, which must again fashion by the same technological processes and from the same limited variety of raw materials a cultural environment which seems unchanging.'

Religion often emphasized this continuity by relating the individual to the still live forces of the ancestors. Sometimes little distinction between the living and the dead was made when referring to people: the dead had merely changed state and were still a potent force.

Social practices also served to counter the hazardous nature of existence; to cut down the disruptive elements in society to a minimum, and to bind the community together for strength. Stress was laid on conformity rather than innovation; loners, adventurers and risk-takers (characteristically the architectural innovators) were discouraged. Emphasis was placed on achieving the basic accoutrements of life: a house, a family and the respect of old age. Proverbs and superstitions underlined this feeling. This is well illustrated by the Tallensi of Ghana. A Tallens' whole life revolved around his homestead; all his possessions and livestock were kept within its walls and its importance is seen in two proverbs. *'U ku nye yiri'* ('You will not see, that is, have, a house') was the worst curse that could be put on children, while, *'I na nye yiri'* ('You will have a house') was the most propitious blessing a diviner could convey to a man from his ancestral spirits.[2] Among the northern Hausa of l'Ader, uninhabited bush was a place of malevolent forces, while the village was kept secure by magical protection. Within the village the best place to live was the secure centre rather than the vulnerable periphery.[3] The village symbolized the strength of the community and of the known world in contrast to the menacing world outside.

Ostentatious individual behaviour was often suspect, and threats of witchcraft were used to safeguard the ideal of equality and conformity to the norm. A man of the Gwari tribe of Nigeria who got better crops from his farm than other people was suspected of being a wizard.[4] The Hehe of Tanzania believed that if a man behaved in any way differently from his neighbours a jealous warlock would kill him by witchcraft.[5] Similarly the Chewa of Malawi believed that deviation from the social norm would bring retribution from the forces of evil.[6]

In many rural societies no great social privilege was attached to wealth and its accumulation was frowned upon. Social practices often meant it was immediately dissipated in the form of extra dependants such as more wives, 24 or in entertainment. Among the Heiban, Laro and Koalib people of the Sudan, a man who succeeded in filling a granary was obliged to entertain guests by killing an animal and providing plenty of beer to celebrate his success.[7]

The egalitarian attitude fostered in these societies did not always manifest itself in community production. Totally collectivized production was not common, although informal cooperation between neighbouring families at peak times and the sharing of food and grazing land was fairly common. Some societies, however, appear to exhibit ritualistic vestiges of a former, more highly cooperative state. An interesting example of this is the ceremonial hunting expeditions of the Lele of Zaïre, for whom hunting is no longer of any significant economic importance.[8]

It has been customary to classify rural African peoples according to four broad economic categories: agriculturalists, pastoral nomads, mixed farmers and hunters and gatherers. Often the pastoralists utilized land which was unsuitable for agriculture, but sometimes the sedentary farmers' holdings were an obstacle to the free movement of the pastoralists and the consequent enmity became a major force in the shaping of settlement patterns. Apart from fishermen, the hunters and gatherers, such as the Tindiga of Tanzania, the pygmies of the Zaïre Basin and the bushmen of the Kalahari Desert, are now only found in small pockets of land into which they have been forced by the expansion of agriculturalists. Even the pygmies, however, no longer rely completely on hunting and gathering and have set up a trading relationship with neighbouring settled villagers who are agriculturalists. Relationships of this sort between peoples with different economic systems have by no means been uncommon, sometimes approaching an almost complete symbiosis. The interaction between the 159–60 pastoral Fulani of West Africa and the settled tribes is well known and well documented. The original basis of the relationship, which was the exchange of grazing and cultivated crops for manure and dairy products, has, however, tended to disappear as the agriculturalists increasingly take up animal husbandry themselves. This sort of economic diversification has taken place all over the continent and the pastoralists and hunters and gatherers are now very much in the minority.

The various traditional systems of agriculture found in Africa contained some remarkably fine adaptations to the problems of the environment. Many African soils were and are poor; most rural societies did not have slave labour; and the systems that were used produced just enough food with the minimum of labour. These systems varied widely and included the intensive 28, 41 cultivation of hillside terraces using manuring and crop rotation, the shifting cultivation of the edges of the forest and the remarkable dry-season cultivation of the semi-nomadic Shuwa Arabs who, on the southern edges of the Chad Basin, produced guinea-corn without a drop of water falling on the stalks by planting at exactly the moment when the water table was at its highest, so that the root growth followed the water down.[9]

If the agricultural systems were carefully geared to the environment, so were the family structures geared to producing the requisite labour requirements. Sedentary farmers needed only a small amount of manpower, but they needed it continuously, whereas shifting cultivators needed much larger labour forces but for shorter times. This difference was reflected in family structure. Sedentary farmers tended to live in small nuclear family units and shifting cultivators lived in larger extended families (see, for example, Netting[10] on the Kofyar).

26

The pattern of settlement was also influenced by the nature of the crops grown, slow maturing crops tying their owners to one plot of land for many years. Moreover, if times were uncertain, it was necessary for these crops to be within the defensive schemes of the village. The Kongo-Mayombe people live in the Zaïre Basin and one of their main crops used to be the oil palm. Oil palm trees have a life of up to a hundred years, which makes them very fixed capital assets. The Lele, also of the forest areas, cultivated the raffia palm, using it for fibres and wine. The drawing of wine kills the palm and its life is only about five years. Allowing time for the preparation of land, the Lele therefore only kept each clearing open for a maximum of about seven years.[11]

The seasonal migrations of the pastoral nomads were, except in a very few areas, not haphazard and followed fairly specific routes. Their patterns were very closely adapted to climatic conditions as well as to social cohesiveness and animal ownership, and almost every group had a pattern peculiar to themselves. Some, especially the camel owners, moved only horizontally along the plains, while others moved up and down the hills; some moved almost continually throughout the year, while others moved only once a year from a dry-season to a wet-season camp. The distances involved varied enormously. The Masai had permanent homes next to dry-season wells and migrated to temporary pastures in the west season often only about 100 km away. In parts of the Sudan migrations covered as much as 700 km annually.[12] There was a great variation in the size of mobile units, but on the whole the longer migrations were associated with the largest groupings. Among the Nuer the grouping size changed during the year. At their dry-season camps several families, who lived in villages of 50–100 people at their permanent bases on knolls, formed camps together consisting of as many as 700 people.[13]

154–6

237

The pastoralists who moved most frequently had houses which were very easy to dismantle and transport, usually tents. Some of those who only made one major move a year had permanent houses in one or other of their camps.

151–3
159–60

In all societies kinship was an important determinant of the structure of settlement pattern. It was usually expressed by physical nearness: all members of one clan would live in a clearly defined piece of territory. Within this were any number of family units, whose size and composition varied enormously across the continent. The traditional Bemba family consisted of parents and children and the daughters' husbands and children. The Kongo-Mayombe family, on the other hand, included all the sons of one mother (though not the mother herself) and their wives and children, her daughters' sons and their wives and the daughters' unmarried daughters. All these people—sometimes up to about three hundred—would live in one village and own land in common. The mother's eldest son would be the head of the household. In some societies, for example the Bemba again, one could even have a limited choice of allegiance, so popular families sometimes sprouted accretions.[14] In such cases, shifting agriculture meant that when villages were rebuilt every four or five years there could be a general re-shuffling.

Village Layout

The word 'village' is in many ways a misleading one in African terms. In most areas villages were conceived of as groups of people rather than groups of buildings. In some places, villages were not at all apparent on the ground and yet certain homesteads definitely belonged together, being lived in by one clan or kinship group. The earliest colonial officers in Buganda reported that there were no villages, only scattered homesteads. Closer examination, however, has shown that the countryside was divided up into named areas which were looked upon as villages to which people belonged.[15]

African villages usually expressed physically the social structure of the group of people living in them. Of course the actual relationships varied from year to year as people were born, married, divorced or died, but the general structure remained fairly constant. The relatively impermanent nature of the buildings meant that there could be a quick response to changed circumstances. On the domestic level, a man taking a new wife would usually build a house for her in his compound, while at the village level in some societies the death of a chief brought about a gradual reorientation of the village as new houses were built to face the new chief's house. Villages and houses were built round people and their groupings; there was no question of people adapting themselves to fixed houses and villages, which may have been unsuitable or inadequate.

There was nevertheless a good deal of careful planning often based on sound practical principles, but sometimes related to religious beliefs and taboos. It was quite well appreciated in some societies that some relations were better kept separate: in the Kaonde villages sons-in-law and mothers-in-law belonged to different sections of the village.[16] The villages of the Kaonde, like others in central Africa (for instance, Lele, western Lunda), were divided into two age sections by an invisible line, proximate generations building separately and alternate generations building together, but both sections acknowledging the rule of one headman.[17] This example underlines the difficulty of just studying the ground plans of villages, since invisible boundaries were not uncommon. The Tullishi of the Sudan lived in six crowded hamlets which described a rough circle.[18] They appeared on a plan to form a corporate unit, but in fact they were divided by an invisible line cutting across the circle which had no physical features and was related to their myth of origin. This line effectively divided the hamlets into two isolated communities and it was reinforced by threats of witchcraft from which only very old men were immune. Invisible forces too were sometimes at work influencing the selection of new village sites. For example, the Kikuyu avoided any grave site, battlefield or place connected with an ancestral curse or taboo,[19] and Lango villages were never built on hills because they were associated with an omnipresent spirit called Jok, and close association with Jok was thought to be dangerous.[20]

The ideal layout of some villages was often said to be entirely symbolic. The Dogon, who live on the rocky Bandiagara escarpment in what is now the Mali Republic, base their philosophy, it is claimed, on the idea of germinating cells vibrating along a spiral path to break out of a 'world egg'.[21] The spiral and 36 the egg shape therefore had special significance. Each village was laid out either in a square to represent the first field cultivated by man or in an oval with a hole at one end to represent the world egg broken open by the spirally vibrating cells. In either case it also represented a person lying in a north-south direction with the smithy placed at the head and certain shrines at the feet, while huts used by women during their menstrual period were the hands and the family homesteads the chest. The anthropomorphic nature of the village was further expressed by a conical foundation shrine and by a hollowed stone for grinding which signified the male and female sexual organs. The surrounding fields fitted into the system. It has however been pointed out that generally 'the nature of the country, the contours and the siting of the water courses necessitated compliance with this rule'.[22]

Many of the village configurations were quite formal or symmetrical, for example the circular plan with houses arranged round the circumference and 171, 183, 226 an open cattle space in the middle, found in southern Africa; or the axial or horseshoe or square plans found in central Africa. This formality did often imply conscious planning, but the mere plan means nothing without a knowledge of the invisible boundaries and social forces recognized by the inhabitants. Among the Bemba, for example, the domestic group and the physical compound groups did not overlap. The domestic group was composed of a man and his wife and his young married daughters and their children, whereas physical groups consisted of separate nuclear families whose houses were not fenced off from each other in any way. A mother's house and those of her married daughters, for example, might or might not be adjacent even though the daughters were still not given their own granary or cooking place for one or two years after marriage and all their cooking was done in their mother's compound.[23] They still belonged, in fact, to the domestic family centred on their father. The physical groupings of the Asante of Ghana also did not always reflect the domestic family. It was not unknown for the husband and wife after marriage to go on living among their own kin; in fact a survey in one town in 1947 showed that about three-quarters of the wives stayed with their kin but would of course cook for their husbands. At sunset small boys would be seen running from one house to another with plates of hot food, carrying it from the wife to the husband.[24]

In societies where there was age differentiation, this was often reflected in settlement patterns. The Nyakusa, who lived in the highlands north of Lake 50–4 Malawi, had an interesting system of age grouping. All the boys of a certain age, usually about twelve years, would go off to form a new age-village. They were joined in subsequent years by four or five successive cohorts of younger boys; but then recruitment would stop and future generations went to new villages. These villages were the permanent place of residence of the peer groups concerned and when they married, their wives joined them.[25] Amongst the Masai young men became warriors at a certain age and during the period of military service they lived together in one section of the kraal. Other pastoralists had similar systems.

As has already been pointed out, formal and informal social forces served to foster a relatively egalitarian climate in many, though by no means all, rural African societies. Villages were therefore an arrangement of more or less equal buildings. In societies with traditional monarchs, the chief's houses were often only distinguished from the rest, if at all, by their central placing or by their slightly exaggerated proportions. They were not usually barricaded or set apart from the rest of the buildings (see Chapter 4).

Homestead Layout

Attention has so far been mainly concentrated on the arrangement of family units within villages; but each unit, compound or homestead also exhibited its own internal plan. Domestic families were, as has been demonstrated, not all equal in size, but a larger family would have had a homestead or compound which was quantitatively rather than qualitatively grander.

The physical layout, just as in the village plan, did not always reflect the social groupings. Similar buildings and plans could sometimes house fundamentally different social groups. This was the case among the Nuba for

22 example, where Moro and Korongo-Mesakin house types were almost identical but their social structures quite different. Moro wives would each have their separate homesteads, whereas Korongo-Mesakin wives would have their own separate buildings within the family homestead, which also sometimes housed children of the head's sister, his own children having gone to live with a maternal uncle.[26]

The requirements of the family were simple and mainly similar in all agricultural societies: a place for each member to sleep; a place for cooking; places for food storage and somewhere to protect animals at night, such as cattle, goats and chickens; a place to eat and a place to sit and talk in the day and practise craftwork, basket making, spinning and weaving. In most parts of Africa, for a greater portion of the year, the weather is warm and when it is dry many activities can be performed outside. So a demarcated space was often sufficient for some activities, and this must be considered as much a part of the homestead as the buildings. In parts of Uganda the men preferred to sit at the gate of their compound under shady trees to talk and eat their food. In northern Ghana and northern Nigeria the women liked to cook outside in the dry season in an unroofed space, partly surrounded by a low wall for shelter from the winds. The trees, their shade, the cooking stones and their surroundings thus became rooms of the homestead.

Amongst only a few peoples was a single homestead building the norm. It
98, 103 was found mostly where the buildings were square or rectangular rather than where they were circular. There were circular buildings which were
189, 254 divided inside into areas for sleeping, cooking, storage and space for small animals at night, but usually each wife still had a building of her own.

The more usual arrangement was that each compound consisted of many
11, 19, 21, 26, 170, 210 separate buildings, each one in effect a 'room' of the homestead with one specific purpose, be it as a kitchen, a man's bedroom, a wife's bedroom or a grain store. Dual-purpose rooms were, however, not at all uncommon. Small
22–3 boys were frequently put to sleep on top of granaries, while wives' sleeping quarters often doubled as kitchens, as it was well appreciated that a grimy layer of soot on the underside of a roof was a good deterrent against insects. Physically, often little distinction was made between one building and another in a compound or homestead and the sleeping hut and the storage hut could look quite alike from the outside. The buildings used for the more

important activities of life, such as sleeping, were not specially elaborate, and the cattle often got as good as the father. Sometimes, especially in the drier regions with short growing seasons, the granary became the largest and most prominent building in the compound. In Gobir granaries with diameters of up to 5·2 m, which means a girth of about 17 m, were built.[27] The cattle house of the Dinka of the Sudan, with a diameter of 12·2 m, was the most prominent building in the household group.

237

Conclusion

In conclusion, it must be stressed that even the simplest settlement as we see it today is the product of a whole multitude of economic, social, political, physical and technological forces. Appearances can easily be deceptive and even a detailed analysis of manifest spatial layout is quite insufficient for a thorough appreciation. Each settlement is a finely balanced solution to a problem of habitation and needs to be seen as a physical reflection of the way of life of its inhabitants.

REFERENCES

1. Lienhardt, G., *Divinity and Experience: The Religion of the Dinka* (Oxford, 1961)
2. Fortes, M., *The Web of Kinship among the Tallensi* (Oxford, 1957)
3. Echard, N., L'Habitat Traditionnel Dans L'Ader', *L'Homme*, 7, 3 (1967)
4. Nai'ibi, S., and Hassan, Alhaji, *Gwari, Gade and Koro Tribes* (Ibadan, 1969)
5. Davidson, B., *The Africans* (London, 1969)
6. Marwick, M. G., *Sorcery in its Social Setting: A Study of the Northern Rhodesian Chewa* (Manchester, 1965)
7. Nadel, S. F., *The Nuba* (Oxford, 1947)
8. Douglas, M., 'The Lele of Kasai', in Forde, D. (ed), *African Worlds* (London, 1963)
9. White, S., *Dan Bana* (London, 1966)
10. Netting, R. McC., 'Household Organisation and Intensive Agriculture: The Kofyar Case', *Africa*, 35 (1965)
11. Douglas, M., *op. cit.*
12. El Arifi, Salih A., 'Pastoral Nomadism in the Sudan', *East African Geographical Review*, 13 (1975)
13. Evans-Pritchard, E. E., *The Nuer* (Oxford, 1941)
14. Richards, A., 'The Central Bantu' in Radcliffe-Brown, A. R., and Forde, D. (eds.), *African Systems of Kinship and Marriage* (Oxford, 1950)
15. Richards, A., *The Changing Structure of a Ganda Village* (Nairobi, 1966)
16. Watson, W., 'Kaonde Village', *Rhodes-Livingstone Institute Journal*, XV (1954)
17. Douglas, M., *op. cit.*
18. Nadel, S. F., *op. cit.*
19. Cagnola, C., *The Akikuyu* (Nyeri, 1933)
20. Driberg, J. H., *The Lango* (London, 1923)
21. Griaule, M., and Dieterlen, G., 'The Dogon of the French Sudan' in Forde, D. (ed.), *African Worlds* (London, 1963)
22. *Ibid.*
23. Richards, A., 'The Central Bantu' in Radcliffe-Brown, A. R., and Forde, D. (eds.), *African Systems of Kinship and Marriage* (Oxford, 1950)
24. Mair, L., *An Introduction to Social Anthropology* (Oxford, 1965)
25. Wilson, M., *Rituals of Kinship among the Nyakusa* (Oxford, 1956)
26. Nadel, S. F., *op. cit.*
27. Schweinforth, Dr G., *The Heart of Africa* (London, 1873)

Illustration Section II

30 *Eritrean house, Ethiopia, about 1930*. The roof of this house would have been covered with grass thatch.

31 *Tigrean house, Sokoto, Ethiopia, 1940s*. Two-storey round houses were found in the Axum and Adua areas of Tigre province and also round the Sokoto area of Wallo province. Between 2000 m and 2500 m high, this land consists of high plateaux; it is sparsely populated and dominated by clumps of giant euphorbia.

32 *Tigre chief's house, Tigre province, Ethiopia, 1940s*. In Tigre province, the chiefs' houses were round in plan whereas farmers' houses were rectangular. Styles there seem to have been remarkably persistent: the farmers' houses were very similar to a fifth-century clay model of a house excavated near Axum in 1959 and, in plan, the chiefs' houses were very like the remains of some ancient Axumite houses. The ceilings of chiefs' houses were sometimes in the form of a cupola and sometimes, especially near Axum, they were made of coloured reeds arranged in a kind of mosaic over beams.[6] The foundations were built of black basalt, which did not absorb water (compare no. 79).

33 *Dogon village, Ireli, Mali, about 1950*. The Dogon appear to have lived on the Bandiagara escarpment for at least 500 years. A piece of their sculpture has recently been carbon-dated to the fourteenth-century.[7] Their traditions say they replaced earlier, so-called Tellem people whose possibly Early Iron Age cave buildings can still be seen. It seems quite possible, on the evidence of material culture, that the Dogon are the direct descendants of this Early Iron Age people.

34 *Dogon village, Bandiagara escarpment, Mali, about 1950*. A close-up of the village shown in no. 33.

35 *Dogon village, Amani, Mali, about 1950*. Notice the stone terraces on which the houses were built.

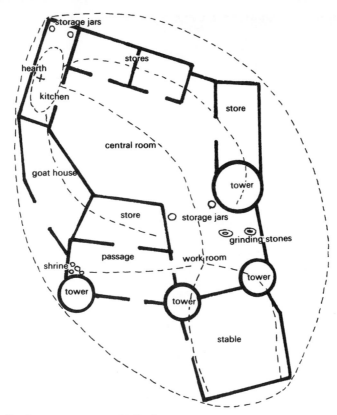

36 *Plan of Dogon house, Bandiagara escarpment, Mali, about 1950.* Despite the apparent lack of planning (see nos. 33, 34), the layout of Dogon villages and houses is highly organized and expresses physically a complicated cosmology. Each house is said to represent a man lying on his right side in the position adopted in the womb and in the Dogon marriage bed, and the component parts of the house represent individual organs of the body. Sexual and reproductive symbolism also pervades the explanations of village layout. Each village is twinned with another village, the two apparently representing heaven and earth.[8]

37 *Dogon houses and granaries, Bandiagara escarpment, Mali, about 1950.* The building with the cellular facade is usually said to be a *ginna* or to have a *ginna* style.

38 *Dogon door, Bandiagara escarpment, Mali.* This door was taken to France in 1952.

39 *Dogon granaries near Mopti, Mali, about 1950.* These multi-storey granaries were built under overhanging cliffs at the highest point in the villages. They were made of mud and small pieces of stone.

40 *Drawing of Tellem tomb cave situated between Sanga and Ireli, Mali.* These buildings are very similar to the Dogon granaries shown in no. 39 and were built in a similar way. Carbon-14 dates obtained in 1965 suggest that the Tellem culture was Early Iron Age, perhaps contemporary with Nok.

41 *Shona (?) stone terracing, Inyanga, Rhodesia.* The Inyanga Mountains lie along the borders of Rhodesia and Mozambique. They were apparently first settled in the Early Iron Age, but the thousands of kilometres of stone terraces like those seen in this photograph were apparently not constructed until at least the ninth century and possibly much later, when a Shona people moved into the area. Many of the terraces are now abandoned (possibly because of the nineteenth-century Ngoni raids, see no. 202), but some, for example near Pemalonga, are still worked by a Shona people. Some of these Shona build stone and mud round-plan houses with conical thatched roofs.

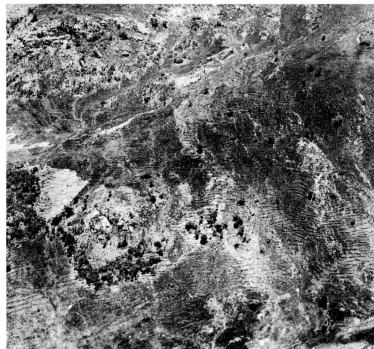

42 *Entrance to Shona 'dug-in' building, Inyanga, Rhodesia, about 1930.* The agricultural system of those present-day Shona who live in the Inyanga Mountains is broadly similar to that practised in the Mandara Mountains (see no. 25). Cattle are now kept in open stone-walled enclosures rather than in cattle houses, although oral tradition and archaeology show that in the highest settlements stock were previously kept for part of the time in stone-lined caverns.[9] This photograph shows the entrance to what may have been one of these caverns.

43 Zimbabwe *or chief's house, Great Zimbabwe, Rhodesia.* The house was surrounded by a massive wall about 10 m high and, on average, 3 m thick, enclosing an area 90 m by 65 m. The outer wall was constructed in dry stone, dressed granite blocks facing a rubble core. Near the top, thinner slabs of stone were worked into a double chevron pattern and large soapstone bird sculptures once looked outwards from the flat top. (See Chapter 6 for more details of the stone walling.) Inside, there is another wall and a tall solid conical tower and remains of several circular stone structures. The houses inside the enclosure appear to have been round in plan and built of wattle and mud with thatched roofs.

44 Zimbabwe *or chief's house, Great Zimbabwe, Rhodesia.* At Great Zimbabwe there are two main groups of ruins. One on the hill appears to have been a temple or priest's house while nearby in the valley there are ruins of a chief's house, as shown in this photograph. Excavations have shown that the earliest stone buildings at Zimbabwe date from about 1100. It was considerably enlarged in the fifteenth century when it became the centre of the empire of Monomatapa. In the sixteenth century the outer stone wall and tower were built; by this time it was the centre of the Rozwi empire. As such it remained for 300 years, surrounded by a network of towns which together organized the gold and ivory trade with the East African coastal states. In these smaller towns lesser chiefs lived in lesser *zimbabwes* such as Dhlo-Dhlo, Khami and Nalatale.

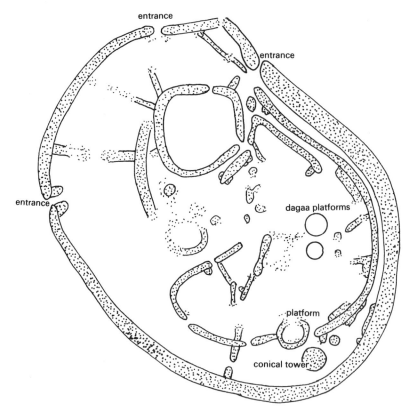

45 *Plan of* Zimbabwe *or chief's house, Great Zimbabwe, Rhodesia.*

0   50
m

46 Zimbabwe *or chief's house, Great Zimbabwe, Rhodesia*. A view inside the main wall showing the solid conical tower. The function of this tower is not known for certain, but it may have marked the graves of the chiefs or have been (as Garlake suggested[10]) a symbolic grain bin, as grain was a common form of tribute to Karanga chiefs.

47 *Rozwi (?) stone retaining walls, 16th–18th century, Khami, near Bulawayo, Rhodesia*. The Khami ruins consist of a group of houses on hilltops set above stepped retaining walls or terraces faced with dressed granite blocks sometimes arranged in a chequer pattern. The houses which were sometimes dug into the hillside, were round in plan and had wattle and mud walls and thatched roofs. Their diameters were 3–10 m. The whole settlement was built between the sixteenth and eighteenth centuries and would have been part of the Rozwi empire. (See Chapter 3.)

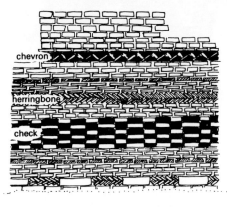

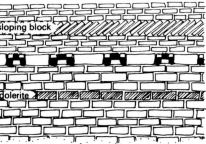

48 *Drawing of stone wall, Nalatale, Rhodesia.*

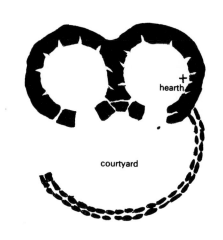

hearth

courtyard

0 _____ 5 m

49 *Plan and cross-section of Ghoya house, South Africa.* There are extensive remains of settlements of corbelled stone houses on the flat hill tops of the northern Free State (country formerly occupied by the Ghoya) and in Lesotho, where the Ghoya now live. These houses have been well documented by Walton.[11] There are three types which seem to represent an evolutionary sequence. This shows the earliest type, possibly pre-1830, built of dolerite or sandstone boulders. The entrance to the house was only about 30 cm tall.

0 ____ 1 ____ 2 m

Drawings after James Walton, **African Village**

3 States and Towns

There is no generally agreed definition of a town or of urbanism. This problem has exercised not only geographers and administrators but also historians and lawyers over a long period of time. Although there have been some attempts at producing a globally applicable set of defining characteristics, no satisfactory consensus seems to have emerged. However, one or more of the following attributes have been identified as the deciding factors: the existence of a separate economy; of specialist merchants and craftsmen; of writing; of heterogeneity in the population; of physical distinctiveness; or simply of large dense concentrations of people. Some writers have identified developmental stages in terms such as 'incipient towns' or 'quasi-urbanism', but there is no common pattern of nomenclature.

Mabogunje[1] has tried to relate criteria developed in other continents to the situation in his own. The task is extremely difficult, partly because such criteria are often themselves poorly defined and partly because in the areas he is dealing with the impact of European colonization has so profoundly altered the pre-existing economic and political equilibrium that reconstructing a picture of what things were like before is necessarily a rather conjectural operation. Political instability can often cause towns to decline or disappear altogether.

The Sudan Zone of West Africa

To people outside the continent, probably the most famous towns of Africa are those of the desert areas of the western Sudan, a chain of major urban centres stretching from Tekrur in the west through Audoghast, Oulata, Timbuktu and Gao to Agadez in the east. They grew up in the European medieval period at a time when international trade between the Mediterranean, Europe and the Far East was expanding rapidly.

Map 5
260–1, 265, 266–8

These Sudanese towns were in fact almost certainly a vital part of that expansion, supplying amongst other things the gold which became the principal unit of currency in Europe and much of the Mahgreb. Further south, other urban centres backed up these towns orientated on the desert, supplying them with the commodities on which the northward desert trade was based. These were gold, pepper and slaves, all of which originated in the forest zone. In exchange for these goods the Saharan towns received salt, silver, copper, cloth and beads from the northern edge of the desert. It is interesting to note that the southern belt of towns, which included Segou, Djenne, Ouagadougou, Katsina and Kano, closely follows the northern limit of the tsetse fly and therefore the effective southern limit of the camel. Further south goods were transported to and from the forest zones on foot.

262–4, 273–83

This may give the impression that each of the towns in these two belts was in some sort of political alliance with the others, which was in fact far from the case. They were often in conflict and the rise of one town was frequently associated with the decline of another. At their zeniths the towns often held considerable sway over large areas of country, and some of these hegemonies developed the characteristics of fully fledged states. Ghana, Mali and Songhai are probably the best known of these. Like the towns on which they were based, these states prospered at different times. Mali, which gradually eclipsed Ghana, was itself superseded by Songhai.

Let us take a closer look at one of the northern towns, Timbuktu. It is not entirely typical, for a variety of reasons which we shall consider, but having been touched by all three major empires of the western Sudan its history is rather better documented than many of the other towns. Also, it has captured the imagination of Europeans for centuries, and in Britain, at least, its fame has become permanently enshrined in some idiomatic expressions still current in everyday language usage. Known widely as the 'golden city', its appeal to Europeans was enhanced by the highly coloured descriptions of Leo Africanus in the sixteenth century and more recently by the even more sensational accounts of Felix Dubois among others.

Being situated near the point where the River Niger reaches furthest north into the desert, Timbuktu was at the intersection of land and river traffic routes. This of course was clearly an important factor in its growth. It was probably founded on the site of a dry-season camp for nomadic Tuareg and their cattle and grew into a trading centre as firstly people from the empire of Ghana and then later the Songhai from the east settled there. In the fourteenth century it came under Muslim Mandinka control as the empire of Mali prospered. Then it was freed again as the Songhai themselves created their empire. Finally it was crushed by the Moroccan invasion in the sixteenth century, since when it has remained a small 'provincial' town.

Timbuktu reached its zenith under the Songhai empire in the sixteenth century. By this time its commercial prosperity had brought it wealth which was displayed in fine palaces, mosques and houses, commissioned from architects brought back from Mecca. And with the wealth, a flourishing of culture at the University of Sankore and in the mosques turned Timbuktu into the intellectual centre of the western Sudan.

Its shape and character seem to have been determined by two main factors. One was that trade was seasonal: in the dry season the desert was too hot for caravans and the river too low for boats. Transient traders were therefore only in Timbuktu for some of the year and yet they were very much a part of the life of the town. Its permanent settled population was therefore not the same as its functional size. For instance, an area of the town, Abaradyu, was always kept to accommodate the five thousand or so camels and their men who made up the salt caravans coming to the town in the wet season. Secondly, it seems that Timbuktu was a place where it was believed a quick fortune could be made. The business class of Timbuktu as in other Sudanese towns seems to have been partly made up of Arabs who hoped they were in Timbuktu for a season. Even today some of the sons and grandsons of those who did stay still hope one day to return to Morocco or wherever their forebears came from.[2]

Part of the reason why the Arabs did not identify very closely with the town may have been that the inhabitants, not even those deriving from local stock, were never involved in governing it. Timbuktu was never itself a

Map 5

266–8

151–3

capital and this is further reflected in the fact that it was never walled, apart from some hasty breastworks thrown up by the Mandingo and Moroccan conquerors. Its strength and its weakness was that the only common bond of its inhabitants was always trade. Even this was divided up between the Arabs and the Songhai. The Arabs organized it while the Songhai were the real producers and provided most of the services except camel transportation.

The Arabs clearly regarded themselves as something of an élite, living apparently in the finest houses and in a separate quarter of the town from the Songhai. The Bela, who were the Tuareg slaves and who were the other inhabitants of the town, also lived in a separate quarter. Within these quarters each group apparently retained its own extended family ties and folk culture and the only area of the town in which these groups intermingled and treated one another impersonally was the market.

In contrast to the trade between the northern and southern chains of towns (which was based on the camel, the horse and the river) that between the southern towns and the forest zone was, as we have seen, largely conducted on foot. In the western part of this area, defined for this purpose as west of a line from Djenne to Accra, this trade was in the hands of Mande merchants. These merchants set up staging points along their routes, many of which developed into permanent settlements. These settlements were usually sited next to towns or villages of the local population and so in effect twin towns developed. It is tempting to see as the prototype for these towns Kumbi, the capital of Ghana as described by El-Bekri in the eleventh century. He depicted two separate towns, roughly 10 km apart, one housing the Muslim traders and the other the home of the pagan ruler and his court. The Mande traders, who were Muslims, also became marabouts or travelling priests and so were responsible for transmitting Islam further than the main Sudanese towns where it first took root. Many of them were also not without political ambition and seized power at convenient times in some of the twin towns. There seems to be some evidence that the Mande influenced the formation of the Akan states right down in the south of modern Ghana and even the state of the Bariba on the Niger in Borgu (where a Mande dialect is still spoken).

In what is now Nigeria this pattern of twin towns did not entirely persist. The settlement patterns in the larger towns were markedly different from those in the west. And although the trans-Saharan trade was extremely important economically (and it was organized along similar lines to the trade further west), it does not seem to have been trade that provided the original impetus for the development of the towns in this area. Examining the layout of these towns in detail, some writers[3] have postulated a military or colonial origin. The common features included town walls of great length (Kano, 22 km; Ibadan, 16 km; Old Oyo, 25 km), a large area of unbuilt land and a high hill or artificial mound within the town walls. In a potentially hostile environment the high ground would have been used for the first settlements and the unbuilt land within the subsequent walls for sheltering outlying farmers in times of siege (see also Chapter 5). It is remarkable how this pattern is evident in both the Sudan and forest zones.

Apart from layout one can also find similarities in less tangible features like mythology. A comparative study of the monarchical traditions shows a widespread reliance on the idea of divine kingship coexisting with legends of origins to the north-east. This gives support to those who maintain that divine kingship was diffused from Pharaonic Egypt. Any such diffusion need not of course have involved mass migrations, and as will be demonstrated (Chapter 9) such Nilotic influences are only some of many.

Hausaland is the name given to a cluster of states which grew up around several of these towns north of the Niger–Benue confluence. They seem to have been founded before the eleventh century, although they did not develop into important trans-Saharan trading depots until the early fifteenth century; the same time that camels are said to have been introduced into the area.

The major towns of Hausaland were, as we have seen, situated at that time at the ends of the international trade routes. However the sites of the smaller towns were influenced by the local trade which later on became as important as the international trade.

Although the states acted autonomously over many matters, and in fact at times openly vied with one another for a bigger share of the Saharan trade, some of the larger states appear to have had specialist functions serving Hausaland as a whole. For example, Zaria seems to have been the chief slave supplier; Gobir in the north aimed to defend Hausaland as a whole from attackers such as the Tuareg from the desert; Kano and Katsina were the main trading centres. By the nineteenth century slaves had become the most important item of northbound trade and Barth, who visited there in the 1850s, estimated that about five thousand left Kano annually. The marauding armies of Zaria must therefore have been of considerable force.

The states were further united by a common culture. This urban Hausa culture was based on the Hausa language (which was written in Arabic script and owed much to Arabic) and on Islam. The principal mosque was one of the
274, 293 most prominent buildings in a Hausa town and, as well as being a religious centre, disseminated education and literary skill, the latter an important aid to efficient trading practices.

Although Hausaland as a whole was united by this common culture, each of the larger Hausa towns attracted a heterogenous collection of inhabitants. Merchants from many parts of North Africa, from Ghadames and from Agadez, were to be found in the towns and each of these groups usually had its own quarter. The residential areas of the towns were further divided into occupational zones: craftsmen were organized into guilds and guild workers were grouped together into definite places. The political and spatial foci of these towns were the emirs' palaces. The emirs were the rulers in charge of the armies; they personified the stability which was so necessary for good trading, so that their powers had an economic as well as a political base.

Hausa towns were, therefore, made up of radial residential sectors hung around the three main institutions of the town: the palace, the mosque and the market. They were defended not only by armies, but also by impressive
278–81, 296 walls often up to 15 m high. Entry was through gates from which wide avenues led to the centre of the town. These broad thoroughfares not only coped with market traffic efficiently, but facilitated the easy passage of troops to the walls in time of attack and the enormous political processions which accompanied the main religious festivals. They would also have impressed visitors and perhaps discouraged them from wandering off into the narrow and tortuous lanes and alleys between the houses.

One striking feature of Hausa town architecture is its physical

distinctiveness from that of the surrounding countryside. House and boundary walls and roofs in the towns were built of mud, whereas in the
291 villages the roofs were almost always of grass and boundary walls were of matting or corn stalks; the basic house walls were often made of mud. (The possible origins of Hausa town architecture and its relationship with the architecture of the Upper Niger towns is discussed in Chapter 6.)

The Chad Basin, the crossroads of Africa, has perhaps the longest tradition of continuous urbanism in the whole continent outside the North African littoral and the Lower Nile. The empire of Kanem–Bornu, established in the ninth century, controlled virtually the whole of the Chad Basin by the sixteenth century. It stretched from Tibesti in the north to the Zaïre Basin watershed in the south and from the Aïr Mountains in the west to Darfur in the east. Traditions point to a gradual peaceful infiltration of peoples, from Darfur and the cities of the Nile and from North Africa, who came to live alongside the early inhabitants of the Chad Basin; the mixture produced the earliest state. The basis of the empire was trade between the forest zone and North Africa, Darfur and the Nile. A network of cities administered the empire and organized the trade. The earliest capital, Njimi, has yet to be positively located, but the remains of Ngazagarmo, which was the capital from the fifteenth century to the early nineteenth century, and Kukawa, which became the capital in 1814, can still be seen. In the seventeenth century, at the height of its power, Ngazagarmo covered about 1500 ha and contained about a quarter of a million people. An account of the city written in 1658 says that it contained four Friday mosques and 'six hundred and
301 sixty roads cleared and widened called Le'.[4] Barth[5] visited Kukawa and described it as follows:

> it is in two distinct towns, each surrounded with its wall, the one occupied chiefly by the rich and wealthy, containing very large establishments, while the other, with the exception of the principal thoroughfare which traverses the town from west to east, consists of rather crowded dwellings, with narrow winding lanes. These two distinct towns are separated by a space about half a mile broad, itself thickly inhabited on both sides of a wide open road which forms the connection between them.'

The style of Kanem–Bornu houses and the defensive arrangements of the towns are discussed in Chapters 5 and 9.

The Forest Zone of West Africa

The states in the forest zones to the south of Hausaland grew up more slowly. No exact dates for their foundation have been advanced, but certainly until the introduction of iron the forest areas may not have been capable of sustaining any very large populations. After the fifteenth century, trade with Europeans along the coast and, more importantly, trade with the Muslim areas to the north almost certainly encouraged their growth.
138–147 The Yoruba towns all exhibit a remarkable similarity of plan and it seems likely that they were all conscious imitations of the major towns of Ile-Ife or
141 Oyo. Their dominant features were the palace of the oba and the principal market next to one another in the centre of the town; the main grove or temple; and two wide roads crossing at the centre. Also noteworthy was the

lack of any specialist areas: all craft work was carried on in houses and people practising the same craft were not grouped together in any way. Perhaps this was to ensure that no one group became powerful enough to be disruptive. The minor roads of the towns divided them into 'quarters' and each quarter had a chief to whom all the heads of compounds in his quarter were responsible, and who in turn was responsible to the oba. These quarters were arranged round the palace in a sort of satellite formation, making each area of the town fairly homogeneous.

This spatial arrangement lends support to the idea of colonial dominance discussed earlier in the chapter. Today many of the towns have lost their distinctive spatial arrangement and are composed mainly of farmers. This is a result of the troubled years of the nineteenth century when many farmers fled for safety into the towns and built houses for themselves in between the existing ones. But long before this latest change the towns had developed into trading centres when the Hausa towns to the north prospered after the fifteenth century, supplying them mainly with kolanuts.

The Coast of East Africa

Just as the revival of international trade with the Mediterranean area in medieval times seems to have affected the growth of states in parts of West Africa, so along the East African coast a similar effect was observed. In East Africa the demand was not only for gold but also for tortoiseshell and ivory, the latter finding its way to India and China. The ports along the coast quickly responded to the increased demand and a network of trade routes grew up from the gold mines and hunting areas of South-East Africa to the ports. At the ports the goods were loaded onto the dhows of Arab sailors and ships of Indian and, on occasion, Chinese merchants who sailed south down the East African coast from port to port with the monsoon winds between December and March, and back north again (as the winds changed) from April to October.

These trading cities, it seems, were initially founded by Muslim traders, possibly from Arabia, settling along the seaboard and marrying local women. By the thirteenth century they had become thriving city states with a distinctive Muslim Swahili civilization of their own. Mogadishu, Mombasa, Zanzibar and Kilwa were probably the most prominent and well known. Each of these states was ruled by a king who levied heavy tariffs from visiting merchants and much of this wealth seems to have been spent on embellishing palaces, mosques and houses. All contemporary descriptions of 310–324 the towns refer to the fineness, grandness and wealth of the buildings. Such, indeed, was the wealth of the towns that many of the goods that were imported in exchange for the gold and ivory were luxury items such as Chinese and Persian porcelain, Indian cotton and glass beads. So much porcelain was imported that fragments still litter the beaches of the coast.

In contrast to the hegemonies of the empires of the Sudan, the city states of the East African coast never sustained hegemonies over the hinterland. In some cases they controlled smaller ports along the coast, for instance, Kilwa controlled Sofala, the outlet for gold traffic, but otherwise they remained perched and isolated on the edge of the sea, prosperous crossroads of the land and sea traffic. Their inhabitants were neither sailors nor manufacturers, but mostly shrewd middlemen, with perhaps a few craftsmen fashioning goods in gold, ivory and probably copper for home consumption.

Portuguese intervention in the late fifteenth and early sixteenth centuries did much to interrupt the trade of these towns and this, compounded with the effects of the migrations of the Galla from the north and the marauding Zimba from the south in the late sixteenth and early seventeenth centuries, finally brought about the downfall of many of them, including Gedi. Some settlements revived with the onset of new trading links after the expulsion of the Portuguese in the mid-seventeenth century, but by the early nineteenth century most had come under the direct rule of the Omani Arabs of Zanzibar.

Most of the towns were undefended until the eighteenth century apart from some poorly constructed town walls, because the inhabitants relied on cooperation with the hinterland. Although the physical appearance of the towns would seem to indicate a dichotomy between Swahili merchants and the local townspeople, as some houses were constructed of stone while the majority were of mud and timber, recent research at Lamu[6] has indicated that there was much social mobility between the two sorts of houses and that the homogeneity in the population documented in the late eighteenth and early nineteenth centuries was probably present much earlier.

Inland East Africa

The trading demands of these coastal states naturally influenced the political organization of peoples at the inland end of the trade. This was most noticeable in central Africa, and also further north the Nyamwezi became highly efficient organizers of the ivory trade with powerful chiefs. Possibly, too, the large stone-built ruined town of Engaruku on the slopes of Ngorongoro, with its many hundreds of round stone-built houses stretching over 5 km on terraces above the Rift Valley, was once the centre of a state which traded with the coast. In central Africa, the Shona, who organized goldmining and ivory collecting between the Zambesi and Limpopo rivers, established first the kingdom of Monomatapa and later the Urozwi empire. Within these empires a network of towns grew up to organize the trade. The most famous was Zimbabwe with its great stone temple and palace (see Chapter 4).

43–8

Inland in East Africa the formation of states did not always result in the growth of towns and was not always stimulated by trade. Many small states seem to have developed to cope with problems rising from a population growing because of the introduction of new technology, such as iron working, and new crops like maize.

More complex societies with significant physical centralization sometimes seem to have formed when there was an interaction between these small states and newcomers, especially pastoralists, from outside the area. Many legends mention immigrants from 'the north'. For instance, by about 1300 Hima pastoralists had reached what is now Uganda and the relationships they established with the agriculturalists already there produced the powerful Chwezi kingdom. The Hima chiefs seem to have ruled from large fortified towns such as Bigo and Kabengo. These towns were surrounded by defensive ditches sometimes cut right into the bedrock, and within the towns the chief's house and cattle kraal were also surrounded by ditches. The towns were often more than 1 km across and within each there was a central mound. It is interesting to note here the similarities with the West

African Hausa and Yoruba towns: they were also large and fortified; they contained a central mound; and it has been conjectured that they were also founded by immigrants.

It must be noted that the influx of pastoralists did not in all areas result in the development of states. Sometimes quite the reverse took place. For example, the state of Engaruku seems to have been completely destroyed by invading pastoralists.

Towards 1500 other groups of pastoralists moved southwards, eventually displacing the Chwezi rulers and being formative in the foundations of the
192–201 kingdoms of Bunyoro–Kitara, Ankole, Buganda, Ruanda and Burundi. These kingdoms all had one thing in common: they were dominated by pastoralists who ruled and defended the kingdoms while the agriculturalists were the food producers. Most of these kingdoms persisted until the twentieth century and something is therefore known about the layout of their towns.

By about 1750 Buganda was the largest and most powerful kingdom northwest of Lake Nyanza. Trade with the east coast (via Karagwe and Nyamweziland) was an important source of its wealth, and the state had become highly centralized with the kabaka (or king) wielding enormous power.

The capital of the Ganda kingdom was organized on a radial basis like the Yoruba towns described above. The palace was the focus of the main roads
199–200 leading to the various districts and the houses of the chiefs were on the side of the capital nearest their own districts. The one fundamental difference between a Yoruba town and a Buganda capital was that the latter was impermanent. Each new kabaka built a completely new capital on a new site on his accession and sometimes also during his reign as well. Similarly, Ankole rulers built new capitals every few years. It seems possible that both the Ganda and Ankole, although settled, were displaying features of the pastoralist origins.

Central Africa

In west central Africa a similar process of state formation took place from as early as the fifteenth century. Here the pattern was similar to Buganda and Bunyoro–Kitara with a small powerful group of invaders fusing with an already settled cohesive group, producing centralized states which then entered into trading relationships. By the fifteenth century, when the
57–9 Portuguese first arrived at the River Zaïre, the Kongo kingdom was flourishing with a large capital city at Mbanza. In the eighteenth century the most powerful state was the Lunda under Luba chiefs, who organized the ivory trade, while in the nineteenth century Kazembe became the most important. Antonio Gamitto, who headed a Portuguese expedition to Kazembe in 1831, described its capital as 'perhaps the greatest town of central Africa'. Unfortunately little is known of the social and spatial organization of these towns, although their splendour always impressed European visitors.

Conclusion

In the context of this book the economic, political and social parameters of the development of large-scale societies are naturally relevant only in so far

as they can be shown to have influenced the built environment. Taking transportation as one factor, it seems clear that many towns were situated at the interface between one mode of transport and another and included provision for the marketing and storage of goods. The mode of transport must have affected not only the spatial organization of the towns but also the nature of individual buildings. Merchants' houses in the Swahili towns of East Africa, for example, had to handle and securely accommodate the large and valuable cargoes of the seasonal dhow traffic and inspire confidence in
319–24 their trading partners. Their large coral houses right on the seaboard provided for both these functions. In a somewhat analogous way, the urban architecture and planning of the West African Sudan zone can be seen as at least partly influenced by the requirements of the camel/porter interface.
260–2, 267 High walls and two-storey building provided not only security but also gates
269–71, 294–5 large enough to admit camel caravans. (Security in both these examples naturally includes fire protection, which is discussed in detail on p. 161.) Transport factors are of course just one component of classical location theory, and yet even they offer scope for much more detailed exploration than it is possible even to hint at here (in relation to the size and spacing of settlements, for example).

In addition to the fully-fledged traditional towns, one can identify in Africa settlements which, largely due to European colonization, appear to have been temporarily frozen at a quasi-urban developmental stage. It is tempting to speculate that, given a few years of independent existence,
71–85 settlements like the small kingdoms of the Bamenda highlands might well have begun to exhibit a wider range of urban characteristics. The study of
105–12 such areas (and there are several, including arguably Iboland) could advance in interesting ways the interrelationship between architecture, history and urbanization theory.

The coverage of this chapter has inevitably been somewhat patchy but, as throughout the book, information on many other specific examples appears in other chapters and more particularly in the captions to the illustrations, to which this material can be seen as a commentary.

REFERENCES

1. Mabogunje, A. L., *Urbanisation in Nigeria* (London, 1968)
2. Miner, H., *The Primitive City of Timbuktu* (Princeton, N.J., 1953)
3. Fage, J. D., 'Some Thoughts on Migration and Urban Settlement' in Kuper, H. (ed.), *Urbanisation and Migration in West Africa* (London, 1965)
4. Quoted in Hogben, S. J., and Kirk-Greene, A. H. M., *The Emirates of Northern Nigeria* (London, 1966)
5. Barth, H., *Travels and Discoveries in North and Central Africa 1849–1855*, centenary edition (London, 1965)
6. Allen, J. de V., 'Swahili Culture Reconsidered', *Azania*, IX (1974)

Illustration Section III

50 *Nyakusa house, southern Tanzania, about 1900.* The Nyakusa live in the Rungwe Mountains which rise to 3000 m at the northern end of Lake Malawi. It is an area of a high rainfall of over 2500 mm a year. The extremely fertile soils are volcanic in origin and can grow a wide variety of crops. The Nyakusa were originally cattle owners and fixed cultivators who practised green manuring and crop rotation. Their homesteads, each surrounded by a banana grove, were built compactly in groups with the main fields on the fringes of the villages. Their remote valleys were scarcely touched by the upheavals of the nineteenth century and their villages remained unfortified. Their houses were built of bamboo which was indigenous to this area. It was used for walls, roof structure and doors. The doors of Nyakusa houses were unusual in not having a high threshold.

51 *Nyakusa house, southern Tanzania, about 1900.* Nyakusa[12] houses were often divided into two rooms. In the bedroom the bed was a framework of bamboos with a log for a pillow, the whole covered with many layers of mats of decreasing fineness towards the bottom of the pile. Notice the bamboo chairs in the foreground of the photograph.

52 *Nyakusa house, southern Tanzania, about 1900.* This building doubled as a cattle house and house for the cowherds. The door was made of narrow bamboo canes, which were lashed to delineate the chevron pattern. The door was then plastered with ochre mud and alternate spaces were painted white.

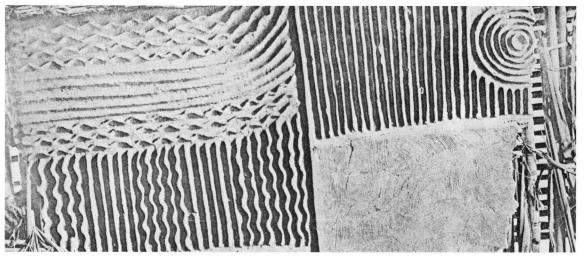

53 *Nyakusa chief's house, southern Tanzania, about 1900.* The spaces between the bamboo uprights of the walls were packed with small pebbles. The interiors were then plastered with red mud. This photograph, which was taken inside, shows how the plastered surface was sometimes worked into a swirling relief pattern.

54 *Nyakusa house, detail, southern Tanzania, 1966.* Notice how the upright bamboos have been slashed to straighten them.

41

55 *Nyasa village, Mbamba Bay, south-western Tanzania, about 1900*. This shows a fishing village right on the edge of Lake Malawi. The houses would have been well sheltered from the often severe lake storms which can blow up suddenly there. Nyasa is a term which covers many small groups of fishermen (including some twentieth-century immigrants) who live along the lake shores. Fishermen were among the more mobile sections of the population; they moved frequently from one lake to another in East Africa. (In West Africa they travelled huge distances along the coast recently helping to spread cholera.) Pile dwellings were built characteristically by fishermen in many parts of Africa.

56 *Ijo village, southern Nigeria, about 1925*. The Ijo, who are made up of some forty sub-groups, live in the Niger Delta and along neighbouring creeks and islands. Their economy was originally based on fishing and salt boiling but from early times they were engaged in trading and transportation as well, forming themselves into small 'village states'. Bonny, for example, was already well established when the Portuguese sea captain, Pereira, visited it in about 1500. Ijo houses were rectangular in plan with walls of mangrove poles, palm midribs or cleft planks, the interstices occasionally filled with mud, and with roofs of palm mats. The houses were divided internally into two or three rooms with the kitchen at one end over which were racks for storing or smoking fish. Many houses were raised on stilts as in this photograph. The rainfall is over 4000 mm a year and the vegetation is mostly mangrove swamps.

57 *Kongo house, Angola, about 1910*. The Kongo peoples, whose empire was powerful for several centuries before the late seventeenth century, occupy a large area in the north of Angola and a small part of south-western Zaïre. Their territory covers both the plain and part of the uplands which rise to 1060 m and runs almost from Luanda to Kinshasa, including much land which is not forest. The house walls were of palm fronds and the roofs of palm or reed thatch. The villages were formed of groups of houses arranged in a square around a central open space.

58 *Kongo granaries, Angola, about 1910.*

59 *Kongo door, Angola, about 1910.*

60 *Ngongo house, Zaïre, about 1910.* The Ngongo comprised a small community living on the borders of the forest and savannah in undulating country.

61 *House under construction, Bolobo, Zaïre, about 1910.*

62 *Kuba chief's house, Bushongo, Zaïre, 1928.* The Kuba live between the Kasai and Sankuri rivers in central Zaïre. Their houses were constructed in a similar way to Kongo and Ngongo houses although much finer and more decorative tie mats faced the framework, especially in the chiefs' houses. Each homestead was surrounded by tall matting fences and the entrance to the chief's house was through a gate hinged at the top and over a high threshold.

63 *Kuba house under construction, Zaïre, about 1910.*

64 *Kuba chief's house, detail of walls, Mushenge, Zaïre, 1949.* These 'mats' were made by tying split palms to closely spaced reeds.

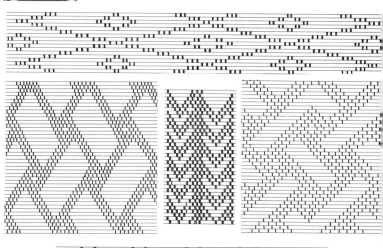

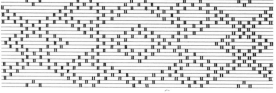

65 *Drawings of Kuba wall mats, Zaïre, about 1910.* Torday and Joyce identified fifteen different patterns used in the wall mats.[13]

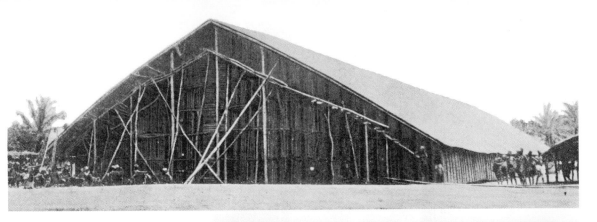

66 *Mangbettu assembly hall, Zaïre, about 1910.* In contrast to the round houses (see no. 238), the Mangbettu assembly halls (and chiefs' houses) were immense rectangular buildings sometimes as large as 90 m by 50 m in plan and 15 m high. They were built from polished palm fronds with walls of woven matting.

67 *Mangbettu assembly hall, Zaïre, about 1950.* The Mangbettu assembly halls are no longer built in quite the same way as in no. 66. The new style has a steeper saddle-backed roof resting on a row of open posts and with an inset thatched gable at each end. The photograph shows the interior of one of these new types. The geometric and figurative mural paintings are similar to those found on the walls of houses (see no. 238).

68 *Yako house under construction, south-eastern Nigeria, about 1935.* The Yako live on the southern borders of Nigeria and Cameroon. They traditionally built their houses of palm fronds with a palm thatched roof. Palm mats (described in Chapter 6) can be seen in front of the house. These houses were much more similar to houses in the southern Cameroon and the Zaïre Basin than to the houses of their neighbours to the west and south.

45

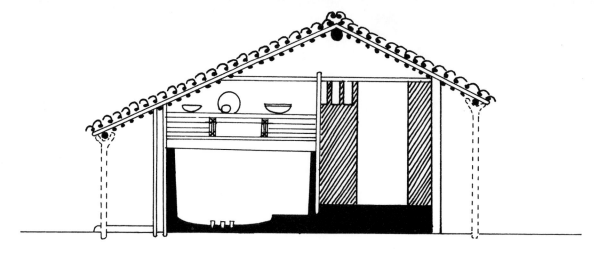

CROSS-SECTION A–B

0 1 2 m

69 *Plans and cross-section of Yako houses, south-eastern Nigeria, about 1935.*

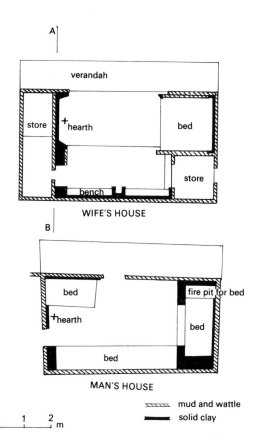

verandah

store + hearth

bed

store

bench

WIFE'S HOUSE

bed

+ hearth

fire pit for bed

bed

bed

MAN'S HOUSE

 mud and wattle
solid clay

0 1 2 m

70 *Interior of Yako woman's house, south-eastern Nigeria, about 1935.*

71 *Bamileke chief's house, Bana, Cameroon, about 1914.* The dissected plateau over 900 m high of largely volcanic origin in western Cameroon has a big rainfall (about 2500 mm a year) and supports lush grassland vegetation with forest remnants in the valley heads. The Bamileke live in this area in dense clusters of houses forming large villages (and formerly small kingdoms).

72 *Bamileke homestead, Bana, Cameroon, about 1914.* Notice the porch on the building on the right of the photograph.

73 *Bamileke doorway, Bana, Cameroon, about 1914.*

74 *Diagrams of a Bamileke house, Cameroon.* These diagrams show the elaborate framework necessary to make a conical roof sit on square walls. The walls of the houses were built of palm fronds or bamboo infilled with mud. The platform of the roof was made on the floor and then lifted to the top of the walls.

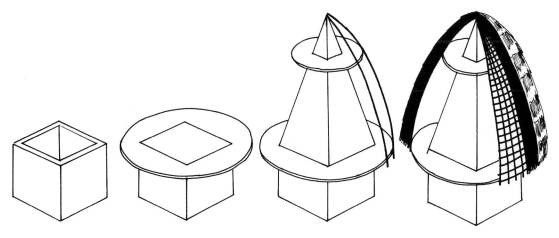

75 *Bamileke boy's house, Bandjoun, Cameroon, about 1965.*   **76** *Bamileke granary, Cameroon, about 1965.*

77 *Plan of Bamileke homestead, Cameroon, about 1960.* Notice that the house belonging to the head of the household was ringed by pillars to form a kind of verandah. In a village these homesteads were grouped around the homestead of the chief.

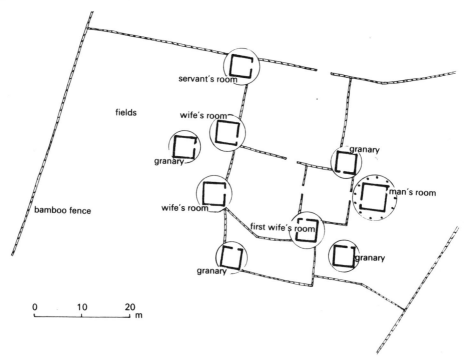

78 *Plan of Bamileke chief's house, Batoufam, Cameroon, about 1960.*

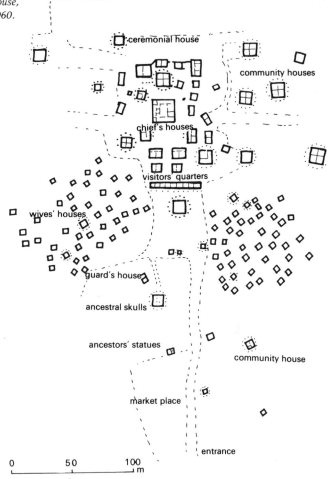

ceremonial house

community houses

chief's houses

visitors' quarters

wives' houses

guard's house

ancestral skulls

ancestors' statues

community house

market place

entrance

0   50   100
m

79 *Tikar palace, Bafut, Cameroon, about 1960.* The town of Bafut covers an area almost eight kilometres long and is divided into twenty-six wards by hedges dotted with scarlet hibiscus flowers. This building was the Achum (shrine) of the Fon (chief) of Bafut. It was built in about 1907 after an earlier one had been burned down by the Germans. It rested on a base of vertical black basalt columns. The basalt is found in veins in the nearby volcanic granite hills. The quantity of grass needed for thatching such a building is considerable and every year the Fon used to organize a grass gathering ceremony when villagers cut enough grass to thatch the palace buildings in return for victuals and entertainment.[14]

80 *Tikar house, Bali, Cameroon, about 1965.* Each building in a Tikar house was generally about 4 m square and divided into two rooms. In this plate the whole building rests on a stone platform. In some areas round houses were built (see no. 249).

81 *Tikar ancestor house, Bamenda, western Cameroon, about 1958.* The western Cameroon grasslands present rather a difficult cultural and social picture. Some commentators have divided the people into small village states each with its own separate name, whereas others have conceived of them as belonging to one of the three major clusters, the Bamileke, Bamoun and the Tikar. Neither system entirely coincides with architectural style. This house is similar to the Bamileke houses shown (nos. 71–9) but has a square roof plan.

82 *Tikar council hall, doorway, Kumbo, Cameroon, about 1949.* This building was 21 m long and 11 m wide. The high pitched roof was covered with thick grass thatch.

83 *Bamoun chief's house, Cameroon, about 1914.* Like the Bamileke, the Bamoun live in the grasslands plateau but further north. The elaborate friezes under the eaves were made of small bundles of grasses, some dyed, fixed into a lattice framework.

84 *Bamoun houses under construction, Cameroon, about 1914.* As in Bamileke houses (see nos. 71–81), the roofs rested on platforms built on top of the walls.

85 *Bamoun town gate, Foumban, Cameroon, about 1965.*

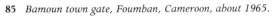

4 Sacred, Ceremonial and Community Buildings

Tropical Africa has been so rich in sacred, ceremonial and community activities that outsiders might expect a wealth of buildings especially designed for these purposes. In fact, however, the weather is generally so warm and the rain so predictable that many such activities can be performed in the open air. One should not, however, make the mistake of supposing that no importance was attached to their locations. A piece of apparently empty and unused land often turns out to have a special significance and a visit may reveal it to be the site of parliamentary or council meetings, of certain religious ceremonies or the village dancing ground. Often such places are demarcated only by a hedge or fence (as in Galla villages) or by proximity to a certain tree or trees (in one Nandi village, six wild fig trees).[1] (Intriguingly, Henrici has identified the fig tree as a component of the flora of the proto-Bantu-speaking peoples, using statistical methods on linguistic data.[2]) A survey of these places would be extremely interesting, but a small book on architecture is not really the place to launch into it. We shall concentrate here upon what are essentially the exceptions.

Indigenous African Religions

African religions have often been dismissed as 'pagan' or 'animistic', but they cannot be described or explained so simply. There was an enormous diversity in beliefs, but one can trace certain broad similarities. Religion permeated almost every part of life. It was man's concern with an assembly of forces both inside and outside the community—single gods, pantheons, ancestors, natural forces, for instance—who could lend assistance in every part of life from birth to death. Religion was by no means a way of escaping from the harsh realities of this world, but was very much a part of living. However the various supernatural forces were thought of, they had to be contacted in some way. These acts of propitiation, invocation or worship took many individual and communal forms throughout the continent, and whereas actual buildings for the participants were uncommon, shrines were much less so. Among the Bini, Yoruba, Asante and Kipsigis, for instance, shrines were altars inside ordinary dwelling houses. More commonly, a place, perhaps under a shady tree, was kept sacred and maybe embellished with ritual objects and occasionally roofed over.

133

The Ibo constructed an unusual *mbari* building which can perhaps be called an elaborate shrine, in that it was connected with worship. It was, however, really more of a religious monument since it was not frequently visited as most shrines are, and once built was left to decay. Here it was the act of building or the act of creating which was the act of worship, and once put up the building was ignored. Everything in it, as well as the structure itself, was completed in the best possible way and much more attention

110

seemed to be lavished on it than on an ordinary dwelling place.[3] Until quite recently the *mbari* shrine was often the only building in a village to boast a tin roof, but this was not put on to increase the building's longevity but because it was considered that a tin roof was superior to thatch.

Before the appearance of corrugated iron, these shrines were roofed with a striking tall pyramid of palm thatch which was in distinct contrast to the lower hipped roofs of ordinary houses. This pyramid rested on four stout square pillars elaborately moulded and painted in geometrical shapes. The side walls were open so that the almost life-size figures inside could be seen from the outside.

Temples seem generally to have been built only where worship involved one or more intermediaries or priests. These priests would then be responsible for the upkeep of the temple. Some Ganda temples had up to four priests as well as mediums and women servants. Other peoples who built 122–3 temples were the Asante, Sogo, Shona, Sonjo and Yoruba. The Asante temples were built on the courtyard pattern, with four distinct buildings joined in a square. Three of these buildings were usually open to the courtyard, while the fourth was partially closed with openwork screens or windows and an opening or door.[4] But even with these temples the ceremony was sometimes performed in the open air in the courtyard while the three rooms which opened onto the courtyard housed drummers, female musicians, spectators and supplicants and the fourth closed room was a shrine, the 'potential abode of a supernatural presence',[5] and the domain of the priest or mouthpiece of the God. Yoruba 147 temples were often floored with decorative mosaic pavements (as were some of their sacred groves).

Christianity

What has been said above refers of course to the indigenous religious beliefs of sub-Saharan Africa and not to Islam or Christianity. Christianity was established while still in its infancy over much of North Africa, Egypt, Sudan and Ethiopia, but it survived only in parts after the Muslim invasion of the seventh century.

Coptic Christianity had apparently gained acceptance in Axum by the fourth or fifth century. Most of the monumental Christian churches which remain date from after the Ethiopian capital had moved to Lasta and the Amharic empire was flourishing between the tenth and the fifteenth or sixteenth centuries. Broadly speaking there were two types of ground plans and two types of building techniques. Most churches had between three and five aisles and were either basilican in plan with a western arcaded porch and an eastern sanctuary or they had a 'cross-in-square' plan with a well-marked transverse axis. Some churches were constructed in wood and stone using 328–9 Axumite building techniques (see Chapter 6), while other more remarkable 325–7 ones were hewn out of solid rock. In the early ones roofs were flat, resting on lintels between piers and walls, whereas later on barrel vaults, domes and arches were used.[6] These were the monumental churches of the towns. In the rural areas the churches were more modest. Today most of these rural 212 churches are round in plan with conical thatched roofs and walls of wattle and mud or stone. But it seems that the round plan has only become popular in the last hundred years. Even the rectangular churches have lost all traces of the basilican plan. Previously, it seems, rural churches were nearly always

329 rectangular in plan with stone walls and flat roofs, raised to a higher level over the sanctuary.[7]

It was not until the nineteenth century and the arrival of many missionaries from Europe that Christianity really began to take root in middle Africa. Although from the fifteenth century Portuguese Catholics had worked along the west and east coasts, their work did not penetrate to the interior or to any sizeable number of Africans. Christianity demands regular communal worship by its members in a consecrated building. Although the churches which have been built over the last century in the new Christian communities have often utilized purely local materials, most were built to emulate European prototypes and are therefore not discussed here.

Islam

Islam swept across North Africa and down into the Horn of Africa within a century of Mohammed's death in 632, encountering and fighting the already established Christianity which it superseded everywhere except in Ethiopia and Nubia. With the organization of the Muslim empire, trade routes were established down the east coast of Africa and across the Sahara into West Africa and with the traders went their religion and its obligation of communal Friday prayer in a mosque.

Although Islam dictates that followers should worship communally on Friday it does not specify that the mosque should be anything more than a dedicated space set aside for the purpose of worship and oriented towards Mecca. Along the coast of East Africa today, the most common mosque is simply a clean brushed space, rectangular in plan with an apse shape at one end and demarcated by a row of stones. In Egypt it seems that roofs were not put on some of the mosques until the fourteenth century. Until then they remained walled courtyards no doubt similar to the one in which the Prophet first led public prayers. In many parts, including West Africa, prayers on days of the week other than Friday are still often conducted in open-air mosques.

Along the east coast the fusion of Arab and local culture produced the Swahili civilization with its own language and architecture. Although the city states which flourished there have long since vanished, much of the architecture survives as it was produced in durable coral and cement. One of
310–5 its most beautiful buildings is the Great Mosque perched on Kilwa Island just off the mainland of Tanzania. It is built on a square plan divided into square bays, and each bay is roofed with a dome resting on pillars edged with dressed coral. The mosque was obviously altered and enlarged several times, but the present building seems to date from the fifteenth century. Although many other 'medieval' Swahili mosques have survived up and down the coast, none approximate to the size and grandeur of the one at Kilwa. Most are rectangular in plan with an arched mihrab at one end; the arches are sometimes trefoil, sometimes three centred, and are often edged with dressed coral.

In West Africa the main feature of the larger traditional mosques is the minaret or tall tower, which is conspicuously absent from the mosques of
265, 274 East Africa. These minarets all taper towards the top and are on a square base; inside a staircase leads to the top platform whence the muezzin calls.
263–5 The mosque building is usually basically rectangular and divided into square

268, 272, 293 bays, the roof being supported in the centre on square pillars. Sometimes the roofs are exceedingly low, as in the Agadez mosque, giving barely enough room for a man to stand upright. Minaret and mosque are sometimes both contained within a walled courtyard.

Tradition attributes the flat roofs and tapering minarets of Sudanese mosques to the celebrated El Saheli whose legendary influence is discussed again on p. 163. It is difficult to say what exactly he did or did not do, but it is certain that all mosques concerned have been rebuilt many times since the fourteenth century. (The one exception may be a mosque in Gao, which is now flattened but whose foundations are still visible.) Leo Africanus visiting
268 Timbuktu in the early sixteenth century described the Jingereber mosque as 'a most stately temple with walls of stone and lime'.[8] This mosque was subsequently demolished and rebuilt in 1570, but is is possible that the building Leo Africanus saw could have been built in El Saheli's time.

Secular power

The position of the monarchy in tropical Africa has already been touched upon briefly in earlier chapters. In rural areas, chiefs' houses were rarely specially walled or fenced off. Indeed often they were only distinguished by their focal position in the village. In almost all societies the chief's house was not distinctly different from the commoners' houses, but was rather a larger, grander or more elaborate version of theirs and built using the same materials.

The way a chief's house was distinguished depended to a large extent on the environment and the building materials. A fairly common arrangement in those forest areas where houses were built from puddled mud and erected in courses of defined height, was that custom reserved certain numbers of courses for nobles and chiefs, and commoners were obliged to build their houses with fewer courses. This scaling-up process was quite widespread.
71, 78–9 For instance in the Bamenda grasslands the main palace buildings were constructed of exactly the same materials, lashed palm walls and grass thatch, as ordinary houses, but they had walls as much as 10 m high. As the chiefs had many more wives than commoners did, the buildings in the palaces were also much more densely grouped than in commoners' compounds. Elaborate decoration in the form of carved hardwood verandah posts and door frames was also reserved for the main palace buildings.

In the kingdom of Buganda it was the custom (as we have seen) for each new kabaka to build a completely new capital, including a palace on a new
199 site when he came to power. These palaces were composed of over four hundred buildings, all like ordinary houses but very much larger. They were always organized in a similar fashion with the buildings facing roads laid out on a grid pattern, and they contained not only buildings for the king, his wives and retainers, storehouses, stables, kitchens and a bath house, but also court houses in which the kabaka tried cases of appeal. Ankole palaces were
201 built in the same sort of way with each new ruler establishing a new palace on a new site.[9]

The Shilluk occupy a densely populated strip of land along the clay plains which border the White Nile. Villages were situated on low natural knolls. At Fashoda, the royal capital, the king's house was built like the commoners' houses but was elevated on a large imposing artificial mound, about 3 m

234 high, known as *Aturwic*.[10] This immediately distinguished his house from the others which were built round it on more or less level bare ground.

In south central Africa, in the old empires of Urozwi and Monomatapa, are
43–8 the spectacular remains of the stone built *zimbabwes* or palaces. When analysed they can be seen to be translations into stone of more humble houses. The outer walls and cattle kraals were built of dressed stone while the main buildings within the walls retained the mud and wattle construction. Here, then, dressed stone seems to have become a royal prerogative.

In Yorubaland the houses were built on a courtyard plan: four rectangular units faced one another with the roof on the courtyard side supported by pillars. The palaces were multiplications of this basic courtyard unit. The
142 supporting roof-posts were also more elaborately carved than in ordinary houses and adorned the outside as well as the inside of the building. A special
144–5 raised and projecting gable feature, known as *kobi*, was reserved for the houses of obas and high chiefs. These Yoruba palaces were surrounded by a mud wall which usually enclosed a large area of forest land as well as the palace buildings. Clapperton reported that the palace of Old Oyo covered an
141 area of about 260 ha of land. Today the largest palace is at Owo and its land covers 44 ha of which 40 ha is forest. Palaces sometimes had as many as a hundred courtyards, each one of them often of enormous size and far larger than in an ordinary house. The largest one at Oyo was said to be about twice as large as a football field. Each of the courtyards was reserved for a special function. The biggest was used for public assemblies or dancing at festivals, while the smaller ones were reserved for the oba's private use. In a few
147 palaces these courtyards were paved with quartz pebbles and potsherds. The palaces have been very well described by Ojo.[11]

The palace of Benin was first visited by the Portuguese in 1472 and between then and its sacking by the British in 1897 many visitors published descriptions of it. Some are tantalizingly vague and others mutually contradictory, but altogether they reveal a large and fascinating building which like palaces anywhere else in the world fluctuated in size and grandeur as the fortunes of its kingdom rose and fell.
126 One of the earliest drawings of the palace was published by Dapper[12] in 1668. It shows several tall rectangular buildings with hipped roofs surmounted in the centre by tall turrets crowned with models of birds. Two of the palace buildings appear to be thatched with shingles and one with palm leaves. Dapper himself did not visit Africa and the picture he published is often considered to be largely a flight of fancy. Close examination of it, however, makes it seem as if the artist—whoever he was—went to great pains to represent certain features accurately (though admittedly the background seems to be non-African). The way the groins were finished on the thatched turret is carefully shown; and this was done in exactly the same way as on the pyramidal roofs of many Ibo *mbari* shrines. Also the thatch on the hipped roof was secured with palm fronds bent over the ridge in a way
127 which is identical to hipped thatched roofs still seen in southern Cameroon. Many writers commented on the size of the king's palace and Burton[13] said it was supposed to accommodate fifteen thousand people. It seems that many of
129–34 the palace buildings were similar to the impluvium houses of the ordinary people of Benin, but how these buildings were organized into a palace is not clear. Both Dapper and Nyandael mention a particularly long gallery resting on fifty-eight square pillars which Dapper says were covered with 'bronze'

plaques. It seems the turrets, crowned with 'bronze' birds and faced with 'bronze' serpents, were the prerogative of the king and his chiefs, as was horizontal fluting applied to the mud walls. Another distinction was that the king was allowed up to seven building courses, whereas commoners were only allowed three and nobles five.

Recent excavations at Ife[14] on a fourteenth-century site have produced a most interesting terracotta pot. On one side it has a relief model of a rectangular house, with what appear to be three carved pillars holding up the saddleback roof. Entwined round the neck of the pot with its head over the centre of the house roof is a large snake. In view of the tentative connections that have been made between Ife and Benin art this is of considerable interest (see also Chapter 7).

In considering the palaces of centralized societies it is important to remember that they housed not only the personal residence of the ruler but also the seat of government. In Hausaland some of the emirs' palaces were almost towns within their own right. The Kano palace occupied over 13 ha and was surrounded by a wall 9 m high. Dr Barth[15] described it as a 'real labyrinth of courtyards provided with spacious round huts of audience, built of clay, with a door on each side and connected together by narrow intricate passages'. Notice he mentions round huts. Round houses are not now common in Hausa towns. One wonders how much these were due to the influence of the Fulani emirs who came to power after the Jihad at the beginning of the nineteenth century. An earlier visitor to Kano, Denham,[16] described how the palace contained a mosque and also 'several towers three or four stories high . . . . It is necessary to pass through two of these towers in order to gain some of the inner apartments.' Most of the Hausa palaces were built like houses, but with the individual courtyard units multiplied many times. The surface decoration was, however, given much more elaborate treatment than in houses. At Kano some of the walls were inset with small pieces of mica, which glinted in the light, and the vaulted ceilings were painted all over with elaborate geometrical designs and sometimes inset with plates.

In each of the Swahili towns of the East African coast there was usually one stone building that was substantially larger than the rest. In nearly all the towns except Kilwa, these palaces were not substantially different in plan from the houses; they were grander in size rather than in quality. They had a central core similar to a house with rooms opening onto a courtyard and beyond that similar quarters for courtiers' wives, and so on. The one exception was the palace of Husuni Kubwa at Kilwa. Perched on the edge of the cliffs this thirteenth-century building was quite unique. Although it did contain a domestic core resembling later houses, it also had as its main axis a central corridor, roofed with elaborate domes, and leading from it various arcaded courts, pavilions and an octagonal swimming pool. It was on a scale and plan never subsequently emulated and it appears to be a completely alien intrusion on the East African coast scene.

In societies with less autocratic constitutions, most decisions were taken in the open air. Where specialized meeting halls existed, however, it is interesting to note that they tended not to mirror the form of ordinary houses. The enormous Mangbettu assembly halls were rectangular in plan while the houses were circular; Tikar council chambers were oblong while the houses were square or round in plan; Bende Ibo club houses were rectangular and under one roof while the houses were built on the courtyard pattern. The Poro houses of Sierra Leone and neighbouring Guinea, built by members of the Poro secret society whose members were drawn from the Loko, Limba, Mende and Temne peoples, had elaborately arched roofs with a steep drop in thatch at the front above a wide verandah and were in distinct contrast to the round plan conical roof buildings of the homesteads.

Conclusion

Summing up this chapter, it is well worth observing that, whereas palaces were almost invariably built in precisely the same idiom as ordinary houses, the churches and mosques clearly maintained strong elements of their non-African antecedents. In rural Ethiopian churches there is evidence of some stylistic assimilation after 1500 years. One might expect that shrines would show a similar or even stronger tendency to remain unchanged in form and, if it is accepted that they could represent a relict style, a detailed study of their architecture might provide useful evidence on earlier styles of housing. Bobo Fing and Gwari ancestor houses are mentioned in this context elsewhere. Could the meeting houses mentioned above be seen in this light too? A more general discussion of stylistic shift appears in Chapter 9.

REFERENCES

1. Adamson, J., *The Peoples of Kenya* (London, 1967)
2. Henrici, A., 'Numerical Classification of Bantu Languages', *African Language Studies*, 14 (1973)
3. Beier, U., *African Mud Sculpture* (Cambridge, 1963)
4. Swithenbank, M., *Ashanti Fetish Houses* (Kumasi, 1969)
5. *Ibid.*
6. Buxton, D., *The Abyssinians* (London, 1970)
7. *Ibid.*
8. Quoted in Hogben, S. J., and Kirk-Greene, A. H. M., *The Emirates of Northern Nigeria* (London, 1966)
9. Roswe, J., *The Banyankole* (Cambridge, 1923)
10. Seligman, C. G., *Pagan Tribes of the Nilotic Sudan* (London, 1932)
11. Ojo, G. J. A., *Yoruba Palaces* (London, 1966)
12. Dapper, O., *Description of Africa* (Amsterdam, 1668)
13. Quoted in Roth, L., *Great Benin* (London, 1903)
14. Garlake, P. S., 'Excavations at Obalara's Land, Ife: An Interim Report', *West African Journal of Archaeology*, 4 (1974)
15. Barth, H., *Travels and Discoveries in North and Central Africa, 1849–1855*, centenary edition (London, 1965)
16. Denham, D., Clapperton, H., and Oudney, N., *Narrative of Travels and Discoveries in Northern and Central Africa (1822–1824)* (London, 1828)

Illustration Section IV

86 *Ngelima village, Yambuya, Kisangani, Zaïre, about 1905*. Both the Ngelima and Nalya (no. 88) live between the Aruwimi and Lindi rivers, tributaries of the River Zaïre. This humid district is at the heart of the high rain forest where there is over 100 mm of rain most months of the year. Each of the houses in the village was about 2 m square. The walls, rising to about 1·5 m, were of wooden poles, while the pyramidal roof was carried to about 6 m. It was thatched with large leaves fastened in horizontal rows against a frame of basketwork.

87 *Ngelima house, Yambuya, Zaïre, about 1912.*

88 *Nalya village, Zaïre, about 1900.* The Nalya
arranged their houses in long straight avenues, devoid
of trees, while the neighbouring Panga, who built
almost identical houses, arranged them in quite a
different way. Such Panga houses were in small groups
round compounds interspersed with smaller
saddleback roofed houses and shelters supported on
polished wooden pillars. Their compounds were
enclosed by leaf screens and trees were left standing in
the compound and also along the paths connecting one
homestead to another.

89 *Bangi ngumba or meeting house, Bolobo, Zaïre, about
1880.* The Bangi live along the River Zaïre near the
Equator. Their territory covers both the thick swamps
and the forest margins further south. The rainfall
averages 1800 mm a year. Houses in Bangi villages
were arranged in a square around a central open space.
They were sometimes surrounded by stockades.
Individual buildings measured about 7·5 m by 2·5 m
and men with many wives sometimes possessed as
many as twenty of these long buildings. In all the
larger Ngala villages and in neighbouring Bangi and
Ngombe villages there was an ngumba, a guest or
meeting house as in the picture. These were about
20 m long and 6 m wide; the roofs were supported by
carved king posts; the sides were usually open.

90 *Sangi house, south-eastern Cameroon, about 1913.*
The Sangi live near the conjunction of Cameroon, the
Central African Republic and Zaïre in the dense humid
tropical forest in an area of very low sunshine and a
rainfall of 1500 mm a year. Their houses were built of
horizontal planks fastened to a framework of vertical
palm fronds. Villages were formed of long parallel rows
of houses facing each other across a wide street.

91 *Ibo house, Oratto area, south-eastern Nigeria, about 1925.* For general notes on Ibo houses see no. 105. This house was built in the forest area and had walls of roughly cleft planks.

92 *Ibo carved panels, Awka, eastern Nigeria, about 1959.* Carved panels and doors on Ibo houses, like these at Awka, seem to be confined to the Onitsha and Degema areas.

93 *Ibo carved door, Awka, eastern Nigeria, about 1959.* The carved posts on either side of the door are said to commemorate valour in war.

94 *Ngoni (?) storehouses near Songea, Tanzania, about 1900.* These buildings were probably part of an Ngoni military camp north of Songea, an outlier of Chief Schabruma's Ngoni state. (See no. 202.)

95 *Mbugwe house near Madukani, Tanzania, about 1955.* The Mbugwe live just west of Masailand and south of Lake Manyara on very flat bare open plains. Their main enemies were the Masai spearmen. They originally built their houses in the middle of the plain where the Masai warriors could easily be seen approaching and fought them with their own weapons, spears. The Masai respected the Mbugwe as enemies and called them *il mangati,* true enemies, rather than the contemptuous *il meek* reserved for the Chagga, Rangi, Sandawe, and so on.[15] Mbugwe houses were similar to Gogo houses (see nos. 96–9) but much lower and larger, being sometimes 24 m by 23 m. Mbugwe fields were often as much as 6 km away from their houses, as the flat open plain was of little use for cultivation.

96 *Gogo house, Tanzania, 1965.* The Gogo live almost in the centre of Tanzania on the flat arid plains at the southern end of Masailand where the dry season lasts eight months. The Gogo successfully halted the slow southern advance of the Masai at the end of the last century. They were mixed farmers and built their homesteads either singly or in clusters at a considerable distance from one another. Their houses are sometimes known as 'tembes'. They were built round four sides of a cattle kraal. Walls were of woven or upright wattles and the flat or wagon shaped mud and wattle roofs rested on forked uprights along the walls. The walls were mostly plastered on the inside only, but occasionally, as in this photograph, they were plastered on both sides.

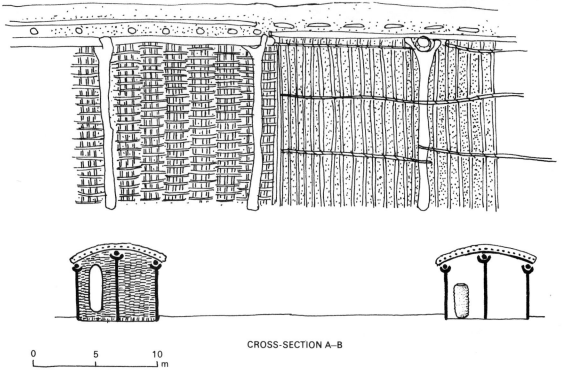

CROSS-SECTION A–B

0   5   10
|—————|—————| m

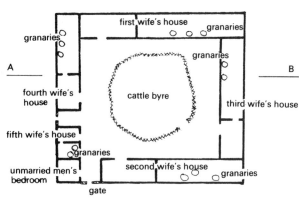

granaries

first wife's house
granaries

granaries

A   B

fourth wife's
house   cattle byre

                     third wife's house

fifth wife's house

                     second wife's house
                                    granaries
granaries

unmarried men's
bedroom

gate

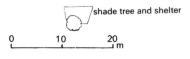
shade tree and shelter

0   10   20
|—————|—————| m

97 *Drawing of walls of Gogo house, Tanzania, 1965.* This illustrates two types of walling found in Gogo houses, sometimes, as here, on the same house.

98 *Plan and cross-section of Gogo house, Tanzania, 1962.* The main door of the house was always oriented towards the west.

99 *Diagram of construction of Gogo house, Tanzania, about 1900.*

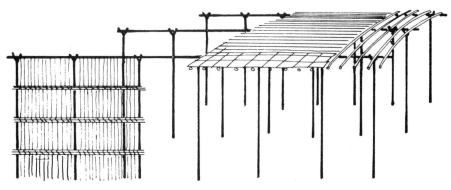

100 *Arab house, Tabora, Tanzania, 1966.* Dr. Livingstone, during his stay in Tabora, is reputed to have stayed in this Arab merchant's house, which has been preserved. Inside the verandah the doorway had a carved 'Zanzibar' door frame (see no. 323). The house was built round four sides of a courtyard. The mud walls were whitewashed on the inside.

101 *Bena (Hehe) fortified village, Iduna, Tanzania, about 1900.* Until the mid-nineteenth century the Hehe were a loosely associated group of chiefdoms in central Tanzania practising mixed farming. After 1850, as a result of the threat of Ngoni raids and the slave traders from the coast, about thirty Hehe chiefs united to form the state of Uhehe, later absorbing much of Ubena. Under King Mkwawa they successfully resisted the German advance. This photograph shows an Ubena village fortified with a palisade and thorn-lined ditches.

102 *Hehe house near Iringa, Tanzania, 1965.* Hehe houses were built round three or four sides of a rectangular courtyard. The walls were mud, the waggon roofs resting directly on them except on the entrance side of the house. The roofs were constructed of poles, brushwood and mud and were covered with a thin layer of soil, upon which grass took root.

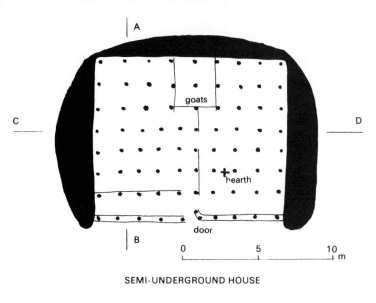

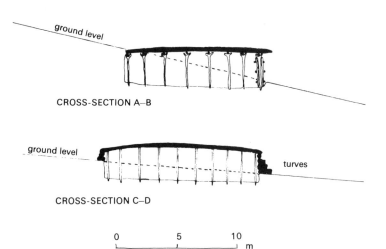

A

goats

+ hearth

door

B

0   5   10 m

SEMI-UNDERGROUND HOUSE

C

D

ground level

CROSS-SECTION A–B

ground level

turves

CROSS-SECTION C–D

0   5   10 m

UNDERGROUND HOUSE

103 *Plan and cross-section of Iraqw houses, Tanzania, about 1950.* The Iraqw are the largest of a group of four allied peoples in northern Tanzania, the Iraqw, Gorowa, Alawa and Burungi, who split up about ten generations ago. Linguistically they are completely isolated. The Alawa and Burungi lived in 'tembe' houses similar to the Mbugwe and Gogo (see nos. 95–9). The Iraqw and Gorowa, however, who live to the west of Lake Manyara on top of the Rift wall at an altitude of 1650–1850 m, had very distinctive 'dug-in' houses. They were square in plan and were either half or completely underground. The type that was half dug-in was built on a slope with the back wall completely excavated, the front wall built up of wattle and daub and the side walls built up of turves. The roof was of wattle and daub supported by posts. In this century the settlements were not nucleated, but examination of abandoned houses suggests that previously they were.

104 *Tigre house, Eritrea, northern Ethiopia, late 1930s.* This house, dug into the hillside, is typical of northern Tigre hill houses. The flat roof was of compacted earth over round beams. The house was either divided internally by a stone wall or by a row of granaries. It consisted basically of two rooms, one for living and sleeping and the other for storage and cooking.

5 Defence

All traditional African societies were characterized by very great economic risk, despite social and cultural measures seeking to minimize its effects. The smaller the scale of the society, the greater the subsistence element and the less the risk was spread. On the other hand, larger and more complex societies inevitably had more delicate political equilibria to maintain and in particular were easy prey to outside aggression. Neither, as has been demonstrated, set much store by accumulated wealth, so in both the protection of food supplies for consumption (or in some cases for trade) was of paramount importance.

This emphasis on protection may seem to contradict some of the notions of a pre-colonial Utopia. Many historians believe that the upheavals which the Europeans witnessed when they began to penetrate the interior of the continent at the turn of the eighteenth and nineteenth centuries resulted from some rather special circumstances. Their arguments cannot be detailed here; but the causes of the individual upheavals seemed in some way to be linked as symptoms of a more general malaise affecting every society: the old order was breaking down because it could not adapt to innovations which 94, 171–6, 202–3 were pervasively infiltrating the continent. The Ngoni civil war in southern Africa, which displaced several branches of the Ngoni people, who fled north and lived as bandits, was perhaps only an expression of inner tensions and strains. Similarly the civil wars in Yorubaland appear to have been the result of social changes that were brought about there following the introduction of firearms.

In comparison to all this turmoil, the age before must indeed have seemed peaceful. But to think of it as Utopia would be misleading. Scarcity of resources must at times have caused fairly intensive competition between neighbouring peoples, which might end up with local wars or migrations. These forces inevitably had an effect on settlement patterns in general and in particular on the defensive arrangements.

Small-scale Societies

Analysis of the methods of defence is difficult, because with the relative stability of colonial rule many of the physical barriers disappeared except in the largest towns (to be considered later). In the rural areas it was neither politically nor logistically possible to create massive barricades. Consequently defences tended to rely for their effectiveness more on ingenuity than intrinsic strength. These sorts of defences perish quickly when not maintained and even oral tradition (in the absence of written records) does not yield much evidence. Nevertheless those that do survive illustrate the lengths to which some communities went.

The splendidly conceived mazes of the plateau area of Nigeria are a

fascinating example of an ingenious defence. Complex entrance tunnels to
12 villages were formed out of live cactus hedges and planned on the principle
of a maze to frustrate any attempts by horsemen to enter either by storm or
by stealth. The tunnel of euphorbia began sometimes over 1 km from the
village.[1] The sides were too close to allow a horse to be turned and there were
many blind alleys and passages which took one back to the place just passed.
So the front sections of a hostile column of mounted men would be brought
back face to face with the rear columns of the force—a perfect ambush. Once
trapped the enemy would have considerable difficulty in breaking out even
with the aid of axes, as the type of cactus used exuded a white juice which
was so caustic that it took the skin off an arm or leg or blinded an eye
splashed with it (and it has recently been found to be carcinogenic).[2]

It seems that a similar arrangement of live hedges planted in a maze was
also found in the region of the cataract and lower reaches of the River Zaïre.[3]
It is not clear exactly which species of plant was used but it was probably
dracena, euphorbia or bamboo.

In south-eastern Zaïre the Bia Francqui expedition in the nineteenth
century reported seeing another type of maze fortification at the village of
Kia Gimen on the banks of the River Lubudi.[4] This village was apparently
defended on the river side by a wall 1 m wide and 3 m high. Protecting
the village from the plain was a concentric series of seven enclosures
joined at each end to the wall. Between adjacent bomas was a ditch 1·25 m
deep lined with pointed stakes and a narrow path. Access was through a
series of gates, but these gates were staggered in such a way that it was
necessary to walk the narrow paths between the fences. All traffic could
therefore be monitored by villagers stationed at strategic points in the maze
and unwelcome guests could fairly easily be disposed of. Concentrically
arranged walls or fences of one sort or another were also used in some other
places. By the nineteenth century, live hedges and palisades, sometimes
178 together with ditches, were probably the most common ways of defending
villages and even towns. The Hehe, who put up the fiercest resistance against
the Germans in central Tanzania, defended their towns not only with
101 palisades and ditches but also with tall wooden watch-towers guarding the
entrance gates.

The terrain frequently provided fairly effective natural defences. Some
hill villages, for example, hardly needed any physical barriers to be
constructed, as often there were only one or two ways up to them. In
143 southern Nigeria, the old town of Semorika had several pathways leading up
the steep hill to it, but all passed through natural rock gateways, two giant
boulders with just enough room for a man to pass between. The Dogon
33–9 villages clinging to the Bandiagara escarpment were inaccessible to the
armed cavalry of the plains. It must be said, however, that it was not always
for reasons of defence that these settlements were on hills (for a more
detailed discussion of this see Chapter 9).

In a few areas, underground houses were built. As with the hill villages, it
is not possible to say that these were always in the first instance constructed
for defensive reasons, but they certainly had defensive properties. Apart
from the more obvious advantage of concealment, they were more secure
103 against fire. In the Iraqw and Kondoa districts of modern Tanzania, where
incendiary attack was particularly feared, the people lived in underground
rectangular pit dwellings roofed with timber covered with mud and foliage.

These houses were approached by a ramp cut into the hillside. It is difficult to know how long these people had been building in this way, but at least in the nineteenth century such dwellings seem to have been the norm.[5]

Underground houses also existed in what is now Upper Volta. Some were similar in shape to the Iraqw houses, while others were apparently bottle-shaped and entered by means of a ladder.[6] It is not clear when these houses were inhabited. Nearby, partly subterranean temples are still in use which look as though they are a last vestige of a pre-existing culture. Among the Bobo Fing, for example, certain underground houses are set aside for the family cult and are reported to represent the home of the founding ancestor of the family. Songs and recitations of the Bobo Fing also refer to ancestors living underground. Frobenius mentioned underground houses near Ouagadougou but the precise location is not clear. The 'Phoka', as he calls them, north-west of Lake Malawi, are said to have built circular houses half underground.[7]

At Inyanga, which is at a high altitude (above 1500 m) in Rhodesia, circular stone-lined underground buildings have been excavated. They had flagged floors and were entered by means of a ramp which had a vertical so-called light shaft at its lower end. It has been conjectured that these buildings were used for penning livestock.

In some parts of the East African highlands, somewhat similar constructions are found, though here they are often larger than at Inyanga. The Chagga, living on Kilimanjaro, used theirs in the recent past as 'bolt-holes' against attack. One at Marangu extended for a total distance of about 50 m underground and consisted of three circular caverns connected by passages. There were two entrance ramps and three vertical light or air shafts.[8] The entrances were hidden amongst houses. Their original purpose and date are unknown.

A bit further south, the Gweno and the Pare constructed much larger tunnel systems. These tunnels cut deep into the mountains and led to large chambers where very many people could hide. Their one disadvantage was lack of ventilation, and the Masai, their most common adversaries, knew that by lighting fires outside the entrance and fanning the smoke into the tunnel with their shields, they stood a good chance of getting the people out. On one recorded occasion, in 1887, it was the German army which was attacking. The chief of Usange retreated underground with the whole of his family, which consisted of a hundred and fifty people, and all were suffocated by the smoke. The only member of the family to survive was a small boy who had been sent out on an errand; as the only descendant he later became the chief.[9]

The competing interests of the settled and nomadic peoples of East Africa led increasingly to the threat of armed conflict and the consequent need for defensive systems. Unlike the almost symbiotic relationship between the pastoralists and the agriculturalists in parts of West Africa, in East Africa each group sought to expand its territory at the expense of the other. The pastoralists seem to have originated in the southern areas of what are now the Sudan Republic and Ethiopia. Over the centuries they spread south in successive waves into areas occupied already in many cases by agriculturalists. Some groups of agriculturalists, for example the Bunyoro, seem to have organized themselves into fairly cohesive states or kingdoms in resisting the pastoralists. In Ruanda the pastoralists installed themselves as a ruling class and turned the agriculturalists into second-class citizens. In the majority, however, the two groups retained their separate identities and the pastoralists have continued their harassment almost to the present time.

Today the Masai are probably the largest group of independent pastoralists in East Africa. They continued to expand southwards right up until recent decades. They appear to have reached the Kenya highlands by about 1600 and the neighbourhood of modern Nairobi by about 1700; they were still pushing further south in the middle of the nineteenth century when the white settlers arrived and alienated much of their lusher grazing land. Nowadays, they are concentrated on the Rift Valley plains, but they have always raided the hills for grazing and for cattle. So, around the margins of Masai territory, the settlements of farmers have always been closely geared to the task of preserving land and checking Masai raids.

Agriculturalists like the Chagga, the Pare, the Iraqw and the Gweno developed, as we have seen, their own special underground defences. Others stood their ground and fought the Masai on their own terms and with their own weapons, spears. The Mbugwe, for instance, lived in a flat, practically desert area near Lake Manyara. These homesteads were deliberately sited in the most exposed and arid places so that Masai raiders could easily be seen approaching. This defensive measure meant that cultivated land was often anything up to 7 km away from the homestead. It seems that the Mbugwe warriors were at their best under these circumstances and despite the hostility there reportedly existed a good deal of mutual respect between the opposing spearmen.

The Sonjo are another example of a people who successfully managed to beat the Masai at their own game. This small agricultural society managed to survive in a pocket of land right in the middle of Masai territory, by barricading themselves into their villages with strong timber palisades, and by having a social structure which reinforced their physical defences. An age system similar to that of the Masai put young men into a warrior class whose sole function was to defend the village, so that they were freed from farming duties and could always be ready to defend the villages.

The Chagga and Pare peoples did not confine their defensive arrangements to bolt-holes; they also built stone forts. Two are known in the Pare area and several from Chaggaland. The Chagga forts were apparently built in random stone on a square plan and were flanked by deep moats and concealed by hedges and spiked stakes. Further south in Rhodesia, at Inyanga, remains of several stone forts can still be seen. Their walls were pierced with loopholes and were often surmounted by a parapet walk.

Protection of food supplies was naturally important for all societies. Underground storage pits have been noted in several parts of Africa but it is by no means certain that they were all constructed for defensive reasons. They are still used by the Shuwa Arabs (near Lake Chad) who store grain at their wet-season homesteads which they abandon in the dry season.[10] The Swazi built bottle-shaped pits beneath their cattle kraals;[11] similar ones have been reported in Bunyoro[12] and from the earliest excavated levels at Kilwa.[13] In Rhodesia, remains of pits have been excavated at Inyanga, Leonard's Kopje and the Khami waterworks site. Some bottle-shaped pits were quite definitely not for grain storage. In the Nuba Mountains[14] and parts of Ethiopia graves were constructed in this way, while in parts of Upper Volta bottle-shaped underground buildings were until recently used by weavers because of their damp atmosphere.[15]

Large-scale Societies

In some places in West Africa, town walls were built of mud and some reached truly gigantic proportions. In some areas almost every town and village was surrounded by a wall by the nineteenth century. As late as 1904, Lugard estimated that there were 40 walled towns within a 50 km radius of Kano and 170 in the whole of Kano province, an area of approximately 28 000 km².

In fact Hausaland is a very good area in which to examine fortification in some detail, especially since the remains of the larger city walls can still be seen today. They remain, however, only a remnant of their former glory. A formidable combination of goats, brickmakers and planners is rapidly bringing about the destruction of the walls and, without annual maintenance, natural erosion accelerates the process even further.

Hausaland consisted of seven main towns each with its own network of satellite towns. The walls round the main towns were built not only to keep out common enemies but also to defend each state from the others. Conflict over economic or political matters often led to internecine wars which were especially prevalent in the seventeenth century. The same century also saw the invasion of the Jukun peoples from the River Benue area. At other times Hausaland had to defend itself against invasion by enemies as various as the Fulani (who of course still provide the ruling families in most Hausa towns), the Gobiri, the Songhai, Kanem-Bornu and finally the British.

The government of each town or city appears to have tried to predict the direction of likely trouble and to have had the walls on that side strengthened accordingly. This was certainly true at the end of the nineteenth century in Kano. In 1903, when the British failed several times to breach the southern walls, they eventually attacked again from the north and found the walls and gates in such a bad state of repair that they managed to force their way in. Extensions were built from time to time and in Kano the main building phases seem to have been in the twelfth, fifteenth and seventeenth centuries.

The walls of Kano appear to have been built in the same way as the house walls in the town they surround, at any rate in their later stages. Pear-shaped bricks of mud and straw were used; the cementing was done with wet mud and the plastering with a mixture of either mud and potash or mud and an infusion of locust bean. The walls seem to have been about 9–15 m high and 12 m thick at the base, tapering to about 1·25 m at the top. They were topped by a buttressed parapet with loopholes in between the buttresses, and surrounded by a big dry ditch.[16] From the drawings it will be seen that the

278–281 walls were squareish in plan with a perimeter of roughly 25 km. The gates were rather ingenious in conception, being slightly skewed and inset. This prevented head-on attacks by any means, as the British discovered when they consistently failed to breach any of the southern gates with cannon fire during the 1903 offensive.

The walls of Hausa cities enclosed large areas of apparently spare land now
276 used for cultivation and housing. This fact led some of the earliest visitors to postulate (taking as their frame of reference medieval European towns) a former 'Golden Age' when the whole area would have been developed. As was discussed earlier, this seems not to have been the case and the land was almost certainly used to accommodate outlying farmers and livestock in times of siege.

Similar walls were found not only in the rest of Hausaland but also in other areas of the eastern part of West Africa, for example Kanem, the states of the Logone-Shari valleys, Borgu, Bussa, Nupe, Yorubaland and Benin. Construction techniques varied from area to area. Even within Hausaland there were very slight variations, the most conspicuous variant being the old site of Zaria at Turunku where considerable amounts of stone were used (see Chapter 9).

In Yorubaland, the walls were built of puddled mud which was sometimes mixed with stone and at times puddled with oil instead of water. Two and even three concentric walls and trenches surrounded some of the towns, especially those outside the thick forest on the plains which were much more exposed to sudden cavalry attack. Gboho (in the extreme north of Yorubaland), for example, had three walls; Ilesha and Ife had two each.[17] Often a thick belt of forest was deliberately left uncut around the walls both to hinder cavalry attack and to serve as a place of refuge in case of defeat. The walls, which rose to about 4·5 m, were surrounded on the outside by ditches, as in Hausaland. However, they were planted thickly with thorn bushes and in the wet season filled up with water to become moats. They were about 4·5 m thick at the base but tapered towards the top.

The introduction of firearms led to certain changes in the design of many Yoruba town walls. They developed a more slender profile, scarcely more than 1 m thick in some places, which allowed gun holes to be pierced. These changes seem mainly to have taken place in the nineteenth century, throughout which Yorubaland was engulfed in civil wars. (Similar circumstances may have been instrumental at about the same time in the introduction of the 'looped parapet' design in Hausa walls.)

In the western part of West Africa, Mandinka town walls in the nineteenth century often exhibited rather more variation than those further east.[18] Some walls described a zigzag course while others comprised a succession of round or square towers joined with short segments of walling. Such devices served to increase the effectiveness of the walls by preventing head-on charges and providing vantage points for guarding against attempts at scaling the walls.

In the more wooded and moist regions, including Sierra Leone, towns of up to five thousand inhabitants were defended not only by walls but by stockades of hardwood.[19] These stockades, accompanied by deep ditches, were outside the walls. An early visitor to one of the towns, Falaba, describes how its defences were much improved by the fact that the stockading had taken root in many places and grown into large trees. The living foliage not only served to conceal the defending warriors but must also have made the town much less susceptible to burning.

An even earlier visitor, Jobson,[20] writes of the Mandingo town of Cassan in the Gambia in 1623:

> It is seated upon the Rivers side, and inclosed round, neare to the houses, with hurdles, such as our shepheards use, but they are above 10 feet high, and fastened to strong and able poles, the toppes whereof remaine above the hurdle; on the inside in divers places, they have rooms, and buildings, made up like Turrets, . . . and . . . on the outside likewise, round the wall, they have cast a ditch or trench . . . circled with posts and peeces of trees . . . so thick that, except in stiles, or places made of purpose, a single man cannot get through . . . and this is as they do signifie to us, to keepe off the force of horse, to which purpose, it seems to be very strong and availeable.

Inside these towns the disordered arrangement of the houses seems to have been a definite defensive ploy: a visitor would soon lose his way and unwelcome ones could easily be trapped. This idea was not confined to Sierra Leone and its hinterland. Tortuous planning seems to have been deliberate in villages as well as towns right across the continent. Baker,[21] for example, writing about the town of Tirangore in the Sudan Republic in 1861, observed that although the main street was broad, all the others were studiously arranged to admit of only one cow in single file in between the stockades surrounding each household, in order to foil any enemies who managed to enter the town. In Kano the twisting narrow streets have been interpreted as insuring Muslim privacy, but they could equally well have served to confuse any unwelcome aliens.

In South Africa during the two decades after 1817, when Shaka, king of the Zulus, began his aggressive policy of annexation against fellow Ngonis, huge Zulu 'war towns' emerged. These were enormously scaled-up versions of the family homestead, except that the cattle were divided between a series of kraals sited between the houses and the central open space. This space was used as a parade ground for the Zulu impi (regiment). The towns were circular in plan and often over 1 km in diameter, containing as many as 1400 houses arranged four or five deep round the circumference. The whole 'town' was surrounded by a wooden stockade.

Conclusion

It is a truism to say that defences were only required by those who felt threatened by external aggression. Whether these defences took the form of an army or fortifications, they required considerable labour inputs which reduced the amount of manpower available for strictly economic activities. Simple, small-scale societies living at subsistence level tried to minimize serious conflict with their neighbours. But even in the absence of armed conflict, some protection was needed almost everywhere from large mammals. The slave raiding which intensified from the eighteenth century and the political upheavals of the nineteenth century meant that few peoples were immune from danger, and by 1900 nearly every village and town in sub-Saharan Africa had some form of defensive cordon.

REFERENCES

1. Mockler, F., *Through Unknown Nigeria* (London, undated)
2. Evans, F. J., and Kinghorn, A. D., letter in the *Daily Telegraph*, 13 August 1973
3. Johnston, Sir H., *George Grenfall and the Congo* (London, 1908)
4. Torday, E., and Joyce, T. A., *Les Bushongo* (Brussels, 1910)
5. Fosbrooke, H. A., 'Defensive Measures of Certain Tribes in North-Eastern Tanganyika', *Tanganyika Notes and Records*, 35, 36, 37, 39 (1953–5)
6. Moal, G. le, 'Les Habitations Semi-souterraines en Afrique de l'Ouest', *Journal de la Société des Africanistes*, 30 (1960)
7. Frobenius, L., *Das Unbekannte Afrika* (Munich, 1923)
8. Fosbrooke, H. A., *op. cit.*
9. *Ibid.*

10. White, S., *Dan Bana* (London, 1966)
11 Kuper, H., 'The Architecture of Swaziland', *Architectural Review*, 100 (1946)
12. Stafford, D. N., 'Bunyoro Grain Pits', *Uganda Notes and Records*, 19 (1955)
13. Garlake, P. S., *The Early Islamic Architecture of the East African Coast* (Nairobi, 1966)
14. Riefenstahl, L., *The Last of the Nuba* (London, 1976)
15. Moal, G. le, *op. cit.*
16. Moody, H. L. B., 'The Walls and Gates of Kano City: Historical References', *Kano Studies*, 3 (1967)
17. Ajayi, J. F. A., and Smith, R. S., *Yoruba Warfare in the Nineteenth Century* (Cambridge, 1964)
18. Meillassoux, C., 'Plans d'Anciennes Fortifications (Tata) en Pays Malinke', *Journal de la Société des Africanistes*, 36 (1966)
19. Siddle, D. J., 'War-Towns in Sierra Leone, A Study in Social Change', *Africa*, 38 (1968)
20. Jobson, R., *The Golden Trade* (London, 1623)
21. Baker, Sir S., *The Albert N'Yanza* (London, 1866)

Illustration Section V

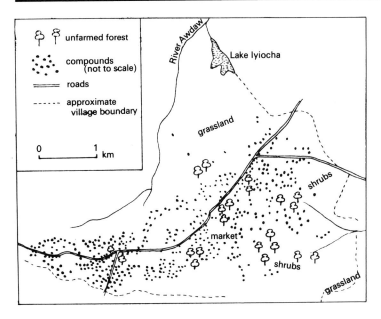

105 *Plan of Ibo village, Oko, southern Nigeria, about 1960.* The Ibo, although thought to be one of the major African groupings, consist essentially of a cluster of about 2000 independent village units whose major common characteristics are language and cosmology. Politically they have been highly fragmented. Originally much of the area would have been forested but, now that the population density is so much higher, forest trees in many areas only survive close to the villages and at spring heads and shrines where they have been deliberately encouraged. In the west of Iboland, villages were not visibly compact but usually extended from a central meeting place into the surrounding countryside for several miles. Fifty years ago many villages were surrounded by earthen walls and a belt of forest.

106 *Ibo house, south-eastern Nigeria, about 1921.* One of the few generalizations one can make about Ibo houses is that they were built within a walled or fenced compound with the entrance through a covered porch. In the south, several rectangular buildings would face each other around a courtyard within the boundary wall. Some of the sides facing the courtyard were left open but the bedrooms were fully walled. The plastered walls were constructed of puddled mud which was sometimes reinforced with lashed palm midribs. The floors were of polished mud and might be decorated with inset palm nuts. Other types of Ibo houses can be seen in nos. 91–3, 107, 108, 116, 136 and 137.

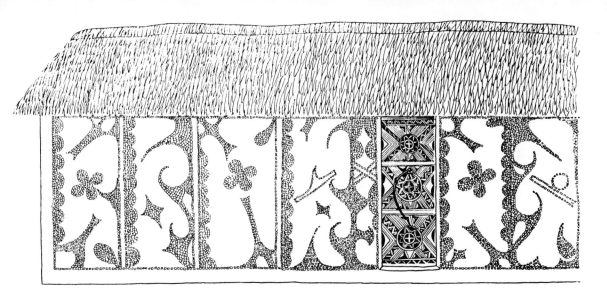

107 *Ibo house, Ikwerri, southern Nigeria, about 1925.* The mud walls of this house near Degema in the far south of Iboland (on the southern margins of the high forest) were inset with cowries and had a carved wooden door.

108 *Interior of Ibo house, south-eastern Nigeria 1956.* The eighteenth-century Ibo writer Equino described the interior of just such a house: 'Our bed consists of a platform raised three or four feet from the ground on which are laid skins and different parts of a spungy [sic] tree called plantain. Our covering is calico or muslin. Seats are a few logs of wood, but we have benches which are generally perfumed to accommodate strangers'.[16] The plantain leaves may have been made into mats. In this photograph the dresser was made out of puddled mud reinforced with poles.

109 *Ibo Ogwa or ancestral shrine, Ika, south-eastern Nigeria, about 1925.* Several aspects of the style of this building including the pillars, their decoration and the front steps are reminiscent of Asante architecture, although the two are separated by 800 km and many different styles. (See especially no. 123.)

110 *Ibo* mbari *shrine, Oratto, south-eastern Nigeria, about 1925.* Unlike many religious buildings, these were not built for meetings; it was the act of building itself which was the religious activity and once built they were left to decay.[17] As well as extensive mural decoration the interiors contained a large quantity of clay sculpture. Notice the palm hipping on the thatched tented roof. *Mbari* shrines are still built, but nowadays they have oblong saddleback or hipped roofs covered in corrugated iron sheeting. This simplification of style following the introduction of new mass-produced materials is quite common.

111 *Ibo club house, Bende area, south-eastern Nigeria, about 1925.* Many Ibo communities and other peoples in southern Nigeria had ritual societies which combined social, religious and political functions. Their principal public manifestations were masquerades. The Bende Ibo produced the Ogbon masquerade. Some of these societies had special club houses. The Bende Ibo club houses are very similar to the Ekoi club houses which are described under no. 115. They were open at one end and against the long interior walls were mud couches covered with incised patterns. The roofs were thatched with palm leaf mats.

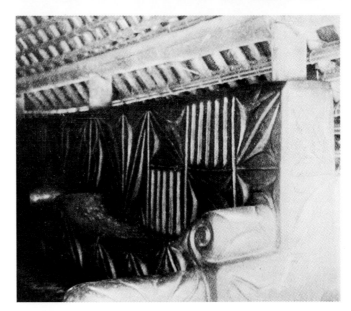

112 *Interior of Ibo club house, Bende area, south-eastern Nigeria, about 1925.*

113 *Yako meeting house, south-eastern Nigeria, about 1940.* Each clan occupied a clearly defined area of the Yako village, and within each of these areas was a men's meeting house where the clan gong was kept.

114 *Interior of Yako meeting house, south-eastern Nigeria, about 1940.* The upright stones and boulders surrounding one of the roof pillars were believed to have supernatural power. The children are sitting on a log bench.

115 *Drawings of detail of murals in Ekoi club house, eastern Nigeria, about 1925.* The Ekoi who live along the Cross River built club houses which were very similar to Ibo club houses (see no. 111). The mud walls were painted in murals in three colours.

116 *Ibo house under construction, eastern Nigeria, about 1921.* This roof was being thatched with palm-leaf mats consisting of two halves of a palm leaf plaited together. The roof was taking the weight of the fourteen people on it without any obvious signs of strain.

117 *Asante palace, Kumasi, Ghana, about 1900*. The confederacy of Asante states emerged at the end of the seventeenth century after several centuries of separate existence. By the mid-eighteenth century the confederacy had become the most powerful state in the forest lands dominating the Gold and Ivory Coasts. The old palace of Kumasi was blown up by the British under Wolseley in 1875 but was rebuilt two years later. This photograph shows the old 'Halls of Justice' in Prempeh's palace after the rebuilding.

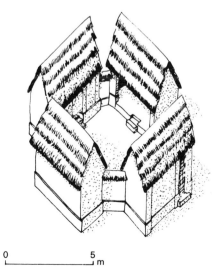

118 *Asante palace, Kumasi, Ghana, about 1900*. The palace was built around several courtyards in the same way as the houses (see no. 119). The mural patterns were marked out on the walls when the mud plaster was still wet by sticking in small slips of cane. These were then 'stitched' together with pieces of grass and the whole plastered over. Finally the designs were painted. Correspondents at the Battle of Wolseley (1875) mentioned colours of yellow ochre and reddish brown.

119 *Drawing of Asante house, Ghana, about 1965*. Asante houses were built around a compound. The walls were made of swish-puddled mud (see Chapter 6) reinforced with stakes and wattle work. Interior and exterior surfaces were then plastered. The raised floors and steps leading to them were constructed of clay and stone plastered over with red earth. Three sides of the house facing the courtyard were left open or only partly enclosed by pillars of palm frond covered with mud. The fourth side, the bedroom, was closed. The screen walls were thatched.

0   5
└────────┴ m

120 *Asante street, Kumasi, Ghana, about 1818.* Two-storey buildings and arcades were apparently common in the capital. The frames of the upper arches were of cane supporting wattle work above. The first floors were given extra support by partition walls below. Bowditch[18] in 1817 described some windows in the palace of open woodwork carved in fanciful figures and intricate patterns and set in a gilded wooden frame. The furniture was equally impressive. Doors were of cotton-wood reinforced with nailed battens.

121 *Asante street, Kumasi, Ghana, about 1818.*

122 *Asante temple, Ghana, about 1900.*

123 *Asante temple, Bawjwiasi, Ghana, about 1965.* This temple is one of the finest remaining in Ghana. It was probably built at the beginning of the century and most of the decoration is still intact.

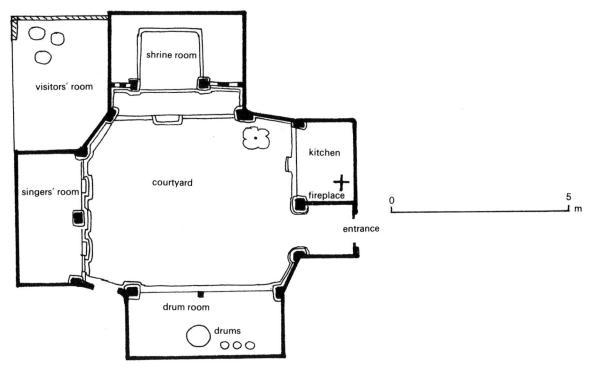

124 *Plan of Asante temple, Bawjwiasi, Ghana, about 1965.*

125 *Asante priest's house, Ghana, 1901.*

126 *Benin palace, southern Nigeria, 1668.* Benin city was destroyed by fire in 1897 after its capture by the British, but many accounts by travellers who visited it from the sixteenth century onwards have survived. By the fifteenth century it was the centre of a powerful state in the forest area immediately to the west of the Niger Delta. Political power became highly centralized in the monarchy and the palaces of the obas were on a lavish scale. Dapper described the palace as 'a collection of buildings which occupy as much space as the town of Haarlem', with numerous apartments and fine galleries 'as big as those on the Exchange at Amsterdam'. These galleries were, he said, 'supported by wooden pillars encased with copper, where their victories are depicted . . .', while the corner of each gallery roof was 'adorned with a small pyramidal tower, on the point of which is perched a copper bird spreading its wings'.[19]

128 *Benin bronze plaque, southern Nigeria, sixteenth century.* Several bronze plaques from Benin were taken back to London by the British punitive expedition of 1897. One in the British Museum shows a tower apparently roofed in shingles (see no. 84) with a model of a snake running down it. See Chapter 6 for a discussion of shingles.

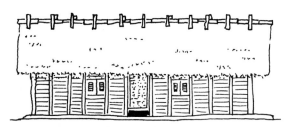

127 *Drawing of Yaounde house, near Douala, southern Cameroon, about 1960.* It is often assumed that Dapper's drawing of the palace of Benin was somewhat fanciful, as the background appears to be a woodcut of a European city, but a comparison of his drawing of the palace roof with a drawing of a roof of this modern house near Douala shows very marked similarities, especially in the treatment of the ridge pole. The drawing of the palace seems to represent exactly the same type of construction as in the house near Douala.

129 *Benin house under construction, southern Nigeria, 1892.* This is one of the few photographs taken in Benin before it was sacked.

130 *Benin tower, reconstructed, southern Nigeria, 1967.* This house has a scaled down version of the sort of tower which apparently adorned the Benin palace before the nineteenth century. Seventeenth- and eighteenth-century accounts suggested they were then up to 12 m high. Several travellers stated that Benin houses were roofed with shingles and this seems to be supported by bronze plaques and boxes from the palace which depict houses with shingle roofs (see no. 128). The shape of the bronze bird is also somewhat conjectural as travellers' accounts differ and only a foot appears to have survived (about a dozen heads, some smooth, some scaly, and two body sections).[20]

131 *Benin house, southern Nigeria, 1965.*

132 *Benin house, southern Nigeria, 1965.* A special case of the court form is the impluvium style. Impluvia are in effect small courts. Sometimes they occur in conjunction with courts and sometimes on their own. Ordinary Benin houses usually had several impluvia and one or two courts. This plate shows one of the former. These impluvia were drained by carefully constructed pipes and tanks. While the house was being built, gutters were dug. Stems of *Carica papaya* (paw-paw), the leaves of which are a powerful anthelminthic, were laid in them and covered with earth. After a few days the paw-paw stems, being very succulent, shrank in drying and were drawn out leaving a drainpipe.[21] The rainfall in Benin itself is 2030 mm a year, but during the dry season there is very little surface water about because of the porosity of the sandy soil. This means that there is an acute shortage of drinking and culinary water and the impluvium tanks were obviously a means of overcoming this (see Chapter 9). Collecting rainfall also obviously helps to reduce the incidence of erosion caused by rainwater running off roofs, which is quite considerable now in the Benin area.

133 *Plan of Benin house, southern Nigeria, about 1890.* The walls were built of swish-puddled mud and the pillars of mud reinforced with wooden posts. Both were finished with plastered fluting and highly polished. The walls were sometimes further decorated with clay figures in niches. The roofs were of palm leaf mats or shingles. In the larger courts decorative trees were grown such as *Newboldia loevis* (the akoko tree) and *Erythrina umbrosa* which has panicles of crimson blossom.[22]

134 *Drawing of roof of Benin house, southern Nigeria, about 1900.* This is an aerial view of the roof of a house with two courtyards and four impluvia.

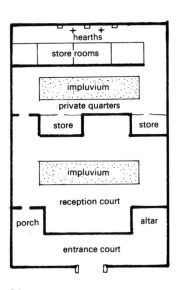

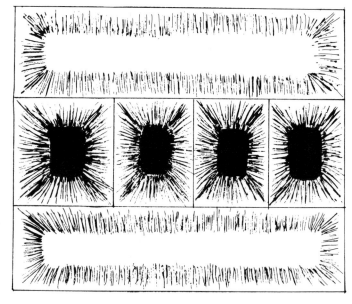

135 *Unidentified village, Forcados River, southern Nigeria, about 1900.* Forcados has for many centuries been an important commercial crossroads, being situated at the confluence of the Niger and Sapele river systems. Much of its trade would have come from Benin and the tower house in the left of the photograph (almost 16 m high) lends strong support to the claims of early visitors that Benin houses had tall towers 12 m high. This particular building, like the others in the photograph, is constructed on stilts to accommodate the 1·75 m tidal range.

136 *Ibo house, Ika, eastern Nigeria, about 1920.* Some of the Ibo in the Ika area have traditions which suggest they migrated from Benin. The house shown here is very similar to Benin houses with its central rectangular impluvium within which is a circular water tank.

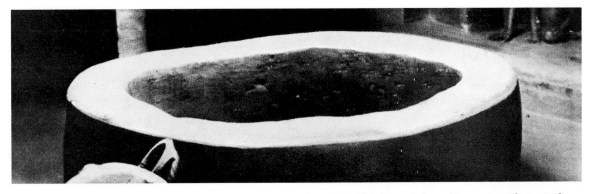

137 *Plan and cross-section of Ibo house, Ika, eastern Nigeria, about 1920.* This house belonged to a man with one wife.

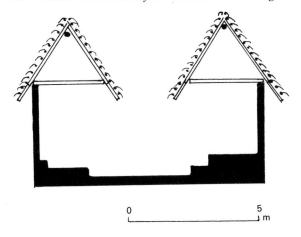

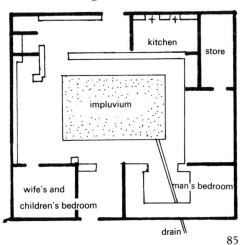

138 *Aerial view of Yoruba town of Ilorin, western Nigeria, about 1950.* Yoruba states, discussed in Chapter 3, varied in size and power over the centuries. Old Oyo, the largest, reached its peak of power in the eighteenth century and Ilorin was one of its most important towns. It was overrun by Fulanis from Sokoto in the nineteenth century. It now has a Muslim emir, but still retains a Yoruba way of life. Outwardly, Yoruba traditional houses looked like Benin classical houses and were constructed in a similar way, but the internal arrangements were different. To accommodate more extended families and craftwork, they tended to have one large central court. There were also impluvia and subsidiary courts for particular sections of the family. Both courts and impluvia can be seen in the photograph as can several buildings awaiting roofing.

139 *Yoruba house, western Nigeria, about 1920.* A view into an impluvium showing how the water was collected in large pots. Some of the impluvia, such as in Ketu, Benin Republic, were drained by underground tanks.

140 *Yoruba house, western Nigeria, about 1925.* Roofs were most commonly supported, as seen here, by wooden pillars made of iroko (ironwood) although plastered pillars similar to those at Benin and elsewhere were also sometimes used.

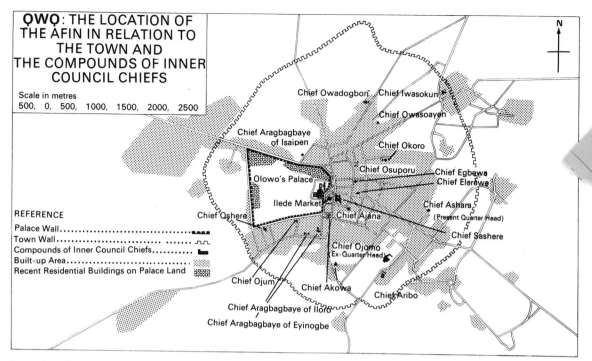

OWO: THE LOCATION OF THE AFIN IN RELATION TO THE TOWN AND THE COMPOUNDS OF INNER COUNCIL CHIEFS

Scale in metres
500, 0, 500, 1000, 1500, 2000, 2500

N

Chief Owadogbon · Chief Iwasokun
Chief Owasoayen
Chief Aragbagbaye of Isaipen
Chief Okoro
Chief Osuporu
Chief Egbewa
Olowo's Palace
Chief Elerewe
Ilede Market
Chief Ashara
(Present Quarter Head)
Chief Oshere
Chief Ajana
Chief Sashere
Chief Ojomo
(Ex-Quarter Head)
Chief Ojum
Chief Akowa
Chief Aribo
Chief Aragbagbaye of Iloro
Chief Aragbagbaye of Eyinogbe

REFERENCE

Palace Wall...
Town Wall...
Compounds of Inner Council Chiefs..........
Built-up Area..
Recent Residential Buildings on Palace Land

141 *Plan of Owo town, western Nigeria, about 1966.* Yoruba palaces, or *afins*, were almost like towns within towns, since the wall often surrounded not only the palace buildings but a large area of forest as well. The *afin* at Owo covered about 44 ha and occupied about 8 per cent of the land within the town wall. Clapperton reported that the *afin* in the town of Old Oyo covered about 260 ha. The *afin* was usually located in the centre of the town next to the principal market, and the compounds of quarter chiefs, who were intermediate in the political hierarchy between the Olowo (king) and the heads of individual houses, were ringed round the *afin*. The *afins* contained numerous courtyards, each one of which had a special function.[23]

142 *Yoruba afin, Old Idanre, western Nigeria, about 1955.* The basic construction of an *afin* was like an ordinary house, with puddled mud walls and roof thatched with palm-leaf mats resting on pillars on the side facing the courtyard. (The *afin* in this photograph would originally have had a thatched roof.) In *afins* (and some chiefs' houses) some features were especially elaborated and all dimensions were on a grander scale. For example, walls were thicker and higher and made from mud mixed with palm oil instead of water; roof pillars were correspondingly taller and thicker and more elaborately carved.

143 *Yoruba town gateway, Semorika, western Nigeria, about 1950.* Semorika was built on the top of a hill of over 900 m, with only one track leading to it. Two large outcrops of rock on either side of the track provided an effective natural gateway which was easily defendable. The modern town of Semorika is at the bottom of the hill.

144 *Yoruba* afin, *western Nigeria, about 1920.* This small *afin* had only two porches. One conspicuous feature of *afins'* and chiefs' houses was the *kobi* or gable projection of the roof into the courtyard forming a porch and their ridge poles were raised only slightly higher than the saddleback roof.

145 *Yoruba* afin, *Oyo, western Nigeria, 1853.* This larger *afin* at Oyo had many porches.

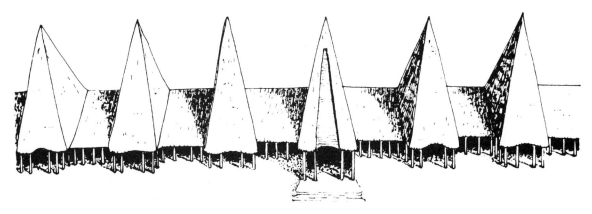

146 *Yoruba doors, western Nigeria, about 1910.* Every *afin* had elaborately carved double wooden doors. These were made from solid pieces of wood carved in relief, and pivoted on protruding pegs at the top and bottom.

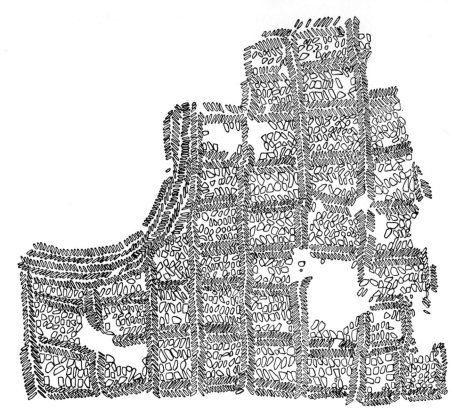

147 *Excavated Ife pavement, Old Ife, western Nigeria.* The floors under the verandahs round open courtyards and in impluvia were sometimes elaborately paved. Here is a detail of a pavement excavated at Old Ife in 1958. It is formed of double lines of potsherds laid on edge in a herringbone fashion to form squares, which were filled in with quartz pebbles. These pavements possibly date from the fifteenth century, towards the end of the time when much of Ife's famous 'bronze' and stone sculpture was produced.[24]

148 *Plan and cross-section of Diola house, Senegal, about 1940.* Outside Benin and Yorubaland impluvia are rare. Examples are, however, found in the Ivory Coast, Senegal and Guinea Bissau but in all cases the impluvia and the surrounding buildings are circular in plan.

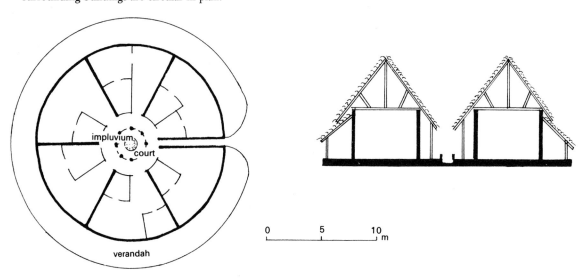

149 *Plan of Manjak chief's house, Guinea Bissau, about 1950.* This shows a plan of a house similar to the one shown in no. 148 but on a larger scale. It was in an area about 100 km north of Bissau. Being so much bigger, the space in the centre of this building should be considered as a court rather than an impluvium.

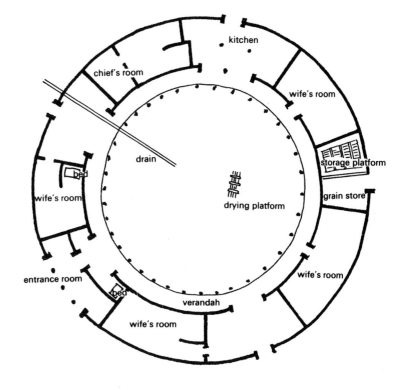

kitchen

chief's room

wife's room

drain

storage platform

grain store

wife's room

bed

wife's room

drying platform

entrance room

bed

wife's room

verandah

wife's room

150 *Diola house, Komobeul, near Ziguinchor, Senegal.* This is a second type of Diola house. The upper storey has a saddleback roof and is narrower than the lower storey which has two lean-to roofs.

0   5   10 m

6 The Building Process

Traditional construction in at least the rural areas of tropical Africa was almost always a highly cooperative venture, as the eighteenth-century account[1] quoted earlier makes abundantly clear. Building would be a major social occasion in which both the men and women of a village cooperated. Thatching was often done by women and ritual jokes about their slowness were made by the men, who of course finished the walls long before the women's roof work was complete. The Kikuyu used to refer to their women as 'sleepy lizards' on these occasions.[2] Elsewhere, similar feelings found expression in the rule that women were not allowed to mark out the ground plan as they would make it too small in order to lighten their work! With the help of neighbours a house could be erected in a day. Indeed, among some peoples, including the Kikuyu, custom was emphatic in insisting that the building must be completed in a day, for leaving it unfinished overnight would be an invitation to evil spirits.[3] This one day would actually be the culmination of perhaps several weeks spent by the man and his family preparing the necessary building materials. In contrast, the Mesakin Nuba took two years to complete a compound.[4] A wealth of custom and tradition surrounded the construction process in almost every society, but it is interesting that the joking and the feigned abuse seem to have been very widespread.

With very little division of labour, with the need to use essentially voluntary manpower, and with every house conforming to type and custom, one would think that construction techniques would have to be extremely simple. In fact, getting any sort of dwelling to stand up using the limited materials available requires a good deal of skill, as anyone who has tried it will know. The fact that buildings of the standard shown in some of the illustrations could be produced under these conditions, indicates clearly that the skills must have been developed carefully over a long period of time. They also suggest that construction skills were passed down from every member of one generation to every member of the next, since few houses outlasted a single lifetime. This must have been a major exercise in frequently non-literate societies. Writing them off as 'primitive', whatever the technical meaning of this term, can be dangerously misleading.

Mud
Similar considerations apply, as I have already argued (see p. 1), to the word 'mud'. One would like to avoid using the word, but in the absence of another expression in common usage (adobe, daga and pise are too limited) readers are asked to try to strip it of its pejorative overtones. The mud used was in fact mostly a good type of 'clay'. In Africa the silt content of most soils is low and this means they are mixtures in varying proportions of sand and clay.

Whereas this is a disadvantage for agriculture, it is an advantage for building. The clay makes the soils sticky and the sand gives them strength; so unless the proportion of one of these constituents is very low indeed, mud can be used in one way or another in the construction process. It is in fact an extremely versatile and strong material, and there is no problem about constructing a two-storey building. Almost any basic shape can be expressed in it and a wide variety of roofing solutions are possible: domes, vaults, shells, flat roofs, etc. If the surfaces of the walls of mud buildings are kept well maintained to prevent water seeping into the cracks, they will sometimes outlive their original builders.

There were various techniques for preparing mud for building. In the far west of the Sudan zone sun-dried mud bricks were made using wooden shutters. The bricks were cemented into place with more mud and the outsides of the walls were plastered over with a mud mixture. In Hausaland pear-shaped bricks were made, and the mud had straw mixed with it. These bricks were cemented into the wall in horizontal rows with their points upwards and afterwards coated with a mud plaster. In the forest areas bricks were not usually made; instead, a technique known sometimes as 'swish puddling' was employed. This was usually done in the middle of the wet season. First a pit was dug and the top soil thrown out; the red clay underneath was then broken into clods; after being softened by a shower of rain, these clods were 'puddled' by stamping. When ready, the clay was left in a heap, protected by banana leaves, to mellow until building started in the dry season. The building would be erected in courses about 50 cm high; each course was laid in a day and then left to harden before the second course was added. Sometimes a mould was made for the swish with two rows of stakes and wattle work; this was filled in and then plastered over. For the palaces of Yorubaland a more complicated technique was used, the mud being puddled with palm oil rather than simple water (see Chapter 4).

The surfaces of a mud building exposed to the weather must be properly maintained to be durable. Plastering therefore had to be renewed regularly. In Hausaland several different types of plastering were practised. To the basic mud and straw mixture was sometimes added potash from the dye pits or an infusion of locust-bean pods or, for the wealthy, mimosa specially imported from Egypt.[5] The plaster was applied by hand, shell patterns were traced in rows along the walls with the fingers. In the Upper Niger areas it seems that rich men used a kind of lime prepared at Jenne[6] and a lime wash was apparently used on some of the more important buildings of Bornu. In parts of the forest areas mud walls were 'washed' regularly to produce a hard almost glossy surface. A new wall was first rubbed smooth with half a coconut shell and then washed with a liquid mixture of rich red earth applied with a pad of rotten banana leaves, or rubbed with a mixture of mashed up leaves of the oil seed tree, or with a stain derived from the locust bean. It was usually the women's task to wash down the walls, except in the palaces where slaves washed them each morning. The polished walls of the palace of Benin much impressed the early visitors. Dapper,[7] writing in 1668, says that the 'walls were made of clay, very well erected, and they can make and keep them as shiny and smooth by washing and rubbing as any wall in Holland can be made with chalk, and they are like mirrors'.

Internal walls, especially in rooms used for sleeping, were often plastered with a mixture of mud and cowdung as this was found to be particularly good for repelling jiggers and other pests. Some Nuba still rub graphite into the walls of their specialized shower buildings, presumably as a water-repellent device.[8]

Most African houses traditionally had mud floors. A mud floor tends to conjure up the idea of something soft and insanitary, but this was far from the case when the floor was properly prepared; it could be almost as hard as cement and quite smooth. A good, hard floor was obtained by beating the mud with a wooden beater while it was setting. The mud was mixed with charcoal, as in Zulu houses[9] or other small aggregate, or with cowdung and then smeared with ashes. In parts of the Sudan the Raik Dinka found that the mud from low ant-hills was particularly good for making a hard practically waterproof, bluish cement. Floors made of mud alone were not in fact completely ubiquitous and mosaics occurred quite widely (see Chapter 7).

Mud roofs were found over a wide area of the western Sudan and in parts of East Africa. Most of them were, in fact, not built of mud entirely but were reinforced with timber. In Mauritania and parts of the Upper Niger region the roofs were practically flat. These terrace roofs, as they are sometimes called, were achieved by laying matting or short poles, arranged in a herringbone pattern, on top of roof beams, and plastering the lot over with mud. The beams were sometimes laid parallel, stretching from wall to wall or pillar to wall. At other times they were arranged in a more complex fashion, the first being laid across the four corners of the room, the next joining two corners to each other and the final ones bridging the square or rectangular space which was left. This design, in particular, enabled a rectangular room to be covered with poles most of whose lengths were shorter than the length of the shortest side. In other parts of the Sudan, Hausaland mainly, mud vaults

283, 287–8 were constructed. On rectangular buildings these looked like 'camels' backs' from the outside, while on round and square buildings they were dome-shaped (though not in fact true domes). All were constructed from mud arches reinforced (within the arches themselves) with short pieces of palm. On the square and rectangular buildings two sets of arches sprang from the walls (not the corners) and intersected at right angles; while on the round buildings several arches sprang from equally spaced points round the walls and intersected at their apexes. The spaces between the arches were filled with short pieces of palm arranged in a herringbone pattern. The whole of the outside of the vault, and sometimes the inside too, was plastered over with mud. The outer surfaces of both flat and vaulted mud roofs were sometimes reinforced with small pebbles beaten into them.

More akin to true domes were the roofs of houses of the plateau area of Nigeria which had domed mud ceilings under thatched roofs. These domes

3 were built of mud mixed with straw without any centring, starting from the top of the round walls and working in layers to the apex. Granaries were often built in a similar way. In Hausaland the enormous Gobir granaries in their arid surroundings were quite spectacular technical feats: almost spherical buildings with diameters of up to 5·2 m built of mud which had a uniform thickness of no more than 7·5 cm.

A particularly interesting illustration of the possibilities of mud

206–8 architecture is provided by the Mousgoum 'shell' houses. These fine buildings, which could be considered as roofs with no walls, were built up in layers of mud and straw into a bell shape and embossed all over with elongated knobs. The purpose of these knobs is not at all clear, but they certainly enabled a man to climb easily to the top of the house, were extremely decorative and perhaps in some way helped to channel water evenly to the ground.

Burnt bricks were known in isolated parts in a band stretching from the Upper Niger areas through Bornu to Darfur and the Nile areas. Legend has it that they were introduced into the western Sudan by an architect brought back by Mansa Musa, king of Mali, after his pilgrimage to Mecca in the fourteenth century (detailed consideration is given to this idea in Chapter 9). Where burnt bricks were used, the walls were load-bearing and the buildings were rectangular in plan with the flat roofs supported in the centre of the building by brick pillars.

Vegetable Materials

Hunters and gatherers and some pastoralists needed houses which could be dismantled and transported. Basically there were four types. The first two were based on a framework of hoops covered with either mats, thatch or 174 skins or a combination of these. In the first type, two sets of arches intersected at right angles, the arches decreasing in height towards the perimeter of the house. The second type consisted of one set of arches all of the same dimension overlapping at a centre point. The third type had a covering of woven hair over a framework of poles laid across forked sticks. 151 The fourth type was a combination of the first and third types. (This description is perforce a simplification; among the Tuareg, thirty different types of tent framework have been distinguished.[10] See pages 99–103).

Most other houses built above ground had a thatched roof. In some parts of Africa this thatched roof reached to the ground forming conical 'beehive' houses. Sometimes the thatching was stepped and sometimes it was plain. Reeds, grass and banana and bamboo leaves were all used as thatching 162–7, 180–205 material. The basic framework for these houses was a circle of long upright poles whose bases were firmly embedded in the ground. The poles were bent inwards until their tops could be bound together. The framework was then strengthened either by tying on hooped formers or by weaving split poles in and out of the uprights. A centre pole—or occasionally in large houses a ring of poles—sometimes further strengthened the framework.

It may be difficult to distinguish from the outside between beehive houses 202–3 and those where the roof rests on walls or forked supporting posts. In some Tuareg beehive houses frameworks were thatched to within 1·5 m of the ground and then a mud wall was constructed within the framework. Also, the dividing line is very slender between a house with a beehive framework with an additional ring of supporting posts and a house where the weight of the roof is taken to be supported on a ring of forked posts, the thatch being continued to the ground.

Houses with thatched roofs above walls had great variations in shape, 213 materials used and construction techniques. Some roofs rested on pillars and 241 were independent of the walls below them, while others were supported entirely by the walls. Saddleback roofs nearly always rested on wall plates 68–9, 114 supported on forked uprights within the walls. The ridge pole was sometimes supported by upright poles but usually rested between the gable 148 ends. Tie beams were only occasionally used. The shape of the roof was usually strictly related to the shape of the walls. Roofs above round walls would be conical, and roofs above rectangular walls would be saddleback, hipped or pyramidal. The Bamileke houses provide a particularly interesting exception because they have conical roofs resting on square walls. This conical roof was constructed round two circular platforms built onto a pyramid structure which rested on top of the house walls.

Almost all conical or pyramidal thatched roofs were thatched with grasses, reeds, stalks or a mixture of these, but one exception was the distinctive tall, narrow, pyramidal roofs found in the Aruwumi River area of Zaïre. These were thatched only with large, broad marantaceous (banana-like) leaves; they were about 6 m high and surmounted short walls of polished planks. However, these broad leaves were rarely the only materials in the thatch; more commonly they were used flat as a first covering which was covered with grass thatch.

The most frequently utilized material for thatching rectangular houses was palm leaves. They were usually prepared by plaiting the two halves of the leaves together to form a stiff mat about 1 m long, which was then lashed to the roof framework. Rectangular houses thatched with palm mats usually had either saddleback or hipped roofs, or very occasionally pyramidal ones. Topologically, it is difficult to imagine how stiff flat mats could be satisfactory, especially in areas of very heavy rainfall, on any other shapes as they cannot be bent to cover curved surfaces. This leads one to speculate that the use of palm may itself have largely determined the shape of the buildings. This question is taken up again in Chapter 9; but from a purely constructional viewpoint it is interesting to note that one way of overcoming the problem of forming watertight groins on saddleback roofs was to inset the shorter sides. This solution produced some very elegant roofs, particularly the very tall ones resting on openwork sides, found at the edge of the Forcados River.

Much discussion has centred on the nature of the roofing materials of the old palace buildings at Benin. Some of the early visitors[12] reported that wooden shingles were used for the king's palace, although not for ordinary houses, while others maintained that palm leaves were used for all buildings. A visitor[13] in 1899, two years after it was sacked, did not see any evidence of shingles, but two pieces of brasswork from Benin which have survived seem to point to the contrary. One is a box and the other is a plaque, but both depict tall entrance towers roofed in shingles. The shingle style could conceivably have fallen out of fashion by the time of the sacking of the town in 1897, perhaps because iron sheeting had found its way there.

Large quantities of nails have been recovered from the old palace of Benin and in 1958 one chief remembered in his youth seeing shingles at Benin.[14] It is interesting, in this connection, that very many iron nails were recovered in a recent excavation at Ife of a fourteenth-century site.[15] These could perhaps have been used for fixing shingles.

Water runs quite cleanly off leaf and palm thatch, and in some places the buildings seem to have been designed to facilitate water collection. In Yorubaland, Benin and parts of Iboland the rooms of the houses were built adjoining four sides of an impluvium or courtyard and the rainwater ran down the corner groins of the roof. It was usually simply channelled into large water pots, although sometimes a more elaborate system of underground storage tanks was employed. In the town of Ketu, which was some way from a river or stream, it was reported[16] that every compound possessed from

74

86–8

68, 116

135

128

132, 136, 139–40

three to a dozen artificial subterranean tanks, covered over with timber and earth and with only a small opening left for the water to run in and be drawn out. This opening was usually covered over with a pot so that a person could walk or stand on a tank without knowing that it existed.

From southern Cameroon through Zaïre and Angola and across to the lake regions of East Africa many houses were built out of palm fronds and bamboo. Both are peculiarly satisfactory materials since they usually grow almost dead straight and with hardly any difference in diameter between one end and the other of a piece, say, 3 m long. They also grow quickly and to a great length: in parts of Zaïre palm fronds of over 20 m are found. Houses of very regular dimensions and of extreme neatness and of sometimes imposing height or length were therefore possible in these areas.

One regulating factor in building with these materials is the property of bamboos and palms that they cannot be jointed: any cutting into the diameter considerably reduces their strength, and they therefore have to be lashed with strips of bark or creepers. In the Zaïre Basin, the outer palm fronds were mostly lashed together horizontally onto an upright framework forming long, fairly low buildings; whereas in the Bamoun and Bamileke areas of Cameroon, tall square buildings were built with the outer palms lashed together vertically. The largest buildings in height and length were the Mangbettu assembly halls built of the giant palms found in that area; they were 'architecture advanced to the point of perfection',[17] immense halls of polished palms almost 15 m high and 19 m long.

In Kuba and Mangbettu halls the lashing on the walls was treated very decoratively and was 'woven' into a pattern between the horizontal palms. Torday and Joyce identified fifteen different patterns in Kuba houses.[18]

This lattice technique was also used further east in many parts of East Africa, but with dicotyledonous timber rather than palm. Walls were constructed of upright poles with horizontal poles tied or woven onto them. They were plastered from the inside with red mud often known as daga. Along the coast this daga was sometimes transported from a considerable distance inland.

Stone

Stone buildings were quite widespread. Basically they are found in four main geographical areas: the East African coast, Abyssinia, the Upper Niger areas and the upland areas (this last category is discussed in detail in Chapter 9).

In some circular buildings the stones were not dressed or were only roughly dressed and set in a bed of mud. In many areas stone was used as a foundation layer underneath mud or mud brick walls. In parts of the Upper Niger area this foundation layer sometimes made up half the height of the building. The rectangular stone buildings of Mauritania were sometimes hard to identify as the stone walls were completely plastered over with mud.

At Zimbabwe and in other ruined Shona chiefs' houses in Rhodesia, the stone walls were built with a dry stone technique. The stone was a local granite which can be formed into flakes between 8 cm and 18 cm thick. The walls were often more than 2 m thick with a roughly dressed stone facing enclosing a rubble core. Three main types of technique have been identified by Whitty.[19] In class 'P' the facing stones were laid in irregular and uneven courses. In class 'Q' the facing stone was dressed into blocks of roughly even sizes and laid in level courses. Class 'R' appears to be the latest style, in which the facing layer was roughly built and uncoursed.

The decorative treatments of the stone buildings of Mauritania, Rhodesia and Angola are all remarkably similar. Perhaps the most common structural pattern, and one that was used in burnt brick and mud buildings as well, was based on a triangular niche or chevron (two pieces of stone sloping to meet at 44, 266 the top). These chevrons, in various arrangements, sometimes in double or triple banks, were found in nearly all the stone buildings. In Mauritania they were complemented by herringbone patterns and by dark stones arranged in layers or singly. In the southern countries most of these same patterns occur 48 as well as some extra ones such as sloping block, chequer and dentelle.[20] In Rhodesia, Garlake[21] has compared a large number of sites and has recognized seven distinctive clusters of decoration, form and function.

310–24 Along the East African coast the Swahili civilization which flourished between the twelfth and nineteenth centuries produced many stone buildings but of a fundamentally different nature from those so far discussed. They have been fully described by Garlake.[22] The building style 322 which evolved there was based on walls and pillars built of coral rubble, cemented together and plastered over with locally produced cement and 312 lime wash. Roofs were either domes or barrel vaults built in the same way, or 316 flat and made of coral rubble and cement resting on mangrove poles. Lintels and the edges of arches were finished in finely dressed coral. The dressed stone—and this was fine-grained living coral from the sea, in contrast to the dead coral rubble from the coastal reef—was finely carved into bosses in intricate interwoven designs and into elaborate panelled surrounds for the mihrabs of mosques (see pp. 120–2). The plastered surfaces were sometimes incised with drawings of ships, though more often they were inset with fine 317–19 Chinese celadon and porcelain bowls. The latter treatment was used especially on domed and vaulted ceilings and on the tall stelae which adjoined tombs. The ship engravings were often done in relatively inconspicuous places, such as entrance halls and small ante-rooms, and they were usually low down on the walls, and it seems, therefore, that they were probably done more as good-luck symbols than as decoration.[23]

In Ethiopia, the earliest stone buildings seem to have been the pre-Axumite temples built of large, irregular, rectangular, dressed stone blocks laid in courses. With the rise of the Axumite kingdom in the first century, a new building technique using both wood and stone became widespread. A core of stone rubble and mud mortar, faced with dressed stone and flat 328 horizontal timbers spaced at regular intervals, was reinforced with timber cross-members projecting out of the wall. This layered technique persisted right down to the twentieth century in some parts of the country. In the earliest buildings, however, flat roofs rested on lintels between columns and walls, and underneath the wooden ceilings were coffered. Later stone arches, 327 barrel vaults and domes were constructed. The interior stonework was richly ornamented with carving and painting.

From the tenth to the fifteenth or sixteenth centuries, a series of remarkable churches were built in northern Ethiopia all in stone and hewn from 325–6 solid rock. In style they often copied the Axumite churches even to the extent of imitating the 'monkey heads' (the name given to the projecting cross members).[24]

In parts of southern Africa, along the tributaries of the Vaal River, small 49 corbelled stone houses were built. Walton[25] has identified three types of construction which seem to represent an evolutionary sequence. The first type, A, was constructed of untrimmed blocks of sandstone or doleritic boulders. In the second type, B, in which the houses were larger, flat doleritic slabs were used. The third type, C, represents a change in shape rather than techniques: doleritic slabs were used in an oval plan.

New Materials

When traditional materials are no longer available (perhaps because of changes in population density, legal rights or a community's location), it is interesting to see how traditional techniques adapt. Often vestiges of the old technique persist as a decorative feature, as in a Mashonaland style where the thick upright wall poles are still plastered over with mud at the base, reflecting an earlier stage when this would have been the only means of attaching the walls to a solid rock surface. (One Kinga style may have a similar background.) The impact of corrugated iron is discussed in Chapter 1; but on the whole it is not inflexibility in the traditional technology so much as competing economic, social and political pressures which have brought the old methods into disuse.

REFERENCES

1. Curtin, P. O. (ed.), *Africa Remembered, Narratives by West Africans from the Era of the Slave Trade* (London, 1967)
2. Kenyatta, J., *Facing Mount Kenya* (London, 1938)
3. *Ibid.*
4. Riefenstahl, L., *The Last of the Nuba* (London, 1976)
5. Kirk-Greene, A. H. M., *Decorated Houses in a Northern City* (Kaduna, 1963)
6. Wargee, 'African Travels of Wargee' in *Africa Remembered* (for details see note 1 above)
7. Dapper, O., *Description of Africa* (Amsterdam, 1668)
8. Riefenstahl, L., *op. cit.*
9. Knuffer, W., *The Construction of the Bantu Grass Hut* (Graz, 1973)
10. Nicolaisen, J., *The Ecology and Culture of the Pastoral Tuareg* (Copenhagen, 1963)
11. *Ibid.*
12. Dapper, O., *op. cit.*
13. Roth, L., *Great Benin* (London, 1903)
14. Goodwin, A. J. H., 'Recent Finds in the Old Palace at Benin', *Man*, 63 (1963)
15. Garlake, P. S., 'Excavations at Obalara's Land, Ife: An Interim Report', *West African Journal of Archaeology*, 4 (1974)
16. Gollmer, Rev. C. A., *Journals*, C.M.S. Archives, CA2/043, unpublished (1859)
17. Meckleburg, Duke of, *From the Congo to the Niger and the Nile* (London, 1913)
18. Torday, E., and Joyce, T. A., *Les Bushongo* (Brussels, 1910)
19. Fagan, B. M., *Southern Africa* (London, 1965)
20. Walton, J., 'Patterned Walling in African Folk Building', *Journal of African History*, 1 (1960)
21. Garlake, P. S., *Great Zimbabwe* (London, 1973)
22. Garlake, P. S., *The Early Islamic Architecture of the East African Coast* (Nairobi, 1966)
23. Garlake, P. S. and M., 'Early Ship Engravings of the East African Coast', *Tanganyika Notes and Records*, 63 (1964)
24. Sauter, R., 'Rock Churches in Ethiopia', *Annales d'Ethiopie*, 5 (1963)
25. Walton, J., *African Village* (Pretoria, 1956)

Analysis of Materials and Technology

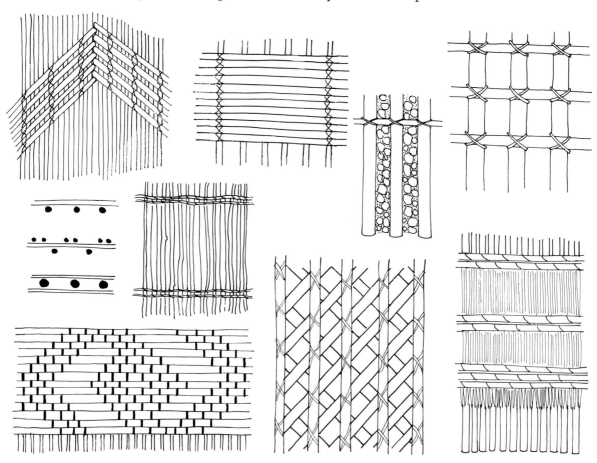

Woven cleft wood, split bamboos, palms, raffias, creepers etc. Often plastered over on inside.

Wood, bamboo palm fronds, grass, bullmores, tied to framework, of wood, bamboo or palm fronds. Stones sometimes used as infilling. Sometimes plastered over on inside or on both sides.

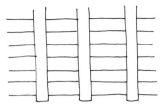
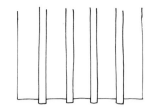

Cleft planks, arranged vertically or horizontally, between upright poles. Horizontal planks sometimes lapped.

Puddled mud laid in courses. Roof supports sometimes embedded in walls.

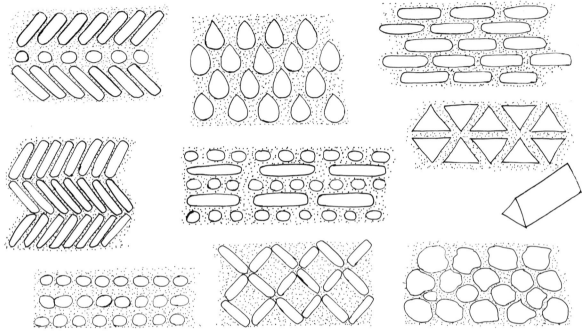

Roughly dressed stones or sundried bricks, either rectanguloid or pear shaped, embedded in mud mortar. Often plastered over on both sides.

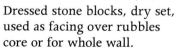

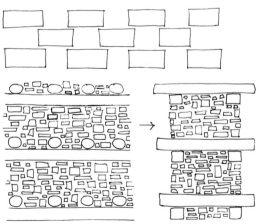

Dressed stone blocks, dry set, used as facing over rubbles core or for whole wall.

Rubble wall set with mortar plastered over on both sides. Openings and corners edged with dressed stone.

Stone rubble walls reinforced with wooden planks held in place by short wooden cross pieces. Solid rock walls sometimes dressed to imitate this technique.

ROOFS

Thatched roofs—circular plan

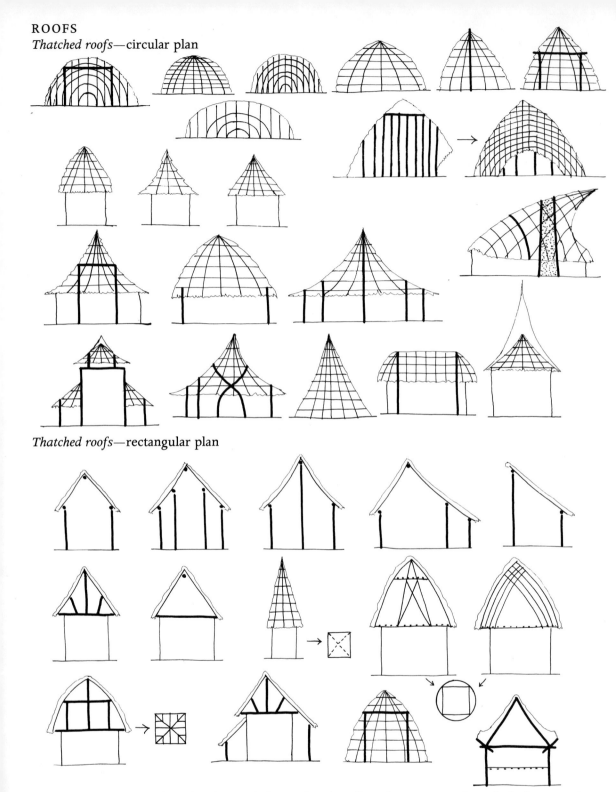

Thatched roofs—rectangular plan

Tied or woven split palms, bamboos, cleft wood or bundles of grass or reeds. Whole framework embedded in ground at perimeter or supported on forked uprights or load bearing walls. Thatched with reeds grass, palm leaves, banana leaves, marantaceous leaves. Sometimes double thatched—e.g. first layer palm, second layer grass. Or covered with skins or mats.

102

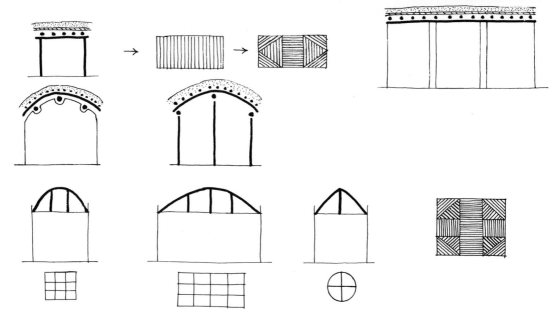

Mud roofs over matting or straw over framework of split wood or palm fronds sometimes thatched over.

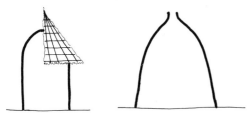

Mud domes, no reinforcement sometimes thatched over.

TENTS

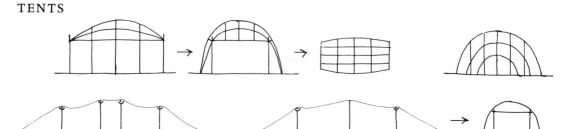

Woven cloth, skins or mats placed or stretched over framework of hoops and/or horizontal poles supported on forked uprights.

STONE ROOFS

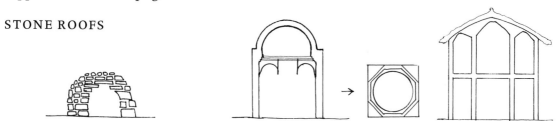

Corbelled stone beehives of either bolders or dressed slabs.
Stone domes, and barrel vaults, of coral or granite rubble and lime cement or rock hewn.

103

Illustration Section VI

151 *Tuareg tent, Air, Niger, about 1960.* The Tuareg, who conducted the trans-Saharan trade, cover much of the eastern Sahara, from Air in Niger to Ahaggar in southern Algeria and to the Niger bend in Mali. Only the southern Tuareg come within the scope of this book. In the Air mountains, although the annual rainfall is only about 200 mm, some Tuareg (or rather the subordinate Haratini) did grow crops with irrigation of the Wadi terraces.[25] Although it is hot for most of the year the temperatures do drop sharply at night and fall to about 5°C in January in the mountains. Tents were always pitched with the open front facing east to catch the warming rays of the morning sun. The southern Tuareg mostly covered their tents with mats. The average family could pack its house and entire belongings on to the back of two camels and perhaps a donkey.

104

152 *Tuareg tent, Air, Niger, about 1967.* A view of the interior of a Tuareg tent. The leather bags hanging from the frame hold the woman's jewellery, toiletries and personal belongings.

153 *Interior of Tuareg tent, Air, Niger, about 1967.* This photograph shows the man's possessions, including his hat and the camel's saddle.

154 *Masai house, Tanzania, about 1903.* The Masai are pastoralists living in a large area of steppe land in northern Tanzania and southern Kenya. The rainfall over the Masai steppe is less than 500 mm a year. Their houses were semi-portable. The wooden frames were transported on pack animals; on arrival at a new site these were covered by the women with brushwood and a mixture of mud and cowdung. The low height of the house is conspicuous here. But any increase in height would have necessitated an increase in length (to keep the satisfactory aerodynamic profile in the windy steppe land) and a huge increase in the quantity of materials used. For example, to make the house half a metre (or 30 per cent) higher each frame would have had to have been just over two metres longer and the whole surface area would then have been increased by about 60 per cent.

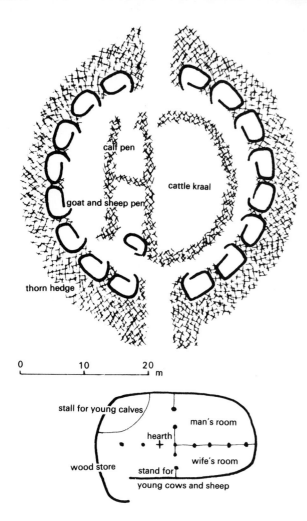

calf pen

cattle kraal

goat and sheep pen

thorn hedge

0   10   20 m

155 *Plan of Masai village, Tanzania, about 1903*. There were two basic types of village: one for the elders (including married men, their wives and children) and one for the warriors, their mothers and younger sisters. Members of the elders' village maintained the herds of cattle while the warriors fought and raided neighbouring tribes for cattle. Cattle kraals near the houses were surrounded by hedges or sticks and the whole village was inside a hedge of dry thorns which acted as a deterrent to wild animals.

stall for young calves

man's room

hearth

wife's room

wood store

stand for

young cows and sheep

0   5 m

156 *Plan of Masai house, Tanzania, about 1903*.

157 *Nandi cave house, south Elgon, Kenya, about 1900*. These houses were situated on the southern slopes of the mountain at an altitude of about 1850 m, usually at the foot of an overhanging cliff and often almost exactly behind a waterfall cascading down from higher up the mountain. The ceiling height of the caves sometimes reached as much as 9 m and some apparently had been artificially enlarged. The entrances of some of these cave houses were closed with wattle screens (as in this photograph), while others had entrance buildings across the mouth of the cave (no. 158) formed of a framework of bent boughs and brushwood plastered over with mud and cowdung.[26]

158 *Nandi cave house, south Elgon, Kenya, about 1900.*

159 *Fulani village, northern Nigeria, 1967.* The Fulani are found all over the Niger Basin from Guinea to Cameroon and they have also pushed into Guinea Bissau and Senegal and the Chad Basin. They were originally all nomadic pastoralists and are thought to have originated in the Futa Jalon upland district of Guinea. With increased population pressure they spread further afield and had reached Hausaland by the thirteenth century. In various places they have become settled either as mixed farmers or, as in Hausaland after the Jihad, as members of the urban-based aristocracy. The architecture of these settled groups is dealt with in no. 213. Those who have remained nomads take their cattle in the dry season over large distances moving from one agricultural settlement to another to graze on the remains of the harvested crops. Instead of taking tentage with them, they utilize materials available on the site and the next picture (no. 160) shows tents built of guinea-corn stalks. In the wet season they return to their villages. At night, cattle were kept in a kraal surrounded by dry thorns with a smudge fire in the centre (these smokey fires, designed to deter insects, give a very characteristic taste to Fulani milk and butter), or were picketed, with the calves tethered separately to a calf rope. The photograph shows a wet-season settlement.

160 *Fulani village, northern Nigeria, 1967.* These houses were built of guinea-corn stalks in the dry season, as the Fulani followed their cattle from one agricultural settlement to another.

161 *Houses, south-western Tanzania, about 1900.* These houses were built in Kinga country but do not appear to be Kinga houses. Kinga country contains many remote valleys and, until not long ago, communications have been minimal. It seems that many small hunting groups may have survived until recent times. These houses may have belonged to one such group. The land around the houses has been terraced.

162 *Dorze house under construction, Chencha, southern Ethiopia, late 1950s.* The Dorze live in the hills west of Lake Margarita. Their houses were constructed entirely from bamboo. The framework is woven from split bamboos and it was then thatched with the leaves of bamboo shoots. The houses often exceeded 8 m in height. They had no central pillar.[27]

108

163 *Dorze house, Chencha, southern Ethiopia, late 1950s.* Notice the small openings on the sides of the house. These served mainly to let out smoke. Similar openings were found in Kanuri houses (see nos. 184, 185 and Chapter 9).

164 *Sidamo house, s*
live on the high pla
framework of their
bamboo wattlework
thatched by weavin
These houses had a central pillar.[28]

165 *Wanji house, south-western Tanzania, about 1900.* This small group of people lived on the Kitulo Plateau, 3000 m up in the Southern Highlands area. The framework of their houses appear to have been conical rather than hemispherical in shape and constructed of straight poles of a similar thickness to the windbreak seen in the next picture, no. 166. (Compare Eritrean houses, no. 30.) The houses were thatched with turves of the peat bog vegetation which is found on the Plateau.

166 *Wanji houses, south-western Tanzania, about 1900.* Notice the windbreak outside the entrance to the house. There is little natural tree cover in the area and at this height the winds can be fierce and cold. Wanji houses were sometimes oval in plan.

167 *Vinza (or Twa) stilt houses, near Mlagarassi, Tanzania, about 1890.* The Vinza (together with a few Twa) lived on swampy lands on either side of the Mlagarassi River. These lands were held in awe by the caravans of east and central Tanzania. The English traveller, Burton, writing in 1859[29] describes the vegetation as 'combining all the disadvantages of bog and swamp, river and rivulet, thorn bush and jungle, towering grasses, steep inclines, riddled surface and broken ground'. The main economic activities of the people in these villages, which contained 40–50 beehive houses on stilts, were fishing and the preparation and sale of salt to passing caravans.

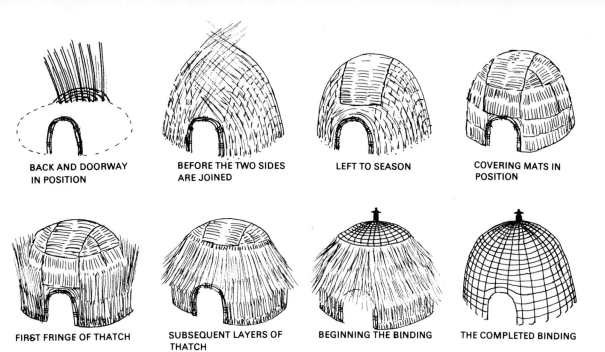

BACK AND DOORWAY IN POSITION

BEFORE THE TWO SIDES ARE JOINED

LEFT TO SEASON

COVERING MATS IN POSITION

FIRST FRINGE OF THATCH

SUBSEQUENT LAYERS OF THATCH

BEGINNING THE BINDING

THE COMPLETED BINDING

168 *Stages of construction of Swazi house, Swaziland, about 1945.* Unlike those peoples who have a regular pattern of transhumance, the Swazi only move when there is some direct social or economic stimulus. When this occurs, the houses are stripped of their thatch and the framework carried to the new site. Unlike neighbouring Hottentots and other pastoralists such as the Masai and the Fulani, the Swazi have not traditionally used cattle as beasts of burden and so the house framework would be carried on wooden posts by 20–30 men. Swazi homesteads were dispersed over the countryside. The terrain is very varied and annual rainfall varies from 450 mm to over 2000 mm. On the plateaux of the middle veld and in the highlands, the villages were built on hills and mountain slopes, whereas in the lowlands, villages were built in clearings in thickly wooded country. An unusual feature of Swazi homesteads were the underground, flask-shaped grain pits built under the cattle kraals[30] (see Chapter 5).

169 *Plan and cross-section of wife's quarters in Swazi house, Swaziland, about 1945.*

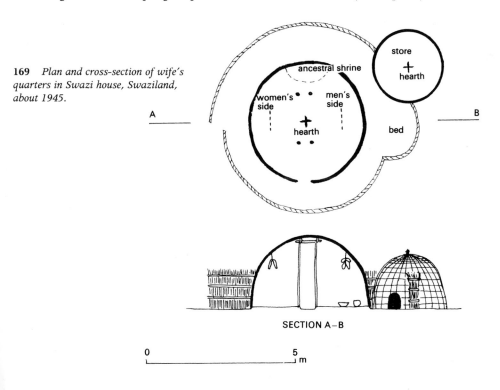

SECTION A–B

0   5 m

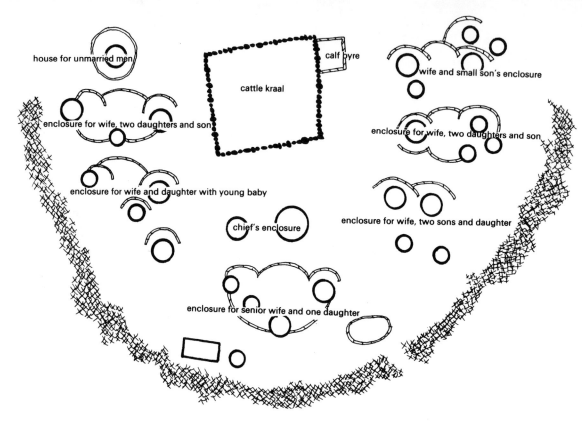

170 *Plan of Swazi chief's homestead, Swaziland, about 1945.*

171 *Plan of Zulu village, South Africa, about 1936.* Until the eighteenth century the Zulus were a loosely associated group of chiefdoms living between the Drakensberg Mountains and the Indian Ocean. After 1818, Shaka and the Zulu Ngonis gradually brought most of the other Ngonis under their influence and built up a Zulu empire. (Zulu villages were surprisingly similar in plan to Teso villages in Uganda, nos. 180–3.)

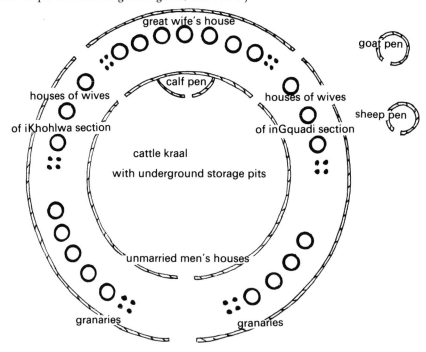

172 *Zulu village, South Africa, before 1956.*
By the mid-twentieth century economic and
political changes had led the Zulu to adopt
mixed farming, and this was reflected in a
reduction in the size of the cattle kraal in
their villages and atrophy of the outer heavy
timber stockade.

173 *Zulu homestead near
Mahlabatina–Ngoma road, South Africa,
1953.*

174 *Zulu house under construction, South
Africa, about 1902.*

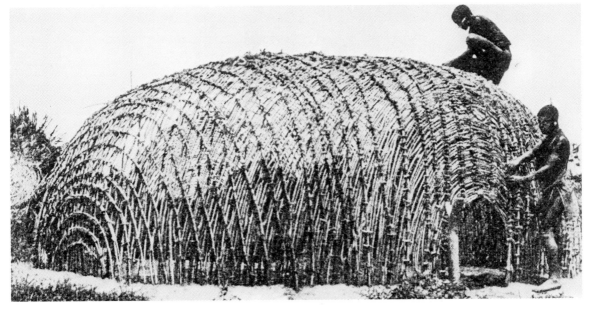

175 *Detail of Zulu house, located between Qudeni and Nqutu, South Africa, 1958.* In this area the thatching was held down with rope lattice work and the apex gathered into a finial.

176 *Tusi house, western Tanzania, about 1930.* Small groups of Tusi and Taturu pastoralists live within Nyamwezi country. (See no. 246 for details of the Nyamwezi.) This photograph shows a Tusi house somewhere east of Tabora. These Tusi are related to the Tutsi ruling class of Ruanda (see nos. 192–4), but in Nyamwezi country they look after their own cattle.

177 *Detail of Zulu house, Cathedral Peak area, South Africa, 1958.*

178 *Nyika fortified village, south-western Tanzania, about 1900.* This village is surrounded by a timber palisade and a mud wall. See no. 101 and Chapter 5 for discussion of the political upheavals which brought about these defences.

179 *Nyika homestead, south-western Tanzania, about 1900.* The Nyika lived in several isolated pockets of land near the shores of Lake Rukwa, in territory shared by the Fipa and Wanda. The Nyika built two types of houses; the second type is seen at the rear of the photograph.

7 Decoration

Isolating the decoration of a building from its form may create a dichotomy which did not exist in the minds of its builders. The distinction can often seem rather artificial even to an outsider; but for a variety of reasons which will emerge, it is convenient in this book to treat ornament or embellishment separately from form.

If, without being overly deterministic, architectural form can broadly be seen as a product of environmental and social circumstance, decoration appears to be much more bound up with a society's value systems. Much as clothing and jewellery, the decoration of buildings can help to establish personal and community identity and signal assertive or protective messages to those who are able to read them. If architecture is the public face of a society, decoration provides the opportunity not only for impressing outsiders, but also for promoting the morale, pride and solidarity of the people. In traditional Africa, decoration was not seen as a luxury. Unlike basic styles, which seem largely to be determined by local factors such as availability of materials, climate and population density, surface decoration is rather more open to variation and change. Whereas a change of building shape, unit size or construction technique would have repercussions on social factors like family size and composition (both in terms of arrangement and extent of accommodation and also of labour requirements), a change in decorative pattern could be made much more simply. It is therefore easier to posit influences from other cultures; and one can imagine that ideas could have diffused fairly easily when trading or travelling took place.

In common parlance, decoration implies conscious effort on the part of the creator to order his materials into a type of design which will be pleasing to the eye. This design may also have some magical or religious significance, but this is of course not always apparent to the outside observer. In western judgement, the suitability of a particular design or decoration is evaluated in terms of whether the creator has been true to his materials. According to this yardstick, most African architectural decoration would gain high marks. But it could be argued that any folk culture founded on a relatively low level of technology and without the stimulus of 'fashion' necessarily produces architectural decoration geared to the structure of its materials. Moreover, African architectural decoration was not the product of one man's imagination: the designs had usually become standardized through generations of use, which would tend to iron out any imperfections in the relationship between the design and its materials.

Many of the designs on African buildings, because of their reliance on texture and relief as well as on shape, could only be properly appreciated by the observer moving about in front of them and understanding their relationship with the prevailing climatic conditions. For example, in the strong clear sunlight of the savannah lands, very lightly incised lines cast a clear dark shadow and show up with great effectiveness. In the forest areas, on the other hand, the light may be equally bright, but the sky is often overcast and hazy and the light does not therefore cast sharp shadows. Under these conditions deeper and wider incised lines look better. Similarly, inside houses where the light intensity is often deliberately low, bold patterns in contrasting colours or deeply recessed panels show up most dramatically. Unfortunately, photographs do not always emphasize this close relationship and in them shape seems to become the dominant characteristic of designs.

Location

Decoration is more commonly applied to some architectural features than to others. In Africa the most common were:

Homestead entrances	Wives' rooms
Granaries and grinding sheds	Doorways
Sacred, ceremonial and community buildings	Inner walls
	Roof pinnacles

Clearly, decoration is of considerable psychological significance, and it is interesting to note that it tended to occur at points of potential social stress. Buildings which, like chief's houses, temples, shrines and club houses (all of which are considered in more detail in Chapter 4) were a power focus for the community, were almost invariably highly decorated. Within the individual homestead, decoration in its psychological warning dimension could perhaps be seen as serving to reduce potential ambiguity and embarrassment by identifying places of special taboo or other significance. Thresholds were everywhere imbued with profound ritual connotations as spatial boundary points.

Changes of state in the lifespan of individuals (*rites de passage* such as birth, initiation, marriage and death) were often marked by ceremonies associated with the process of decoration (which could either be for permanent retention or purely transitory, depending upon the culture and the context). Boran initiates, for instance, moved away from their families into buildings vividly decorated with painted cowhides.[1] Among the Korongo, to take but one further example, young girls at puberty were cloistered in specially designated granaries which they painted outside with essentially ephemeral spindly white human figures[2] (which are, in passing, very similar to the 'late white' rock paintings at Koloo in Tanzania).

Of perhaps equal interest is the observation that decoration also seemed to be applied to points of high structural stress. Apart from obvious critical points like lintels and jambs, it is possible that even the bowls set in the roofs 283 of certain Hausa and Swahili buildings might have originated as early warning mechanisms for potentially unstable roofs. On buildings with conical thatched roofs the pinnacle was a particularly vulnerable point for collapse and leakage. Often (for instance, among the Azande) a finial specially 4, 175 woven in thatch or basketwork was applied, but in some areas the points were covered with upturned pots (e.g. Gwari, Kanuri, Masaba, Nupe), carved 84, 257 posts or figures (e.g. Masaba, Pende), gourds (e.g. Kanuri), or ostrich eggs (e.g. Shona, Nyamwezi, Kanuri). The bird connection is explored further below, but it is perhaps relevant to note here that the distribution of ostrich eggs as roof decoration far exceeded the limits of the ostrich habitat. (Their occurrence in the roof of the Blue Mosque at Istanbul lends weight to the contention, more closely argued in Chapter 9, that many so-called 'Islamic' features may have originated in sub-Saharan Africa rather than, as is so often supposed, have come the other way.)

Dressed wooden door frames, where they occurred, were often much heavier than was needed to support either the door or the surrounding wall. Along the East African coast elaborately carved 'Zanzibar' doors were found, not only on the multi-storey stone buildings but also on the much smaller mud and wattle houses. There the door frame was always the first part of the building to be erected. Apart from the Swahili, elaborately carved doors were executed by, amongst others, the Venda, the Yoruba, the Nupe, the Ibo and the Dogon. The Bamileke, the Tikar, the Suku and the Holo had very elaborate frames but somewhat insubstantial doors.

It is self-evident that the scope for decoration depended to an extent on form, function and the materials of the building concerned. In portable houses the decoration itself must be portable and the fine mats and blankets used by such nomads as the Tuareg and the Somali are good examples. In houses constructed entirely of vegetation there was little scope for painted decoration, but the decorative possibilities of dyeing, tying and weaving plant fibres are discussed in Chapter 6 and in the captions to many of the illustrations. Stone is also more versatile than might be imagined and this too has been brought out elsewhere in the book.

Mud finishes are particularly receptive to mural painting and sculpted and incised decoration. External mud walls also benefit from a protective layer of paint. The graphite treatment of Nuba houses, for example, definitely had a utilitarian function. Similarly, the sculptured mud decoration found round Hausa doorways served to reinforce the edges of the wall openings as well as providing the means of displaying power symbols such as 'magic squares'.

Techniques

Mural painting was found most densely along the Upper Guinea coast and its hinterland and continued in a band east along the coast taking in peoples such as the Kru groups of Liberia, the Toma, Kisi, Asante, Ibo and Calabari.[3] It also occurred further north in Mauritania, amongst the Dogon, in the Hausa palaces, and further east in small pockets, for example, in parts of northern Cameroon, in the Ubangui-Shari and Ubangui-Wele areas of central Africa, in parts of Ruanda and Uganda, in the Nuba Mountains, in Nubia and in parts of South Africa.

The colours used in mural painting were generally confined to black, white, red and ochre. Blue and green pigments were not used until recently when 'blue bags' and commercial paints began to be imported, despite the fact that plants such as indigo were widely cultivated and used for dyeing cloth.

Relief mud decoration was found amongst the Fulani of Guinea, the Asante, the Ibo, in Benin, in Hausaland, in Oualata, in Abomey and in parts of Yorubaland and amongst the Mousgoum and the Nyakusa. Incised mud decoration was mainly confined to a much smaller belt running from southern Upper Volta through Hausaland to the Jos Plateau but also occurred in the Nuba mountains.

324

38, 73, 82, 92–3
107, 145–6, 251
204–5

152–3

54, 62–5, 85
175–6, 194–5, 258

285, 296

110, 118
123, 240, 302–3
260–1
273, 283
67, 238
17, 23–4, 201

56, 106, 111–32
206–21, 285
293–7, 300
7, 8, 211, 282

The practice of pressing natural objects into wet clay was quite
107 widespread. Pebbles were the most common material for this but in Kano
pieces of mica were used inside the emir's palace. Another material was
domestic pottery, either whole or broken, while in a few cases ceramic pieces
216 were specially fired. The walls of Nupe houses were done in this way, and so
147 were their floors. Apart from Nupe-land, Yorubaland and the archaeological
site at Daima, mosaic pavements were constructed by a number of other
16, 18 peoples. The Gwari and the Nuba both equipped their grinding-sheds with
the most durable tessellated floors. The Jaba decorated their front patios
with cowrie shells arranged in a circular or what has been called a dice-cup
pattern.[4]

Conspicuous and grand examples of applied decoration have been found
in Benin, Dahomey and Yorubaland. Inside the old palace of Benin, the pillars
128 and doors were adorned with cast brass plaques (more commonly known as
'bronzes') depicting in low relief the war deeds and battles of past obas.
Outside, the buildings were reported to have been crowned with cast
126, 130–1 'bronze' birds, while down the tall pyramidal towers wound 'bronze'
snakes. Some reports seem to indicate that these snakes were as much as 12 m
long. King, who visited Benin in 1821, described one of these snakes as
follows: 'a copper serpent whose head reached to the ground and whose
body was as thick as that of a man'.[5]

Many of the 'bronze' plaques have survived and can be seen in museums
in Europe where they were taken by the British punitive expedition to Benin
in 1897. A large number of 'staves surmounted by birds with semi-
outstretched wings' were apparently found when Benin was taken by the
British.[6] None are known to have survived intact, although one bird's foot
has come to light in the remains of the city. The snakes were each made from
about twenty-five sections. About a dozen of the snakes' heads have been
found, but only two of the body components.[7] The latter were hollow semicircular in section, about 50 cm long, and look as though they were
threaded onto wooden supports. The exact significance of these snakes, which
were probably pythons, is not at all clear, although the snake as a power
symbol is almost universal. In Yoruba symbolism the snake represented the
power of the Oba. Python cults are common and important among the peoples
of the Niger Delta to the south and south-east of Benin. It is perhaps also
interesting, in view of other connections which have been tentatively made
between the Niger and the Nile areas, that an engraved python winds its way
from top to bottom of the Meroe Lion Temple at Naga.

Much closer to Benin and the Delta, however, is Fika Emirate in northern
Nigeria, where the farmers regularly place a python 1·5 m long in every
corn-bin in order to fend off rats, mice and other vermin.[8] There may be a
somewhat similar explanation for the widespread use of other reptile figures
8, 67, 125 in African decoration. As can be seen from the plates and the drawings,
205, 223, 303 naturalistic and stylized chameleons, geckos and lizards are found in many
parts. They are certainly common elements of the household fauna and must
serve to keep down the insect population.

Modelled birds, although not with outstretched wings, were found
43 surmounting one of the walls of the acropolis at Zimbabwe. It is reported that
they were used by various peoples in southern Africa as a protection against
lightning. Wooden birds on poles have been seen in Lesotho (in the Dilli Dilli
Valley) and amongst the Rokwa peoples of Transvaal. At Vokwe, remains of

Decorative Motifs

Hausa

Asante

Nabdam

Dogon

Nyakusa

Grebo

Sotho

Nyakusa

Zande

Ibo

Mangbettu

Lobi

Fulani

Mangbettu

Bini

Ankole

Lobi

Lafofa

Ankole

Lobi

Ekoi

Nabdam

Dogon

Nyakusa

Dogon

Venda

Ankole

Birom

Lafofa

Nabdam

Bassari

Moba

Mousgoum

Abomey

Heiban

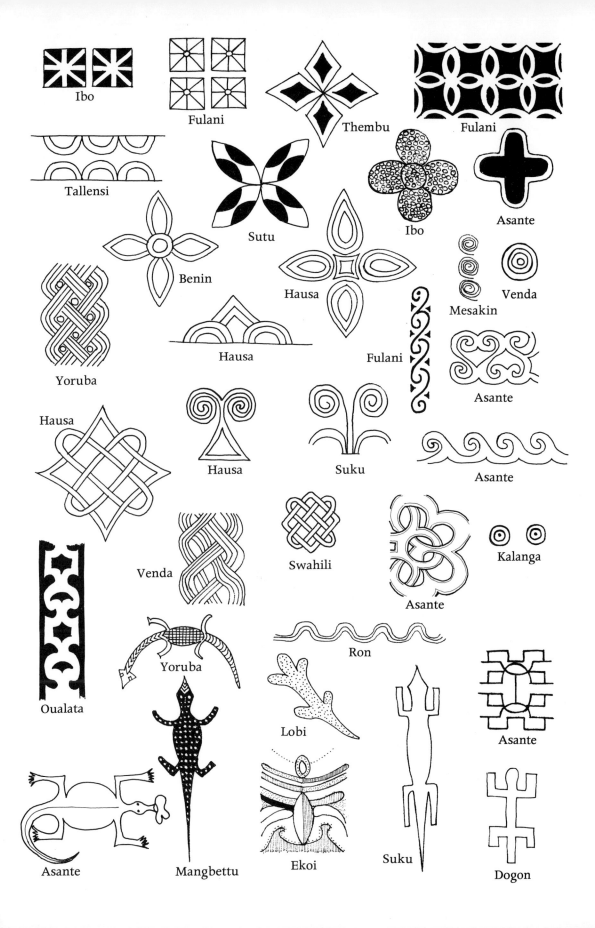

Ibo

Fulani

Thembu

Fulani

Tallensi

Sutu

Ibo

Asante

Benin

Hausa

Venda

Mesakin

Hausa

Fulani

Asante

Yoruba

Hausa

Suku

Asante

Hausa

Venda

Swahili

Asante

Kalanga

Oualata

Yoruba

Ron

Lobi

Asante

Asante

Mangbettu

Ekoi

Suku

Dogon

earthenware birds have been discovered which have holes for poles.[9] The Zimbabwe birds were modelled in soapstone and were of two types; one had a ridge down the front and back which, it has been suggested,[10] could mean that it was copied from a cast metal prototype. The connection of the South African birds with lightning makes one wonder if the Benin snakes together with the birds could have had a more practical value as lightning conductors. (In a recent survey in Rhodesia it was found that in six months over one hundred people died from lightning strikes, including twenty-one people in one house.)[11]

To the west of the Old Benin kingdom, vestiges of low-relief decoration showing affinities with the bronze plaques still survive. In what was Dahomey (now Benin) some of the walls of the Abomey palace are decorated with mud reliefs depicting human and animal figures, but when they are compared with the accounts of early visitors to the kingdom they seem to have been rather heavily touched up and in consequence to have lost some of their original spontaneity. At Ife, the old capital of Yorubaland, Frobenius discovered amongst the ruins a piece of terracotta relief depicting a mud fish. It would appear from this that some walls there were decorated with baked clay tiles. Today in some of the other palaces of Yorubaland remains of mud reliefs can be seen on pillars and walls.

Decorative Motifs

The drawings on pp. 120–1 illustrate some of the more common decorative motifs. These can obviously be analysed in many different ways, but one approach is to think of them as falling into the following two main categories:

1 Cellular design, usually made up of two alternating, serially repeated units, one being the 'positive' and the other its 'negative' (one light, one dark, for instance; or one raised and the other incised). The design is based on geometrical shapes and completely covers the surface on which found.
2 Intricate linear design based on curved lines, often with much interlacing. The design is 'applied' to a neutral ground.

Some would, I suspect, want to identify the second category with the influence of Islam; but the fact that it is also found amongst peoples like the Ibo and the Asante who have almost totally eschewed Islam makes it difficult to accept that view without qualification.

REFERENCES

1. Wingfield, A., Life on Kenya's Abyssinian Border', *East African Annual* (1948–9)
2. Nadel, S. F., *The Nuba* (London, 1947)
3. Haselberger, H., 'Le décor mural chez les Noirs de l'ouest Africain', *Africa-Tervuren*, 9 (1963)
4. Meek, C. K., Tribal Studies in Northern Nigeria (London, 1925)
5. Quoted in Roth, L., *Great Benin* (London, 1903)
6. *Ibid.*
7. Goodwin, A. J. H., 'Recent Finds in the Old Palace at Benin', *Man*, 63 (1963)
8. White, S., *Dan Bana* (London, 1966)
9. Walton, J., *African Village* (Pretoria, 1956)
10. *Ibid.*
11. *Times*, 25 March 1976

Illustration Section VII

180 *Teso house under construction, Uganda, about 1910.* The Teso were pastoralists living east of Lake Kyoga in two separate areas, one just inside Kenya and the other in Uganda. The peak of the thatch of their houses was sometimes ornamented with a buck's horn.[31] Inside, the floor and lower part were plastered with mud and cow dung up to about 0·5 m above ground level. The annual rainfall in both areas is about 1250 mm.

181 *Teso house under construction, Uganda, about 1910.*

182 *Plan of Teso house, Uganda, about 1920.* The bed was a mud platform covered with goat skins.

183 *Plan of Teso homestead, Uganda, about 1920.* Both the cattle kraal and the whole homestead were surrounded by stockades or euphorbia hedges.[32] The layout of this homestead is similar to Zulu homesteads (see no. 171). The granaries demonstrate a greater reliance on agriculture in the last hundred years.

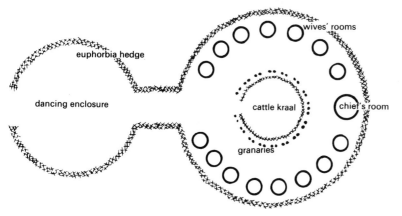

euphorbia hedge

wives' rooms

dancing enclosure

cattle kraal

chief's room

granaries

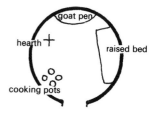

goat pen

hearth

raised bed

cooking pots

184 *Kanuri house, northern Nigeria, about 1965*. In distinct contrast to Bornu towns where the houses were large, rectangular and built of mud (see no. 301), the village houses were mostly round and thatched. They were arranged in compounds surrounded by a fence or a mud wall. On the pinnacle of the roofs, which were often overgrown with gourd tendrils, was sometimes perched an ostrich egg, a bottle-shaped gourd, or an iron spearhead.

185 *Detail of Kanuri house, northern Nigeria, 1968*. The small opening in the thatch served mainly to let out smoke. Similar openings were found in Dorze houses (see no. 163).

186 *Sonjo palisade, northern Tanzania, about 1955*. The Sonjo are a small group of people living right in the centre of Masailand. In 1950 they numbered only 4500 people divided amongst six villages built on the slopes of the escarpment at around 1500 m.[33] They are mixed farmers who manage to get two crops a year from poor land with only about 500 mm of annual rainfall, by irrigating the land in the dry season with water from streams. To protect themselves from Masai raiders they surrounded their villages with heavy timber palisades. This photograph shows the main entrance to a village with a small 'wicket gate' at one side which was constantly manned by guards (see Chapter 5). Their houses were in the beehive style similar to no. 188. In one abandoned Sonjo village, Mej, there are remains of a stone gateway, and in several villages circular stone fireplaces similar to those of Engaruku have been found.

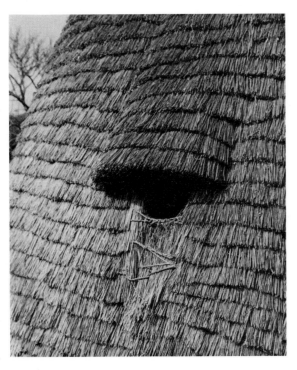

187 *Konjo house, Uganda, about 1900.* The Konjo live on and around the flanks of the Ruwenzori Mountains. Their houses were supported by one post in the centre and thatched with banana leaves, with sometimes an additional grass thatch over the top half of the roof as shown in this photograph.

188 *Sambaa village, Korogwe, Tanzania, about 1900.* The Sambaa live in and around the Usambara Mountains. It is an area of high annual rainfall (over 2000 mm at 1250 m in some places) and lush vegetation. This village, situated on the Pangani River, was at about 180 m in a very humid place. Villages varied in size from ten houses to over one hundred houses. Smaller villages contained just one lineage group, whereas the largest villages had many.[34] The villages were often surrounded by palisades or euphorbia hedges.

189 *Chagga house, eastern Kilimanjaro, Tanzania, about 1900.* The Chagga lived in dispersed settlements set among banana groves on the slopes of Mount Kilimanjaro. They practised mixed farming. Each family homestead in its banana grove was surrounded by a hedge of masale, the Chagga plant of peace and pardon. Each clan area, which consisted of many dispersed settlements linked by paths, was demarcated by a larger hedge or earth bank. The houses in the eastern area (east of the River Weru) were larger than those in the west. Those in Rombo district were the largest of all and had dry stone walls round the homesteads.[35] Inside, Chagga houses were divided into bays by a central passageway. On one side there were stalls for animals, usually four or five cows and calves, and on the other side there was sleeping accommodation. On the first floor children slept on one side and fodder was stored on the other.

190 *Chagga house, western Kilimanjaro, Tanzania, about 1900.* In the area west of the River Weru, the Chagga houses were much lower than those in the east, as is seen in this photograph where the house was thatched with banana leaves. In the far west of Chaggaland their houses were indistinguishable from those of the settled Masai whose territory they bordered. In this far western area the rainfall is only about half that in the east.

191 *Haya house, Uffumi, near Bukoba, Tanzania, about 1940.* The Haya live between Lake Nyanza and Ruanda and Burundi. Most Haya live on the undulating strip of land bordering the Lake where the rainfall is over 1800 mm a year. Until this century they were divided into five mostly small kingdoms. Karagwe, the most westerly, was the largest, comparable in size to Bunyoro. The Haya were settled cultivators and cattle keepers, cultivating mostly in the valleys and hollows in the hillside but also on the shale bands and doleritic dykes on the hilltops. Their land has become extremely fertile with careful husbandry.

192 *Tutsi house, Kissaka, Ruanda, about 1910.* From the fifteenth century until the mid-twentieth century the Tutsi were the pastoralist overlords of Ruanda who kept the Hutu agriculturalists in a state of vassalage (see Chapter 3). Ruanda (like Burundi) consists largely of a massive mountainous block. Population density was high everywhere, but on the land over 1700 m it reached more than 180 persons per km². Settlements were mostly on hilltops. Tutsi houses were usually built by the Hutu as part of their feudal service. (Compare no. 179.)

193 *Tutsi Mwami house, Uyanza, Ruanda, about 1950.* The Mwami was the Tutsi chief.

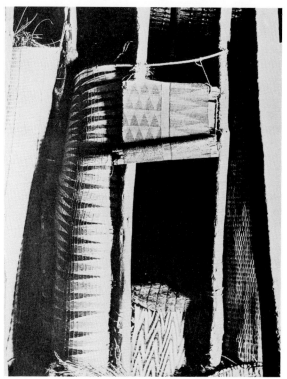

194 *Tutsi house interior, Kissaka, Ruanda, about 1910.* Reed matting made of cane or elephant grass was widely used in interiors of houses in the inter-lacustrine region. In this photograph the screen is used to partition off the platform used for keeping the sacred milk containers. The mats were constructed by sewing dyed reeds onto a woven groundwork of flat split reeds.

195 *Tutsi house interior, Kissaka, Ruanda, about 1910.* Here the screens surround a bed made of clay. Similar bed screens were found in Ganda houses.

196 *Ganda house, Uganda, about 1900.* The Ganda live in a narrow band of country along the west side of Lake Nyanza and in a wider band to the north of the lake. Over most of this fertile country there are gentle hills rising to about 250 m above the lake (which is itself at 1135 m), interspersed with swampy rivers and hollows and with forest remnants along the lake shore. The annual rain is over 840 mm everywhere, falling throughout most of the year. In the eighteenth and nineteenth centuries the Ganda were organized into a powerful state with the Kabaka ruling from an enormous palace on Mengo Hill. Outside the capital, chiefs ruled over dispersed settlements. The homesteads situated on the slopes of hills were surrounded by permanent banana plantations between the top of the hill and the water supply at the bottom, and the cattle grazed on the flat hilltops.

127

197 *Plan and cross-section of Ganda house, Uganda, about 1900.* The roof of the house was made of a network of palm fronds or flexible sticks lined with closely tied canework and supported on circles of pillars within the house. The covering was grass thatch, which was worked into several flounces at the apex, one on top of the other. The walls under the verandah were made of elephant-grass matting which was also used for doors and to surround internal pillars. A large house contained up to five beds, usually made of clay and surrounded by screens (see no. 195). Behind the main house there were smaller buildings for kitchens, latrines and goats' and children's houses, and the whole homestead was surrounded by a tall woven fence.

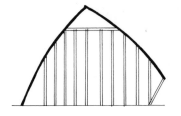
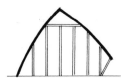
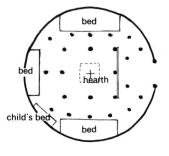
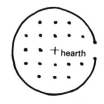

bed

bed

hearth

child's bed

bed

hearth

0   5 m

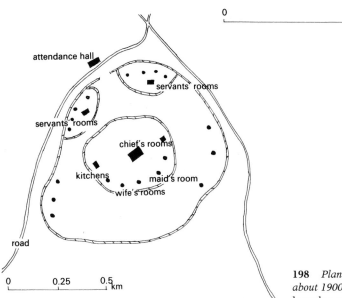

attendance hall

servants' rooms

servants' rooms

chief's rooms

kitchens

maid's room

wife's rooms

road

0   0.25   0.5 km

198 *Plan of Ganda chief's homestead, Kisozi, Uganda, about 1900.* The square buildings in the plan appear to have been a recent innovation.

199 *Ganda royal mausoleum, Kampala, Uganda, 1965.* When the Kabaka (king) Mutesa died in 1884, he became the first Kabaka to be buried in his palace. Before that the Kabaka was buried in two shrines away from the palace, one for the body and one for the jawbone. The shrines of thirty-four Kabakas are still recognized.[36] In 1938 the old mausoleum was replaced by a new one constructed of steel on a concrete foundation. This photograph shows the new building.

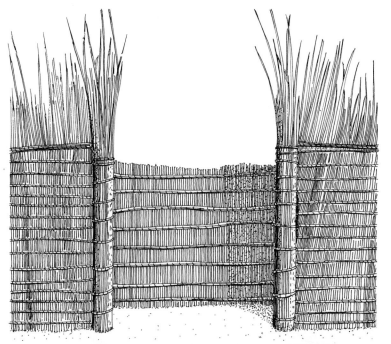

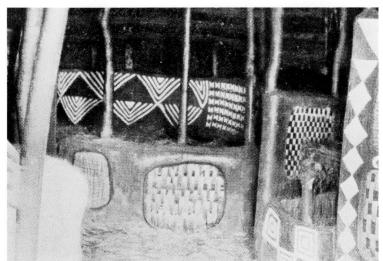

200 *Gate of Ganda palace, Uganda, about 1910.* The palace was surrounded by a tall woven fence about 3·5 m high made of elephant-grass and supported at intervals by stout posts. The posts were cut from wild fig trees and eventually took root. The responsibility for building the boundary fence was divided between district chiefs.[37] As the fences were only reckoned to last about four years this was an ongoing task. The fences built in Buganda were of three distinct types: one type for the Kabaka, one type for chiefs and a third type for commoners. In the palace there were about 450 buildings for the Kabaka and his wives. Besides these there were hundreds of smaller houses and cooking huts. The main buildings were built in a similar way to ordinary houses, but were of much larger proportions and had a much finer and thicker thatch, sometimes as much as 30 cm thick. To build just one, two hundred men would be at work for at least two months.[38]

201 *Ankole house, Uganda, about 1920.* The kingdom of Ankole appears to have come into being at the beginning of the sixteenth century at about the same time as the kingdoms of Ruanda, Bunyoro and Buganda. It was ruled by the Hima pastoralists in much the same way as the Tutsi pastoralists ruled Ruanda (see no. 192). The Hima kings, known as the Hinda, ruled there until modern times. As among the Ganda, each new ruler established his palace on a new site. This photograph shows the interior of a princess's house.

202 *Ngoni homestead, near Songea, Tanzania, about 1900.* After the civil wars in Zululand in the early nineteenth century, several factions of the Ngoni moved north eventually settling in parts of Zambia, Malawi and Tanzania. This last group set up two Ngoni states in Songea and Njòmbe.

203 *Interior of Ngoni homestead, Songea, Tanzania, about 1900.*

204 *Holo chief's house, Kwango, Zaïre, about 1960.* These houses were sometimes round and sometimes square as seen here. The doorway is unusually high and is flanked with squared logs richly carved. The heavy grass thatch hangs to the ground and is cut into steps on the front side.

205 *Suku chief's house, Kwango, Zaïre, about 1960.* The doorway is framed by two upright carved wooden posts decorated with lizards and has a semicircular wooden lintel carved with two spirals. This house and the Holo one shown in no. 204 are both rare examples of a square beehive type.

130

206 *Mousgoum village, northern Cameroon, 1912.* The Mousgoum inhabit that parcel of land between the Logone and Chari rivers just south of Lake Chad, in which the dry season is virtually desert but becomes swampy in the short wet season. (The annual rainfall is about 650 mm.) These houses were built entirely of mud with no formers, that is, they were true domes, albeit pointed, rather than vaults. The significance of the relief pattern in the outside is not entirely clear, but whatever function it may have had it is certainly a most striking decoration. It made it possible to climb to the top of the house from the outside, possibly for defence; it may have added streamlining and strength; and it may have helped to prevent rainwater erosion channels forming down the sides.

207 *Mousgoum homestead, northern Cameroon, about 1912.* The pattern on the walls of this homestead was, it seems, less common that those shown in the other photographs.

208 *Mousgoum homestead, northern Cameroon, about 1912.*

131

209 *Mousgoum corn urn, northern Cameroon, about 1912.*

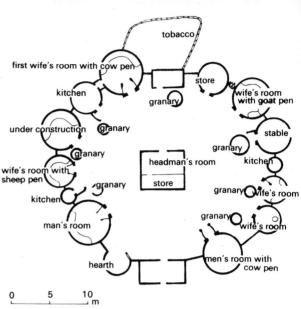

210 *Plan of Mousgoum homestead, northern Cameroon, about 1950.* Notice the passage linking the wife's sleeping room with her kitchen.

211 *Drawings of interior of Mousgoum house, northern Cameroon, about 1950.*

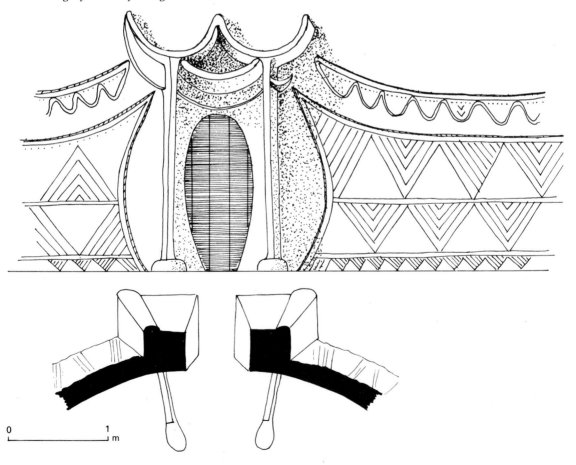

8 A Taxonomy of House Forms

The area covered by the book, as is made clear in Chapter 1, is inhabited by over a thousand different peoples or tribes, which rather vague word really defies precise definition, even using linguistic parameters. Nevertheless, it can be broadly stated that each tribe has a unique material culture, not in every particular of course, but certainly in aggregate. Many tribes have more than one type of house style. Style is defined here as not only the form of individual buildings but also the way they are arranged. Discussion of decoration is in Chapter 7; this chapter deals essentially with form. Looking at these forms alone it is possible to group them into the following main categories.

1 Round plan, free-standing; diameter less than height; walled with mud and/or stone; often with stone foundations; thatched roof (conical or trumpet-shaped); arranged in clusters of buildings, usually on the ring pattern, with buildings part of enclosing wall or fence.

Examples: Koalib, Heiban, Tira, Moro, Mesakin, Korongo, Tullishi (Sudan); Rift Valley wall, Engaruku (Tanzania); Matakam, Kirdi, Kapsiki, Namchi, (northern Nigeria, northern Cameroon); Angas, Ron, Birom, (northern Nigeria); Bandiagara escarpment (Mali); Tamgué Mountains (Senegal and Guinea); Atakora Mountains (northern Togo and Benin); Baya-Kaka (Central African Republic).

2 Round plan, free-standing; diameter approximately equal to height; roof of poles leaning against central framework; poles sometimes encased in dry stone work at base; thatching of grass or turves.

Examples: parts of Eritrea (Ethiopia); Wanji (Tanzania).

3 Round plan, free standing; diameter equal to or greater than height; walls of mud and/or wattle, bamboo or palm fronds; thatched conical roof (convex or concave profile); often with verandah full or part way round; arranged in clusters of buildings within surrounding fence, hedge or wall.

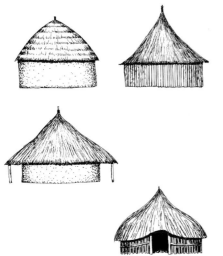

Examples: Kipsigis, Nandi, Luo Kikuyu (Kenya); Mangbettu (Zaïre); Tiv, Nupe, Jukun, (Nigeria); settled Fulani (Guinea, Nigeria, Cameroon); Dourou, Tikar, Toupouri, Massa (Cameroon); Kinga, Safwa, Nyamwezi (Tanzania); Grebo (Liberia); Tonga, Venda (South Africa); Gurage, Galla (Ethiopia); Ila (Zambia); Dagomba, Konkomba (Ghana); Kisi, Susu (Guinea); Azande, Shilluk, Bari (Sudan); Mandinka (Mali, Senegal, Guinea, Ivory Coast); Yalunka (Sierra Leone).

4 Round, oval or rectangular plan with hemispherical or lozenge-shaped profile; basic framework of hoops; covering of skins, mats and/or thatch of grass, leaves or mud over brushwood; can usually be dismantled; often found in association with cattle kraals; usually arranged symmetrically.

Examples: Masai (Tanzania, Kenya); Twa (southern Cameroon, Zaïre); Herero, Ambo (Namibia); Namaquo, Pondo, Zulu, Thembu, Xhosa (South Africa); Swazi (Swaziland); Shuwa Arab (Chad, Nigeria); Somali (Somali Rep.); Gheleba, some Galla, Bileni (Ethiopia); some Tuareg (Niger); Songhai (Mali, Niger); Sotho (Lesotho).

5 Rectangular plan, free-standing; framework of 1–4 parallel arches strengthened by horizontal cross-pieces resting at ends on poles between forked posts; covering of plaited mats; very often used as portable tent; large version sometimes immobile.

Example: Some Tuareg (Niger).

6 Rectangular plan tent; framework of two to four rows of parallel forked sticks surmounted by horizontal cross-pieces; occasionally arches instead of middle sets of poles; covering of skins or blankets under tension.

> Example: Some Tuareg (Niger); nomadic pastoralists (Sudan, Ethiopia, Somali Rep.).

7 Round plan, free-standing; conical roof and no walls; framework of straight sticks (guinea-corn stalks, bamboo); sometimes thatched.

> Examples: Fulani dry-season houses (northern Nigeria); Kinga area (Tanzania); Lutoko (Sudan); some Saho (Ethiopia).

8 Round plan, free-standing; framework of flexible poles embedded in ground at base and tied at top under tension; known as 'beehive' type; usually slightly convex profile; thatch sometimes of banana leaves but more usually of grass or reeds, either stepped or plain; sometimes low perimeter wall inside building; sometimes central support; often divided internally by partitions; same design as house; often with porch.

> Examples: Dinka (Sudan); haya, Chagga, Pare (Tanzania); Ruanda (Ruanda); some Acholi, Ganda (Uganda); Rundi (Burundi); Fulani (Nigeria); Kanuri (Nigeria, Chad, Niger); Dorze, Sidamo (Ethiopia), Kamba (Kenya); Luguru (Tanzania); Tubu (Chad).

9 Round plan, free-standing; two storeys high; walls of roughly dressed stone set in mud mortar; wooden lattice windows; drip course between each story; slightly domed mud and pole ceiling, thatched roof.

Example: some Tigre (Ethiopia).

10 Round plan, free-standing; two storeys high; walls of small round boulders set in mud mortar; second storey reached by external stone staircase; within, walled courtyard with two-storey entrance porch; thatched roof.

Example: some Tigre (Ethiopia).

11 Round plan, free-standing; flat roof; walls of mud or mud and straw; flat roof of poles and mud and straw; found in tight clusters, usually built into surrounding wall; painted and incised decoration on walls common. (Granaries often had thatched covers.)

Examples: some Dogon (Mali); Lobi, Nankanse, northern Ghana; southern Upper Volta (around Po); northern Upper Volta (around Ouahigouya).

12 Round plan, free-standing; 'shell' mud roof and no walls; slightly convex profile; sometimes embossed patterns on exterior; arranged in clusters within surrounding wall.

Example: Mousgoum (northern Cameroon); Tallensi grinding rooms (Ghana); Bangadji kitchens (Chad).

13 Oval plan, free-standing; asymmetrical peaked tha[] [] [] [] roof supported by conical mud pillar and mud arch; walls of mud [] [] [] []

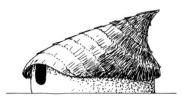

Examples: some Kagoro, Jaba, Ka[] [] [] [] [] [] [] [] (northern Nigeria).

14 Oval plan, free-standing; mud and/or wattle wall[] roof with semi-conical ends; sometimes on stilts.

Examples: pockets of coastal [] southern Liberia, Guinea Bi[] central Ivory Coast , Nyasa [

15 Round or oval plan, free-standing; corbelled stone construction; untrimmed sandstone blocks, doleritic boulders or trimmed doleritic slabs.

Examples: some Sotho-Tswana (Lesotho, Botswana); some Ghoya and Tuareg (South Africa).

16 Round plan: one, two or three storeys in height; built coalescing to form 'tower' houses; walls of puddled mud; flat roof and upper floors of poles, straw and mud.

Examples: Somolo, Ssola, Tambernu, Somba (southeastern Upper Volta, northern Benin, southern Mali).

17 Crown plan, (concentric circles) free-standing; central court or impluvium; mud walls; thatched saddleback roof.

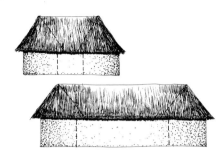

Examples: Diola (Senegal); Manjak, Papcis (Guinea Bissau); Dida, Guro, Gagu (Ivory Coast).

18 Square plan, free-standing; conical roof; walls of mud or mud and palm fronds; thatched roof of grass or reeds.

Examples: Bamileke, Bamoun (Cameroon); Abadja Ibo (Nigeria).

19 Rectangular plan, sometimes free-standing, thatched saddleback or lean-to roof; walls of planks, bamboo, cane, matting or cane and matting; walls sometimes plastered internally; roof thatch of palm leaf mats, reeds, bark, palm fronds, sometimes on stilts.

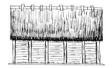

Examples: widespread in River Zaïre Basin, e.g. Wela, Poto, also Nyakusa (Tanzania); Ijo, Yako, Oratto Ibo (Nigeria); forest areas of southern Cameroon.

20 Rectangular plan; often arranged contiguously around a central square open kraal; walls of wattle or stone and mud; flat or waggon-shaped mud and wattle roof supported on forked uprights just outside walls or on walls; can be known as 'tembe' style.

Examples: Gogo, Mbugwe, Alawa, Burungi, Rangi, Hehe (Tanzania); Sabei (Uganda), some Tigre (Ethiopia).

21 Rectangular plan, free-standing; thatched saddleback roof; buildings often arranged facing across a small court with some of the sides facing court open or pillared; walls puddled mud or wattle framework plastered over; relief murals common form of decoration.

Examples: Ibo, some rural Hausa (Nigeria); Asante (Ghana); southern Togo; southern Benin; southern Ivory Coast.

22 Rectangular plan; thatched saddleback roof; units built round court or impluvium having continuous roof; walls of puddled mud or mud and wattle; sides facing court or impluvium sometimes open or pillared.

Examples: Bini, Yoruba, Ekoi (Nigeria).

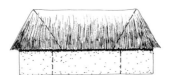

23 Rectangular plan; mud brick walls; flat or vaulted mud roof reinforced with wood or palm fronds; sometimes two-storeyed; buildings arranged within walled courtyards, sometimes forming part of courtyard wall.

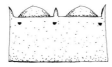
Examples: urban Hausa, urban Kanuri (Nigeria); Upper Niger towns such as Ojenne, Timbuktu (Mali); southern Mali; western Upper Volta; Mauritania.

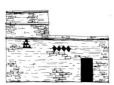
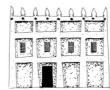

24 Rectangular plan units; one storey high but built coalescing and on top of one another; mud brick or puddled mud walls; flat mud roof reinforced with wood and palm fronds; sometimes found with style 3 built on top.

Examples: northern Ivory Coast, Mali, Upper Volta, northern Ghana, e.g. Bobo, Dagari.

25 Square plan; free standing; walls of poles or palm fronds and mud; hipped roof thatched with grass or reeds.

Examples: Lozi (Zambia); Pende (Zaïre); Tikar (Cameroon).

26 Square plan; free standing; thatched hipped roof framework of flexible poles embedded in ground at base and tied at apex under tension; slightly convex profile; thatch of grass; often with elaborately carved door frames.

Examples: Holo, Suku (Zaïre, Angola).

27 Rectangular plan, free-standing; walls of roughly dressed stone set in mud mortar; reinforced with horizontal wooden beams and short round cross-pieces; flat roof of mud and poles.

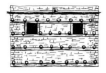

Example: some Tigre (Ethiopia).

28 Rectangular plan, free-standing, with stone rubble and cement walls; thatched roof; multi-storey; often with elaborately carved wooden doors.

Examples: East African coastal towns (Tanzania, Kenya).

29 Rectangular plan, free-standing; hipped roof; thatch of palm leaf mats sometimes with two long sides lapped over other two; walls of wattle and mud; sometimes with carved wooden door posts sometimes on stilts.

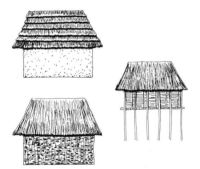

Examples: coastal regions of Kenya, Tanzania, Nigeria, Benin Rep.; lake shores (Zaïre, Tanzania); central Zaïre.

30 Square plan; tall pyramidal thatched roof; thatch of broad leaves.

Examples: Ngelima, Nalya (Zaïre).

31 Cave houses; caves often artificially enlarged; sometimes small courtyard in front surrounded by mud wall or fence; wattle and daub wall sometimes built across mouth of cave.

Examples: Matengo (Tanzania); some Nandi (Kenya); some Lunda, Sango, Lomotwa, upper Wele River area (Zaïre); Kirdi Mountain (Cameroon); Dar Banda, Djebel Mara (Sudan); Teda (Chad).

32 Underground or semi-underground 'dug-in' buildings; rectangular in plan; sometimes with excavated passageway in front; walls of stone in mud mortar, wattle and mud, mud bricks or turves; flat or slightly waggon-shaped roof of earth, mud and poles supported on many rows of forked uprights.

Examples: Iraqw, Gorowa (Tanzania); some Tigre (Ethiopia); parts of the Niger River bend; southern Upper Volta.

Illustration Section VIII

212 *St Michael's Church, Debra Berhan, Ethiopia, 1940s.* In the rural Christian areas of central, south and west Ethiopia, churches were round in plan with thatched roofs. Walls were either of wattle and mud or stone. In recent times the round plan seems to have spread to the north too, where previously the churches were rectangular with flat roofs.[39]

213 *Fulani house, Futa Jalon, Guinea, about 1950.* These houses belonged to those Fulani who settled and became mixed farmers. Although near the slopes of Futa Jalon, these houses bear little resemblance to the archetypal pastoral Fulani houses (see nos. 159, 160). These villages were composed of irregularly arranged houses grouped round the mosque or chief's house. The women's houses were about 10 m in diameter, and mosques and chiefs' houses were usually somewhat larger. In chiefs' houses the hard mud floor was often covered with incised patterns.

214 *Drawing of the interior of a roof on a Fulani house, Futa Jalon, Guinea, 1956.* The apex of the roof was filled with a basketwork panel.

215 *Aerial view of Nupe village, central Nigeria, about 1950.* Nupe territory stretches in a ribbon for over 300 km along the Niger valley, with a side branch along the River Kaduna. The rivers and streams were clearly of importance to the Nupe for as well as helping to cultivate the alluvial valleys, the water was used for transportation of goods between states to the south and the Hausa states to the north. Note the characteristic open irregular layout of Nupe settlements and the complex pattern of footpaths linking the settlements.

216 *Nupe house, Zanchita, near Bida, central Nigeria, about 1960.* The relief decoration found either side of the door of this inner kitamba is stained and hardened with an infusion of locust-bean pods. The design may owe something to that found on mud vaults, where the surface is divided into squares by the ribs of the vault and bowls are sometimes used as bosses (see, for instance, in Kano). The surface round the door is tessellated with baked clay tiles.

217 *Nupe palace, Bida, central Nigeria, about 1920.* In about 1850 Bida became the capital of the Nupe, supplanting Rabba. The photograph shows the kitamba (entrance building) of the palace of the ruling house of Masaba (one of the three houses from which the Etsu or ruler is chosen). Inside the kitamba there were raised clay platforms stained and polished dark brown.

144

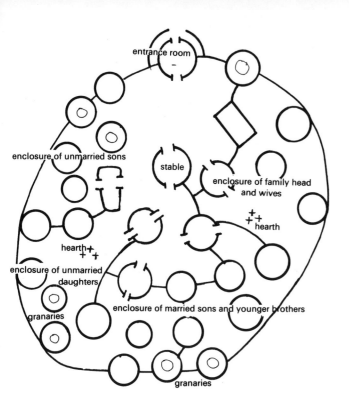

218 *Plan of Nupe chief's house, central Nigeria, about 1940.*

entrance room

enclosure of unmarried sons

stable

enclosure of family head and wives

hearth

hearth

enclosure of unmarried daughters

granaries

enclosure of married sons and younger brothers

granaries

219 *Plan of Nupe house, central Nigeria, about 1940.*

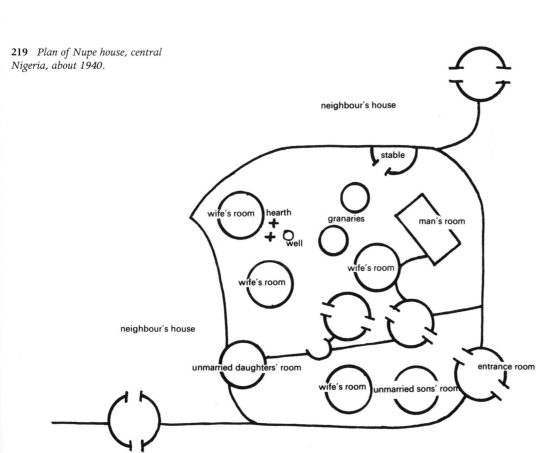

neighbour's house

stable

wife's room hearth

granaries

man's room

well

wife's room

wife's room

neighbour's house

unmarried daughters' room

entrance room

wife's room unmarried sons' room

220 *Nupe granaries, Zanchita, near Bida, central Nigeria, about 1960.* These granaries had just been filled and sealed and would all eventually have been thatched. Notice the saddle-stones.

221 *Nupe smithy, Bida, central Nigeria, about 1955.* There was a distinct division of labour among the Nupe. Transportation and agriculture, iron, brass and silver working, silk and cotton-cloth weaving, bead making in glass and stone, and canoe building were all important. Each of the crafts was organized into guilds, each guild in its own ward in Bida town, and each craft had its own type of specialized building. This photograph shows a smithy on the left and part of a kitamba (see no. 216) on the right. The decorative patterns cut in the wall of the smithy provided light and ventilation. The arrow-shaped doorway is very characteristic of Nupe architecture.

222 *Chamba district head's house, Toungo, north-eastern Nigeria, 1957.*

146

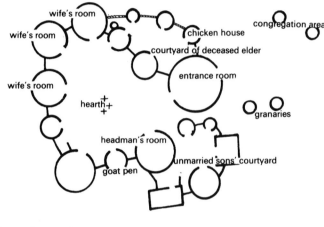

wife's room
wife's room
chicken house
congregation area
courtyard of deceased elder
entrance room
wife's room
hearth
granaries
headman's room
unmarried sons' courtyard
goat pen

0   5   10
⊢⊢⊢⊢⊢⊢⊢⊢⊢⊢⊢ m

223 *Dagomba homestead, northern Ghana, about 1970.* The Dagomba live in nucleated villages with about sixty compounds similar to the one shown here clustered tightly together. The size of the entrance building is associated with its use as a stable for horses as well as a reception room.

224 *Plan of Dagomba homestead, northern Ghana, about 1965.* The only rectangular buildings were occupied by unmarried sons who visited southern Ghana in the dry season and on their return wished to have a tin roof on their houses—and tin roofs cannot satisfactorily be put on round buildings.

225 *Ila village, southern Zambia, before 1944.* The Ila live north of the Kafue River in an area of relatively low rainfall with a seven-month dry season. They were pastoralists keeping their cattle in individual family kraals at night. Their houses and family kraals were arranged in a circle around a central open space and the chief's house and kraal. Other types of kraal arrangements are shown in nos. 171 and 183. This village contains approximately four hundred buildings.

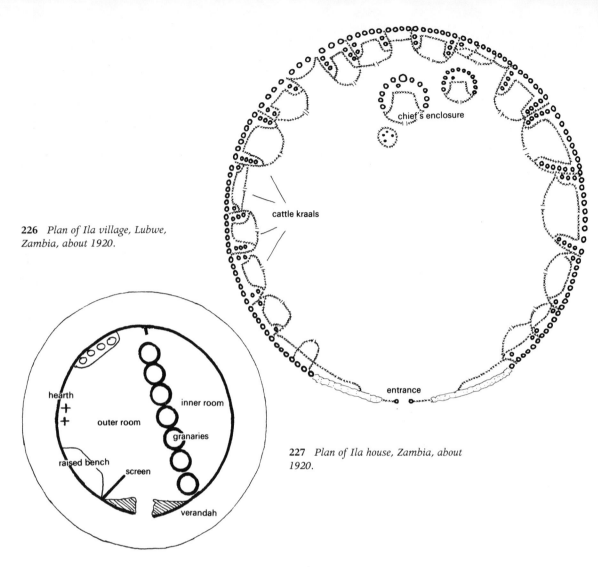

226 *Plan of Ila village, Lubwe, Zambia, about 1920.*

chief's enclosure

cattle kraals

entrance

hearth

inner room

outer room

granaries

raised bench

screen

verandah

227 *Plan of Ila house, Zambia, about 1920.*

228 *Ila chief's house, Nanzela, Zambia, about 1920.*

148

229 *Cuabo (?) house, near Chametengo, Mozambique, about 1900.* Chametengo is on a tributary of the Zambezi River. The area is very hot and temperatures of over 50°C have been recorded.

230 *Interior of Cuabo (?) house, near Chametengo, Mozambique, about 1900.* The platform in the top right of this photograph was a bed reached by the notched ladder. The mud building in the foreground was apparently a lock-up for a mischief maker!

231 *Pare house, north-eastern Tanzania, about 1928.* The Pare live in mountainous country on the edge of Masailand. They were in constant fear of attack by the Masai and other neighbours and their ingenious defensive systems are discussed in Chapter 5. This house appears to have been thatched with banana leaves.

232 *Ibo house, Ikwo, eastern Nigeria, about 1925.* See no. 105 for general notes on the Ibo. Ikwo Ibo houses more commonly had mud walls.

233 *Shilluk village, south-eastern Sudan, about 1965.* The Shilluk live on land bordering the White Nile around the town of Malakal. The river and its tributaries flood in the wet season. The buildings with stepped thatch in the photograph are said to be a recent innovation (possibly derived from the neighbouring Dinka); previously there were only two or three 'steps' at the bottom of the thatch.

234 *Shilluk village, Fashoda, south-eastern Sudan, about 1930.* The larger buildings on the left were communal cattle houses in the rainy season and at other times were used for village meetings or as guest houses. Note the absence of stepped thatch (see previous picture, no. 233).

235 *Shilluk Reth's house, Fashoda, south-eastern Sudan, about 1930.* The house of the Reth (king) was virtually identical to that of an ordinary person but raised on a large artificial mound (*aturwic*) some 3 m high.

236 *Dinka homestead, Sudan about 1930.* The building on the left is the *luak* (cattle-house). See next picture, no. 237.

150

237 *Dinka homestead, Sudan, about 1870.* The Dinka, who number about one million, are cattle herders and farmers living on the banks of the White Nile. The Dinka economy was much bound up with flooding regimes. Their wet-season homesteads were on land rising above the flood water, river levées about 90 m apart. To the Dinka, cattle were in some respects as valuable as humans and they occupied a central place in their religion. This may account for the fact that the largest building in the homestead was the *luak* (or cattle-house), but cattle-houses are also found in communities where cow dung is collected for use as manure on the fields. *Luaks* were sometimes as much as 12 m in diameter; an extra ring of poles inside helped support the roof. The house of the head of the household was distinguished by a double porch. Many Dinka houses were built on stilts and this has been associated with flooding. However, closer examination does not entirely support this thesis as the Raik Dinkas who live nearest the swamps build their houses on the ground.[40]

238 *Mangbettu houses, Zaïre, about 1950.* The Mangbettu live south of the River Wele in north-eastern Zaïre, around the watershed of the Nile and Zaïre rivers and on the margins of the forest. It rains every month of the year and there is over 100 mm of rain every month from March to October. Their houses were about 6 m in diameter. The roofs were thatched with grass and rested on verandah posts and the wattle framework of the walls. The walls were mostly plastered and a space was left under the eaves to allow for ventilation. The mud walls were decorated with yellow clay and charcoal.

239 *Bangadji (?) chief's house, Mayo-Kebbi, Chad, before 1945.* Notice the corn urns on the right-hand side. The buildings with flat mud roofs were kitchens and the small round holes on top acted as chimneys. The kitchen doorways and the corn urns were very similar to those found in Mousgoum homesteads (see nos. 206–11).

240 *Grebo village, Liberia, about 1900.* The
Grebo live in clearings in the high forest
round the Cavally River on the borders of
Liberia and the Ivory Coast. It is a very
humid area with an annual rainfall of over
2000 mm. Typically their villages consisted
of 30–100 houses grouped around a central
open space. Each house had a grain store in
the rafters and few free-standing granaries
were built. Notice the projecting eaves which
deflect the water away from the walls (a
problem with steep pitched roofs) and the
timber walls decorated in black and white.

241 *Jukun houses, Wukari, central Nigeria, 1958.*
The Jukun kingdom of Kororofa was centred
around Ibi on the River Benue. It was mentioned in
the *Kano Chronicle* as early as the fourteenth
century and between then and the nineteenth
century it was continually in conflict with first the
Hausa and Bornu kingdoms and later the Fulani
empire. There are pockets of Jukun people
elsewhere, for example near Abuja and Shendam;
the Igala rulers are of Jukun origin. The building
on the left of this photograph was a meeting house
whose roof rests on a ring of poles; the roofs of
houses rest directly on the mud walls. The insides
of the walls of some Jukun (Kona) houses were
decorated with geometric patterns of red, white and
black.[41]

242 *Nyakusa chief's house, south-western Tanzania,
about 1900.* Most Nyakusa houses were rectangular
in plan (see nos. 50–54). In this photograph notice
the stone infilling and how the interior fluted mud
plastering (seen in no. 53) was carried to the
outsides of the doorposts.

243 *Nyakusa house, south-western Tanzania, about 1900.* See also nos. 50–54.

244 *Kinga house, southern Tanzania, about 1900.* The Kinga, who are the eastern neighbours of the Nyakusa, live in the Kipengere Mountains north-east of Lake Malawi. It is a country of much rainfall, deep valleys and high mountains, and until recently communications were poor. Contrast the walls of this house splayed out at the base and the roofs with very wide eaves with the Nyakusa house (no. 242) with walls splayed out at the top and narrow eaves. Notice the mud podium and the mud door pilasters. These features could be a relic of building on a rock surface, when the uprights cannot be dug into a trench and have to be supported above ground. This technique was also employed by some of the Shona on their rocky land, after they had abandoned stone buildings. Notice the trimmed bamboo roots at the apex of the roof, possibly representing ostrich heads; ostrich eggs were widely used to decorate apexes of roofs and were sometimes (for instance, among the Shona) reputed to act as lightning insulators.

245 *Safwa house, south-western Tanzania, about 1900.* The Safwa live north of the Nyakusa around the town of Mbeya.

246 *Nyamwezi house, western Tabora, Tanzania, about 1930.* The Nyamwezi occupy a large area centred on Tabora. They controlled trade between the coast and Karagwe and other states to the north and Katanga and north-east Zambia to the south. Until the middle of the nineteenth century, when they became united under one leader, they were a loose confederation of small chiefdoms with different cultural traditions and sometimes different origins. Their houses were both round and rectangular in plan and sometimes both styles were found in one homestead. The round houses were divided internally by a circular partition on top of which was a grain store.

247 *Fulani house near Tibati, Cameroon, about 1914.* Here the Fulani are at their easternmost extent on the Adamawa Massif. (See no. 159 for details of other Fulani settlements.) They are now mostly settled mixed farmers rather than pastoralists. This photograph shows the entrance building to a compound. The porch was a characteristic feature though often it was more enclosed with arcading (similar to Nupe houses, no. 216). The twin apex roof was somewhat unusual. A layer of open, diamond-weave matting sometimes covered the roof thatch.

248 *Luyia village, northern Kavirondo (northern Nyanza), Kenya, about 1900.* The Luyia is a general name for a collection of about fifteen different peoples all of whom lived in similar houses. The houses were round in plan with conical thatched roofs and a broad verandah encircling the whole. This village was surrounded by a more or less circular mud wall and a deep moat and was typical of the northern Kavirondo villages north of the Nzoia River. In the more southerly villages euphorbia hedges mixed with aloes carried bright red flowers for most of the year.

249 *Tikar house under construction, Cameroon, about 1914.* The Tikar, a cluster of small chiefdoms speaking similar languages, live north of the Bamileke and east of the Mambila Plateau. In this photograph the internal partition of the house can be seen. The roof would have been finished with a heavy grass thatch and the walls plastered with mud. Notice the finished houses behind, with their 'spire' roofs. Similar roofs were found on Azande houses and in parts of Sierra Leone, Ivory Coast and Liberia. Tikar houses were also often square in plan (see nos. 79–81).

250 *Venda houses, South Africa, about 1955.* The Venda live in the middle Limpopo Basin and the Zoutpansberg Mountains of the northern Transvaal. Until the fifteenth century they appear to have lived north of the Limpopo River and to have been associated with the stone cultures of Rhodesia, especially Khami (see no. 47). When building a new house the Venda used pieces of iron (*pfumo*) to help them locate a suitable site.

251 *Drawing of a Venda door, South Africa, date unknown.* This carved wooden door is now preserved in the Pretoria Museum.

155

252 *Gurage houses under construction, Ethiopia, about 1965.* The Gurage live in south west Ethiopia in one of the most densely populated areas of the country. In contrast to the scattered settlements of the central plateau area, the Gurage live in compact villages. Their houses were thatched with a double layer of thatch with pieces of the bark of the *ensete* or false banana plant sandwiched in between for insulation. The stalk and fibre of this plant were also used in the construction of the house framework.

253 *Kikuyu chief's homestead, Kenya, about 1930.* The Kikuyu live in scattered homesteads in the highlands above the Rift Valley. The annual rainfall varies between 1000 mm and 2000 mm and comes in two seasons. The roofs of their houses were usually supported on four central posts with additional support from the verandah posts at the eaves. The walls were usually of wood and wattle plastered with sheep dung and clay, but in the forest areas the walls were of trimmed planks set edge to edge. The photograph shows granaries in a chief's homestead. The whole homestead was surrounded by a hedge or stockade within which the cattle were kept at night. There is a Kikuyu proverb, *Wega uumaga na mocie*, the quality of a man is judged by his homestead.[42]

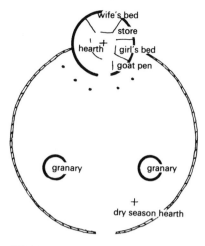

254 *Plan of Kikuyu house, Kenya, about 1930.*

255 *Ibo house, near Abakaliki, south-eastern Nigeria, about 1925.* This house was in the north of Iboland in the grasslands, where the rainfall is less than 1800 mm a year (compare this with the south of Iboland where the annual rainfall is over 2500 mm). Over most of Iboland palm mats were used for thatching, but here grass has been used instead. The roof was circular in plan while the house was square in plan. This style can be thought of as intermediate between round and square. This interface is discussed in Chapter 9.

256 *Bondei house, Ngomeni, Tanzania, about 1900.* The Bondei, who live in the coconut groves of the north Tanzanian coast, where the rainfall is about 1700 mm per annum, exhibit certain features of both the matrilineal and *shungwaya* (bilateral) traditions of inheritance which are separately present in their neighbours.[43] It could be said that this blending is also evident in their architecture. Their oval houses can be thought of as interim between round and rectangular.

257 *Pende chief's house, southern Zaïre, about 1955.*

258 *Interior of Lozi chief's house, Leului, Barotseland, Zambia, about 1930.* The Lozi live in the plains of western Zambia. They were pastoralists who practised some agriculture and fishing. In the eighteenth and nineteenth centuries they were organized into a strong state which had control over most of the Upper Zambezi Basin. Their villages were built on low mounds. Each year when the plains were covered with the floodwaters of the Upper Zambezi, the Lozi migrated by canoe to higher ground. Leului was the low-water home of the ruler.

259 *Drawing, cross-section and plan of Katab house, northern Nigeria, about 1950.* These striking houses occurred in only one small area of northern Nigeria among the Moroa, Katab and Jaba peoples at the foot of the escarpment of a far western outlier of the central plateau of Nigeria. It is interesting to speculate on a possible connection with the architecture of the Iron Age Nok culture of about 300 BC, as its type site was within the area in which these houses were found. Katab blacksmiths' houses were quite different, round in plan with very tall conical roofs, perhaps signifying the importance of iron working.

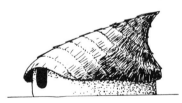

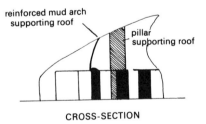

CROSS-SECTION

GROUND FLOOR PLAN

FIRST FLOOR PLAN

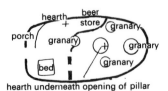

hearth underneath opening of pillar

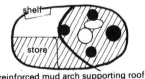

reinforced mud arch supporting roof

9 The Distribution of Styles

Theories about architectural style are almost as much a part of a culture as the styles themselves. Africa has suffered from interpretations, often apparently founded more in ideology or emotion than in careful study, put forward by generations of outsiders.

An example of such a theory is that the continent was originally covered with round houses but that under the influence of foreign contacts these are gradually giving way to rectangular ones. This idea, together with the associated notion that the metamorphosis represents 'development' from a primitive to a more advanced state, has received such powerful advocacy over a period of almost 250 years that it has now to a large extent been accepted as true both by Africans and by non-Africans. Only recently has it been suggested[1] that a circular plan may be 'a sign of nature's rhythm'! This is only one of a number of assumptions which confuse any analysis of styles.

Many theories put forward are highly simplistic and rely on the idea that styles can be 'explained' simply by Portuguese or Islamic influence, for example. The wide diversity of styles illustrated in this book should show that although certain generic characteristics have emerged, most styles were very specific to local conditions. It seems much more satisfactory to think of individual styles as a complex interweaving of many different ideas. In the same way as it is now thought untenable to postulate massive migrations of people across Africa in order to explain the emergence of kingdoms at one time or another, but preferable instead to think of small bands of people, pastoralists or traders for example, moving about and coming into contact with other cultures, so with house types the emergence of any one style was probably due to a fusion of ideas from within and without. A conceptual model to explain this would be a process rather like the assortment of genes and chromosomes which underlies the mechanisms of biological interaction.

Several documented cases indicate that the process of change could be either gradual or sudden and that despite political and economic changes house styles have in some cases remained basically constant. In Tigre in Ethiopia a pottery model of a house dated to the fifth century was excavated in 1959 and shows remarkable similarities with present-day Tigre houses.[2] Yet in other parts of Ethiopia in the thirteenth century there was a decisive break with tradition upon the accession of the Solomonid dynasty when the stone-built capital was replaced by a tented camp arranged in concentric circles, which moved round the country. In Tanzania, the Iraqw appear to have changed their house type twice within the space of a hundred years.[3]

Sudanese Style

An area where a gradual development seems to have taken place is the western Sudan. Here, in the Niger and Chad Basins, courtyard houses with rectangular buildings are widespread, and coincide quite closely with the areas in which people have espoused Islam. This fact has led some writers to conclude quite simply that the rectangular flat-roofed style is an entirely alien one traded across the desert with Islam. One is bound to ask whether the evidence really justifies such an explanation. There is certainly a good deal of similarity in the styles of rectangular buildings over most of the western Sudan area, and at times they have all been labelled variants of a unitary Sudanese style. The central characteristics of this style are said to be a courtyard plan; a flat or dome-shaped vaulted roof, and parapets pierced with gutter pipes or channels. Walls are constructed of mud bricks set in mud mortar; and the mud roofs are supported by palm frond joists and formers.

260–301

Some of these features are of course undoubtedly shared by Muslim domestic architecture in the Mediterranean areas and elsewhere. Principal amongst these is the courtyard plan: it gives privacy to the inside rooms when there is only one entrance and privacy for women is one of the central tenets of Islam. However various features of the Sudanese style are also found, sometimes independently and sometimes together, in other parts of West Africa. Moreover, some of the peoples converted to Islam in the area, the Fulani, Nupe and Khassonke for instance, do not build in this Sudanese style, despite the fact that their contacts with Muslim culture have been as strong as their neighbours who do. One writer, Engestrom,[4] has studied this in some detail and has related the possession of a sort of proto-Sudanese style (including the rectangular plan) by the Dogon, Samo, Bobo and Nounouma to a common linguistic base. He has postulated that these people were the early inhabitants of the western Sudan area and that the rectangular shape must have pre-dated Islam, at least here, and must have been spread later to the peoples converted to Islam.

213–221

33–40

It has been suggested[5] that support for this idea can be found in the shape of underground houses in Upper Volta and Mali. In Upper Volta the ancestor houses of the Bobo Fing are said to represent the homes of the founding families of the villages. These *wasa* are most often underground and rectangular in plan. Archaeological evidence provides grounds for the notion of a pre-Islamic rectangular style. Excavations at Ntereso in northern Ghana have revealed the remains of a rectangular building which seems to have had a flat roof. A date of the second millennium BC has been claimed for this.[6]

Another writer, Prussin,[7] has suggested that what distinguishes the buildings in the Sudanese style from others in the same area is a specialized technique of building in mud bricks. She also suggests that it was the Manding as peripatetic traders and marabouts who diffused this technique throughout the Sudan from an origin outside the area. A further suggestion is that mud bricks allow stronger and taller rectangular buildings to be erected than is possible in puddled mud, and that they may therefore have been introduced to facilitate the building of large mosques and minarets. This sounds quite plausible, but cannot be used to explain the emergence of the Sudanese style, because in some areas the same style was produced in stone and burnt brick: the former notably in Oualata in the west, and the latter in Bornu in the east and Timbuktu in the west. Furthermore in some areas, such as Dinguiraye, large round-plan mosques were built using puddled mud and thatch. Mud bricks may well have been an innovation introduced by the Manding, since there is evidence that indicates that they may have introduced a fair number of other innovations into the area over which they held sway, but there is no *a priori* reason why the rectangular style should not already have been in existence at the time.

Despite a marked similarity over the western Sudan as a whole, these Sudanic buildings do nevertheless show significant variations both in technique and style. In the far west in Oualata some houses were built of stone set in mud mortar and plastered over with mud, whereas in the Upper Niger areas rectangular mud bricks were most frequent. In the Hausa towns pear-shaped mud bricks were almost invariably used while in Bornu (and in one small area of the Upper Niger) until the eighteenth century burnt bricks were common.

An alternative hypothesis to explain the distribution of the Sudanese style is that mud buildings originated as a way of adjusting to some of the hazards of urban life. One of the most frightening of these is fire. This is of course true of any part of the world, but the risk of fire is very great indeed in this area where the annual rainfall is only 300 mm falling in three months, and where for the other nine months an absolute drought prevails and gale-force desiccating harmattan winds are common. John Pepper Clark has written:

And at harmattan, the bamboo walls
Are ready tinder for the fire
That dries the fresh fish up on the rack . . .

(Abiku)

City populations could amount to forty thousand, and all cooking was done outside over open fires in the dry season, so some means of reducing the risk must have been a top priority for the governments concerned. The documentary evidence is very sparse, but there are reports that thatched buildings were forbidden entirely in some towns at various times. Taking an example from outside the area, in Sierra Leone, it appears that despite smaller populations and much wetter climates whole towns were often destroyed by fire.[8]

This idea of the Sudanese style as an urban one rather than a Muslim one would explain why certain Muslim peoples did not adopt it. It may also explain why in the scattered farmsteads and hamlets of Hausaland, for instance, particularly towards its wetter margins, the same basic style incorporates very much less mud and very much more grass (for roofing) than in nearby towns. Similarly in the Chad Basin to the east there is a distinct difference between buildings in the towns and those in the villages. Most of the village houses in Bornu were thatched and on a round plan, whereas until the early nineteenth century many of the urban buildings were of burnt bricks and rectangular in plan.

An account of Mali in the fourteenth century reveals that roof styles at least were different then from those found in the Upper Niger area today. Al-Omari[9] described the roofs as being mostly in the form of cupolas or 'camels' backs' depending on whether the buildings were round or rectangular, whereas today in that area all the houses are rectangular and the roofs flat. However, in Hausaland the type of roofs Al-Omari described are still found, but mostly in the central and southern parts of the area. It would seem reasonable to suppose that the change in roofing in the Upper Niger area is perhaps connected to the desiccation of the area since the fourteenth century. The sequence of roofing found today in Hausaland certainly lends

273   support to this idea. In the north of Hausaland around Daura flat roofs are
289   dominant, in the central area around Zaria roofs are mostly domed, while in
299   the far south around Abuja roofs are domed and thatched. (The annual
rainfall in Zaira is 1150 mm which is slightly more than double that of Daura.)
This contradicts the view recently advanced by Prussin[10] that the domed
roofs of Hausaland were a product of the Fulani Jihad.

    It begins to look as if the Sudanese style (in so far as it exists at all) was
primarily urban and in existence before the spread of Islam, though modified
since by changes in climate and materials. An interesting sequence has been
revealed by the excavations at Tegdaust,[11] which presumably was the so far
unidentified Audoghast. The earliest layers show an eighth- or ninth-
century village, where the houses were made with mud bricks, which was
superseded later in the ninth century by a stone-built town. A later town
was then built on the ruins of this one, using the remains of the stone
buildings as foundations. Elsewhere a similar sequence of stone and then
mud bricks can be seen, but with in some areas the stone persisting for much
longer, even sometimes to the present day. In Timbuktu one of the early
mosques was described by Leo Africanus in the early sixteenth century as a
'most stately temple with walls of stone and lime'; now all the mosques are of
mud brick although until recently the bottom halves of the walls of some
266   houses in Timbuktu and in nearby villages were built of stone. In Aïr the
Tuareg associate stone houses with the Itesan Tuareg, who according to
tradition were the early Tuareg immigrants. In Abelessa an interesting
agricultural village has been described.[12] It was divided into four quarters,
inhabited by people from Tassire, descendants of Tuareg slaves, and in the
other two, Arabic-speaking immigrants from Tidikelt. The first two quarters
consisted of mud and stone houses; the others were of mud brick.

    It is interesting that in the west of the area rectangular mud bricks seem to
have replaced roughly shaped rectangular pieces of stone. Further east in
Hausaland, the building technique was significantly different and pear-
shaped bricks were used. Here again it is possible that these bricks replaced
small round stones. South and east of Hausaland are two highland areas where
just such a technique of mud and stone is still found. And at Turunku, the
296   precursor of Zaria city, many of the remaining houses have stone foundations
298   and the town wall, uniquely in Hausaland, was built of small round boulders
and mud.

    In the Chad Basin burnt bricks have been found on over a hundred sites.
Perhaps this technology was a response to the poor drainage conditions
which were prevalent in the area. This idea is supported by the fact that by
the nineteenth century, when the Kanem-Bornu capital was moved to
Kukawa, burnt brick technology had been abandoned; by this time Lake
Chad had become much smaller and the desert had moved southwards. It is
suggestive, too, that in the Niger Basin burnt bricks were only found in one
small area around Djenne where similar swampy conditions prevailed in
earlier centuries before the desert encroached further south. In 'Ain Farah,
Darfur, there are some burnt brick remains which are generally thought to be
those of a Christian monastery which survived until the fourteenth century.
However, Zienelabdeen, who comes from Darfur and who has studied (but
not so far published on) Nubian Christian buildings, has said that the size of
the bricks at 'Ain Farah is quite different from Nubia and that the remains
are more likely to be an outpost of the Bornu empire.

It is not certain whether the burnt bricks were developed separately in the Chad Basin, but it certainly looks as though the technique was in that region long before the architect El Saheli is said to have introduced them into the Upper Niger area in the fourteenth century.

The major trade and pilgrimage lines across the desert must, of course, have been influential in introducing new techniques and styles. Analysis of rock paintings in the Sahara has shown how traffic in the first and second millennium BC was polarized at different ends of the western Sudan. In the west the routes connected Gao and Libya, while in the Chad Basin connections were with Nubia. This pattern seems to have persisted in much later times and this is reflected to a certain extent in building patterns and techniques. But it must be borne in mind that trade is a two-way affair. The
265, 268, 274 tapering minarets of Timbuktu, Agadez and Tichite, for instance, have certain features in common with the towers of Berber kasbas. Most people have assumed that the kasbas influenced the minarets to the south, but the influence could very well have travelled in the other direction, particularly as tapering minarets are not found in many parts of the Islamic world (in East
126–31, 144 Africa not at all) and as the towers on non-Muslim Benin and Yoruba houses were so remarkably similar to the tapering minarets further north. The decoration around house doorways is perhaps analogous. The moulded relief
260–1 decoration of Mauritania is often assumed to have come from Marrakesh where similar designs are found; but closer examination reveals that in Oualata the craft is confined to women whose ancestors came as slaves from the black areas further south.[13] This surely must give strong circumstantial support to
106, 117–25, influence northwards across the desert, especially as similar decoration is
285, 294–6 found amongst the Hausa, Asante and Ibo (these last two being non-Muslim).

Impluvial Style

In the forest areas in the south, courtyard houses were also constructed, but here four buildings usually faced one another across the courtyard. In all cases the buildings had thatched roofs. Sometimes they were thatched
119 separately and connected by screen walls, for example Asante houses,
132–42 whereas the Yoruba, Bini and Ekoi built a continuous roof round the courtyard. A special variation of this style was the so-called impluvium
132, 134, 136 where the courtyard in fact became a water collecting tank. Examples were found in Benin and among some Yoruba and Ibo. Many people have pointed out similarities between certain features of the West African impluvium style and the impluvia of ancient Egyptian and Roman houses. At first sight the similarities are quite striking and parallels have been drawn between Yoruba and Benin potsherd pavements and Roman mosaics. It has also been
112 pointed out that the clay couches found in Ibibio and Ekoi houses greatly resemble those found in Roman houses even in the colouring, and that the walls and roofs of Latin atria were blackened with soot in much the same way as Edo and Ekoi houses. Similarities have also been found in other aspects of Yoruba and Egyptian material culture, religion and language. Yoruba make-up pallets are a good example.

Such observations are of very considerable interest, and it is perhaps only natural that they should have given rise to a good deal of speculation and been linked with other fragments of evidence pointing to a migrationist interpretation. Excavations at Daima (south of Lake Chad) have revealed a potsherd pavement dated about the twelfth century very similar to the Yoruba style. Fagg has pointed out[14] that Daima lies 'in the approaches to the Lake Chad–Mandara Mountain corridor, through which contacts between West Africa and the Nile Valley would be sure to pass'. Others who have studied the famous Ife bronzes have contended that the bronze casting technique was probably introduced from outside (although not the naturalistic style). Elsewhere in this book (see pp. 33–36) the arguments from settlement geography for postulating a fairly early colonial phase have been stated. One way to make sense of all these discoveries is to imagine a group of technological and stylistic innovators migrating across the eastern Sudan and down the Benue valley to become the overlords of some pre-existing Yoruba culture, although in very small numbers and becoming quickly assimilated with the local inhabitants.

What are the arguments for the development in West Africa of the impluvium style? The mean annual rainfall in Benin itself is 2000 mm, but during the dry season there is very little surface water due to the porosity of the sandy soil, and even that little tends to be saline. This means there is an acute shortage of drinking and cooking water. Impluvia provided a means of collecting water, which was drained into tanks or pots. No really large settlement could have taken place in this area before a means of collecting water had been found. Collecting rainfall also, obviously, helped to reduce the erosion caused by rainwater running off roofs, which is quite considerable now in the Benin area. Ventilation was clearly also an important factor. In the hot, dry savannah, mud buildings are built with one small door and no windows to keep out as much of the hot dry air, dust and bright, white light as possible. In the forest areas where the air is heavy and humid and the light much less intense, a pleasant building is one that shelters the inhabitants but does not restrict the movement of air too much. In a mud building these requirements are most easily met by having one side of a rectangular building or room left open with the roof supported by posts. But to ensure privacy and to make the buildings secure and easily defensible a good arrangement is obviously to put four such rooms or buildings in a square, joining them at the corners and making one entrance to the central court. This was what the Asante did. In the Yoruba, Bini and Ekoi impluvia the four roofs abutted at the corners forming groins.

This presupposes the existence of rectangular houses in the forest areas before the appearance of the impluvium style. This is entirely consistent with what is found elsewhere in forest areas. Most of the tropical rain forest of Africa is found in the Zaïre Basin (an area of over 3 500 000 km²), where nearly all the houses are rectangular and there is no evidence for a pre-existing round style. On the margins of the forest, McMaster[15] has provided evidence of stylistic interaction with the round plan apparently encroaching on the rectangular. In the Mangbettu villages houses are round, whereas meeting halls and chiefs' houses are rectangular. Among the Bira, forest houses are rectangular but those on the plains are round. Both Bamileke and Abadja Ibo houses have rectangular (in fact square) plans, while the roofs are round and thatched with grass. Most of the rectangular houses in the forest are thatched with palm leaf mats. The mats are plaited and their stiffness, close texture and durability makes them a most effective means of roofing in an area of low sunshine, high humidity and almost incessant rainfall. Here grass, even if it were available, would quickly go mouldy, but in fact it is not

238
66
71–8
255

available in any quantity except on the margins, and it is there that intermediate and round styles are found. Topologically grass is much more versatile; with stiff mats there is very little alternative but to make a saddleback roof (the same is true of tin).

So it is quite conceivable that both the rectangular style and impluvia originated locally. Nevertheless it would be foolish to rule out outside influence altogether, which as is known from other evidence percolated inland from the coasts of West and West Central Africa, (for example the spread of certain crops).

At Daima south of Lake Chad, Early Iron Age houses have been excavated. Those in the latest levels, dated to about the tenth century appear to have been made with a puddled mud technique. Somewhat below them remains of a potsherd pavement of a very similar type to Yoruba ones were found.[16] It seems possible, therefore, to think of the Yoruba and Benin courtyard houses as a mixing of a rectangular forest style with a puddled mud technique that may have been introduced from outside the area.

Hill Style

It has often been maintained that hills are a hostile environment in which no one would live except under pressure. Only recently a geographer[17] has remarked: 'hill villages were the expression of the attempts of small or weak groups to survive in the face of holy wars, slave raids or the influx of stronger tribes during the course of tribal migrations'. It is certainly possible that in some areas the upheavals of the nineteenth century caused certain peoples to settle temporarily in the hills,[18] but this view cannot be upheld on a broader perspective. Some hill societies were clearly a long-term response to the particular environment. In many there was a very close integration of technology, social organization and the environment, and the specifically constructional features would have required high labour inputs over a long period of time. It must also be said that in many cases the environment, far from being hostile, is most pleasant. It is perhaps relevant to note that most of the early European settlers made straight for the hills, because of their climatic advantages, good water supplies and absence of tsetse fly.

A surprising result of the analysis of styles (Chapter 8) is the discovery of many similarities not only in building but also in settlement pattern and other cultural attributes of certain peoples who live in the widely scattered highland areas of Africa. A high percentage of the following characteristics commonly occur in these areas:

1. Hillside location.
2. Settled mixed and intensive system of agriculture with stock kept under close management, often indoors.
3. Stone terracing.
4. Some irrigation.
5. High population density.
6. Round-plan buildings with diameters less then height.
7. Cellular homestead plan with high degree of building specialization.
8. Stone used in one or more of the following: house foundations, house walls, terracing, kraal walls.
9. Tessellated decoration on doorways, floors, benches.

10. Saddle-shaped grindstones (with pushers), often mounted on mud benches.
11. Circular wall openings.
12. Painted and incised decoration with dots, wavy lines and chevrons.

The most complete examples of this style are found in the Nuba mountains of the Sudan where they have been well documented by Nadel[19] and by Riefenstahl's photographs.[20] 3000 km to the west in Nigeria, certain peoples of the Mandara Mountains and the Jos Plateau have quite remarkably almost identical architecture. Elements of it can also be identified as far afield as Rhodesia, Tanzania, Central African Republic, Ghana and elsewhere in Sudan and Nigeria.

It seems unlikely that such marked similarities could all have originated separately, but of course much more work would need to be done to prove any connections. It is perhaps significant that the examples cited should be on a line between Nubia and the Niger–Benue confluence, as many writers have conjectured that the technique of iron working could have been spread along this very line to West Africa, as well as perhaps along another route further west. It is illuminating that Daima (see above) lies between the Jos Plateau and the Mandara Mountains.

Terraces are also found in other areas, such as Inyanga where they are spectacular in number and well constructed. These have been tentatively dated to the ninth century. Other areas include northern Togo and central Benin, where terraces, sometimes only very rudely constructed, were found.

At Engaruku on the edge of the Rift Valley in northern Tanzania, extensive remains of terraces can be seen. Excavations have shown that they were used for both houses and agriculture.[21] The terraces extend for some 5 km along the valley and remains of several thousand houses can be seen, as well as what appears to be a dam 30 m long. Radio-carbon dates have given the fourth and eighth centuries for the terraces. It has been said that Engaruku is 'unique both in its construction and in its pottery . . . . Here, if anywhere, it might be permissible to suspect the early infiltration of some northern Early Iron Age tradition, as yet unknown, from the Ethiopian end of the Rift Valley.'[22] In fact the house remains do appear to show marked similarities with those of Eritrea. The only people who until recently built remotely similar houses in Tanzania were the Wanji who lived 2500 m up on the Kitulo Plateau. The framework of their houses (with no stone walls) appears to be similar to Eritrean houses. However, stone fireplaces very similar to those at Engaruku have been reported[23] in Sonjo villages together with the remains of a stone gateway. Sonjo houses are now of the beehive type.

In many parts of East and South Africa there are remains of stone kraals associated with wattle and mud houses. The 'Sirikwa holes' in Kenya which were formerly thought to be the remains of densely grouped stone houses have proved on excavation to be circular cattle kraals, sometimes stone-lined, cut into the hillside, with small circular wattle and mud houses leading out from them.[24] This arrangement, of a circular cattle kraal in front of a circular house, is one which was formerly used by some Kikuyu.[25] Some of the Sirikwa houses seem to have been inhabited until the nineteenth century.

Further south in the Transvaal there are many sites where long stone 'scooped' boundary walls surround stone kraals and mud and wattle houses. One such site was described by Moffat (quoted in Chapter 1). Although some of these remains are apparently comparatively recent, others seem to date back to the beginning of this millennium.

43–7 Similar arrangements of stone walls and mud buildings were found at Zimbabwe, Nalatale and other Shona sites. At Zimbabwe the mud and wattle buildings together with stone enclosures were surrounded by a monumental stone wall, while at Nalatele the mud and wattle buildings surmounted stepped stone terraces.

1 In the last fifty years many hill peoples have begun to move down to the plains often because of the coercion of government officials who found them difficult to manage in the hills. It is interesting to look at these relatively well-documented recent migrations to see the effect they have had on house styles. In Nigeria the Mumoye, who have moved down to the plains from the Mambila Plateau, are typical. Their homesteads have not only become fragmented but individual buildings have become larger in diameter. Exactly similar changes have been noticed in the settlements now

13 built at the foot of the Nuba Mountains, and in Gwari villages on the plains. In the light of these facts, it is possible to suggest a hypothesis that other house types might be hill styles enlarged. For example, the Dagomba in northern Ghana, whose legends say they migrated from the hills to the north-

223–4 east of their present home, built houses on a cellular ring pattern, mostly similar to those of the Nuba but with larger diameters. The doorways of their houses were also decorated with tessellations, although recently these have been carried out with imported pottery. East of the Volta River many other peoples beside the Dagomba traced their origins to groups of horse-borne invaders from the north-east. Many of them came to form what are usually

215–21, 241 called the 'Middle Belt States'. Of these, Mamprussi, Borgu, Jukun and Nupe houses were similar to those of the Dagomba although both Jukun and Nupe buildings were built within an enclosing wall. Nupe houses had doorways decorated with baked clay tessellations.

Beehive Style

Turning now to the so-called 'beehive' style, the main area of concentration

159–205 is the upper basins of the Blue and White Niles, including the periphery of Lake Nyanza. There are interesting outliers on Kilimanjaro and in Bornu and it is arguable that study of these would throw light on questions of

184–5 migration. The Kanuri say they came from the Nile Basin, and significantly their language has recently been shown to have some affinity with the language of Meroitic Cush. In East Africa it seems fairly clear that migrations of pastoralists from the north in the fifteenth century had much to do with the formation of states in Uganda, Ruanda and north-western Tanzania (this is discussed in Chapter 3). In this connection it is perhaps significant that

176 the Tusi, an intrusive group in Nyamweziland who trace their ancestry back to the Tutsi of Ruanda, have persisted in building 'beehive' houses with stepped thatch in distinct contrast to the round plan, pole wall, houses of the

246 surrounding Nyamwezi.

Conclusion

This chapter has darted about somewhat over the continent and over time. Study at this level of generality gives unequalled opportunity for making connections inaccessible to those who concentrate on individual periods or regions. Proof of the validity of the necessarily tentative conclusions must await more detailed research, but it is submitted that a number of testable hypotheses have been advanced. It is often said that one criterion of scientific method is the generability of predictions and it is perhaps worth noting, in conclusion, that some of the ideas developed in this chapter have already proved successful in making accurate predictions on architectural questions when other cultural and locational data have been given.

REFERENCES

1. Mbiti, J. S., *African Religions and Philosophy* (London-Ibadan-Nairobi, 1969)
2. Gebremedhin, N., 'House Types of Ethiopia', in Oliver, P. (ed.), *Shelter in Africa* (London, 1971)
3. Fosbrooke, H. A., 'Defensive Measures of Certain Tribes in North-Eastern Tanganyika', *Tanganyika Notes and Records*, 35, 36, 37, 39 (1953–5)
4. Engestrom, T., *Notes sur les modes de construction au Soudan* (Stockholm, 1957)
5. Moal, G. le, 'Les Habitations Semi-souterraines en Afrique de l'Ouest', *Journal de la Société des Africanistes*, 30 (1960)
6. Davies, O., 'Timber Construction and Wood Carving in West Africa in the Second Millennium BC', *Man*, New Series 2 (1967)
7. Prussin, L., 'Sudanese Architecture and the Manding', *African Arts*, 3 (1970)
8. Siddle, D. J., 'War-Towns in Sierra Leone, A Study in Social Change', *Africa*, 38 (1968)
9. Omari, Al, *Masalik el-Absar fi Mamalik el Amsar* (translated) (Paris, 1927)
10. Prussin, L., 'Fulani-Hausa Architecture', *African Arts* (1976)
11. Roberts, D., 'Les Fouilles de Tegdaoust', *Journal of African History*, 11 (1970)
12. Nicolaisen, J., *The Ecology and Culture of the Pastoral Tuareg* (Copenhagen, 1963)
13. Jaques-Meunie, D., *Cités Anciennes de Mauritanie* (Paris, 1961)
14. Fagg, B., 'Recent Work in West Africa: New Light on the Nok Culture', *World Archaeology*, 1 (1969)
15. McMaster, D. N., 'The Geography of Rural Settlements', in Harrison Church, R. J., *Advanced Geography of Africa* (Amersham, 1975)
16. Fagg, B., *op. cit.*
17. Gleave, M. B., 'Hill Settlements and Their Abandonment in Tropical Africa', *Transactions of the Institute of British Geographers*, 40 (1966)
18. Sutton, J. E. G., 'Habitation Sites on the Liganga-Maganga Ridge', *Azania*, 2 (1967)
19. Nadel, S. F., *The Nuba* (Oxford, 1947)
20. Fox, J., 'The Splendour of a Forgotten Tribe', *Sunday Times*, 12 October 1975; Riefenstahl, L., *The Last of the Nuba* (London, 1976)
21. Sassoon, H., 'New Views on Engaruku', *Journal of African History*, 7 (1967)
22. Fagan, B. M., and Oliver, R., *Africa in the Iron Age* (Cambridge, 1975)
23. Fosbrooke, J., 'Sonjo', *East Africa Annual* (1944–5)
24. Sutton, J. E. G., *The Archaeology of the Western Highlands of Kenya* (Nairobi, 1973)
25. Cagnola, C., *The Akikuyu* (Nyeri, 1933)

Illustration Section IX

260 *Interior of courtyard of Oualata house, south-eastern Mauritania, about 1955.* This decoration was executed by women. There were two main types, white painted bas-relief moulding and flat painted motifs in red on a white ground. The latter appears to be comparatively recent innovations.[44] The decorative motifs were almost exclusively composed of curved lines. Interlacing, which is very typical of decoration of Muslim houses further to the east, in Nigeria, for example, does not appear at all. Doors were constructed of vertical planks of wood supported by transverse pieces and decorated with metal bosses.

261 *Interior of courtyard of Oualata house, south-eastern Mauritania, about 1955.* The walls were of stone plastered over with mud.

262 *Djenne house, Mali, about 1950.* Like Oualata, the towns of the Upper Niger area played important roles in the old empires. They were focal points for the trade in salt, gold and other commodities, and many of their merchants amassed great wealth. Each of the cities had its own distinctive style of architecture which differed not so much in type of construction as in detail. In the Djenne style the principal feature was vertical buttresses crowned with pinnacles; special attention was paid to the entrance. The walls were of mud bricks plastered over with mud which was sometimes mixed with vegetable butter. The roofs were flat terraces built of palm fronds and they were drained by spouts of wood or pottery.

263 *Djenne mosque, Mali, about 1950.* Mosques in the Upper Niger area were built for the most part like the houses (see no. 262). The Djenne mosque, like Djenne houses, had regular buttresses with projecting pinnacles and an imposing entrance with steps. The original mosque was destroyed in about 1830, but was rebuilt at the beginning of this century in a similar style.

264 *Detail of Djenne mosque, Mali, about 1950.*

265 *Songhai minaret, Agadez, Niger, 1968.* The wooden poles sticking out of the minaret support a spiral staircase. The mosque at the foot of the minaret has an exceedingly low ceiling. Both are contained within a walled courtyard.

266 *Timbuktu house, Mali, about 1905.* Of all towns in West Africa, Timbuktu was perhaps the most well known to the outside world in the late medieval period. It was popularly called the Golden City on account of its central position in the gold trade, but it was also a major centre of culture and scholarship. Like Oualata and Djenne it was sacked by the Moroccans in 1591 and the architecture now extant can hardly compare with what was there before. Timbuktu is on roughly the same latitude as Qasr el Barka and Oualata. Although much drier than Djenne, 400 km to the south, it does often have severe storms in August and September which can cause buildings to collapse. The upper part of the walls of this house were built of mud bricks and the lower half of stone.

267 *Timbuktu house, Mali, about 1950.* Small houses in Timbuktu were built round one courtyard and larger ones round two courtyards, one for women and visitors and the other for slaves, kitchens, latrines and horses and sheep. A covered passage gave access from one courtyard to the other. The buildings around the first courtyard were often more than one storey high.

268 *Jingereber mosque, Timbuktu, Mali, about 1950.* Unlike the Djenne mosque the buttresses here were irregularly spaced and did not project above the top of the wall. The mud bricks used in its construction can be seen. Barth mentioned that in his time there was an inscription on the Jingereber mosque indicating it was built in 1327. According to Tarikh al Sudan it was completely rebuilt in 1570.[45]

269 *Bandiagara house, Mali, about 1950*. Bandiagara represents the interface between the Islamic, riverain commercial settlements and the agricultural Dogon of the escarpment (see nos. 33–9). (Interestingly, it is also on the watershed between the Niger and the Volta Basins.) The influence of both communities can be seen in the architecture. Bandiagara houses were distinguished by strong horizontal as well as vertical lines on the frontages which effectively divided them into rectangular modules. This overall effect was very similar to the decoration found on Dogon 'ginna' houses.

270 *Interior of courtyard of Bandiagara house, Mali, about 1905.*

271 *Bandiagara house, Mali, about 1905.*

272 *Nyamina mosque near Bamako, Mali, about 1920.* Nyamina, which is between Djenne and Bamako on the Niger, is half as wet again as Djenne. The walls of the mosque were much lower and there were more and thicker buttresses.

172

273 *Hausa palace, Daura, northern Nigeria, about 1960.* Legend has it that Daura is the oldest of the Hausa cities and it is still in many ways their spiritual centre. This photograph shows a courtyard within the emir's palace which was rebuilt in the mid-twentieth century. The painted decoration is a recent innovation. The building techniques of Hausaland are discussed in no. 286 and Chapter 6.

274 *Hausa minaret, Gobirau, Katsina, northern Nigeria, about 1955.* The Gobirau mosque, apparently originally built in the fifteenth century, was rebuilt in 1702. After the Jihad of 1805 it was not repaired for about 120 years. The strength of its walls has been ascribed to the practice of mixing the mud not only with vegetable butter (*katse*) but also with blood from cows slaughtered to feed the builders.[46] The eighteenth-century minaret is now concealed by the minaret in the photograph.

173

275 *Hausa old city, Kano, northern Nigeria, about 1960*. Kano has throughout its history been one of the major cities of Africa. Even before its rapid growth in this century, the inhabited quarters of the city were densely populated. Originally there were large areas of unoccupied land within the walls (perhaps to fall back upon in time of siege), and it is into these areas that expansion has taken place. The roofscape in the photograph, looking towards Dalla (the central hill on which the city was founded) is thus not markedly different from its appearance in past centuries. Hausa cities are discussed in more detail in Chapter 3.

276 *Plan of Kano city, Northern Nigeria, 1851*. This is a copy of a rough sketch drawn by Barth.[47] It shows a large proportion of the land within the city walls unoccupied. Much of this has now been built on.

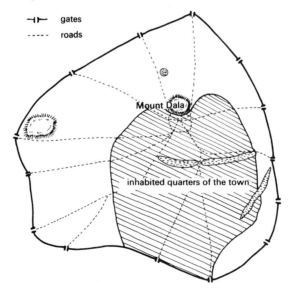

gates
roads

Mount Dala

inhabited quarters of the town

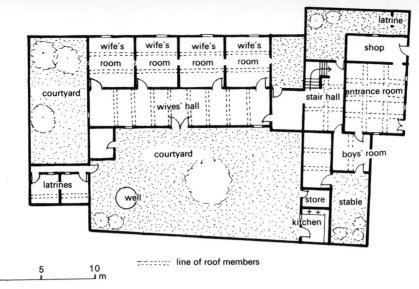

line of roof members

0   5   10
|____|____| m

277 *Plan of Hausa house, Kano, northern Nigeria, about 1950.* This house, which belonged to a merchant in Kofarmata Street, was very similar to the one which can be seen in the foreground of no. 275 (all the buildings this side of the first road). The buildings around the entrance were two storeys high, that is the *zaure* (vestibule), hall and boys' room. The hall rose the full height of two storeys and a staircase at one end of this led to a sitting-room and a bedroom on the first floor, above the *zaure*. In an Islamic community such as this, domestic privacy was important and guests were not invited beyond the *zaure*. In order to prevent visitors from even glimpsing the inside, doors were never arranged opposite each other and it was frequently necessary to approach an adjacent room via an intermediate one. The compound walls were also usually built tall enough to prevent a horseman seeing over. The roofs of this house were flat; there were very few domed roofs in Kano.

278 *Exterior of Hausa town walls, Kano, northern Nigeria, 1903.* The circumference of the walls of Kano in 1903 measured just over 17 km. They date back to the twelfth century when the first and smallest wall was built round the town. The walls were subsequently enlarged in the fifteenth century, when the emir's palace, Gidan Rumfa, and mosque were built, and again in the seventeenth century.[48] The mode of building was the same as for houses: pear-shaped bricks were laid in courses and plastered over on both sides with mud. The rows of small compartments along the top of the wall inside enabled archers and later musketeers to shoot through loopholes in the solid wall. Thirteen gates gave access to the city and these were closed at night with doors of hammered iron on a framework of palm wood. The gates were narrow and recessed into the walls so that any attacking party would be crowded into a small space. Several of the gates were further protected by an outward turn of the wall next to the gate which allowed missiles to be thrown onto the flank of any attacking party.

279 *Interior of Hausa town walls, Kano, northern Nigeria, about 1903.*

280 *Plan of Hausa town walls, Kano, northern Nigeria, about 1903.*

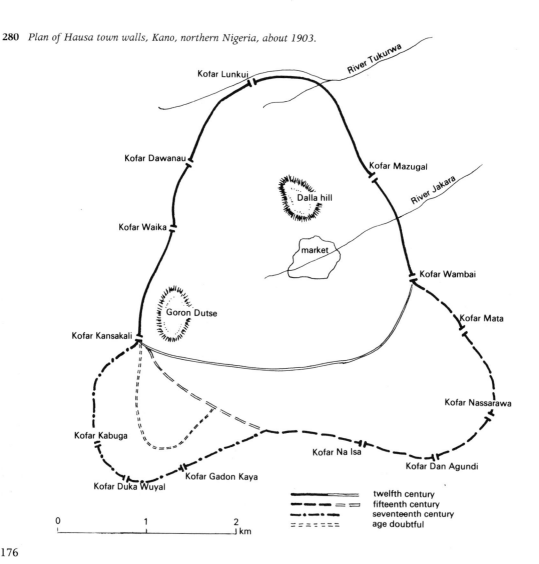

River Tukurwa

Kofar Lunkui

Kofar Dawanau

Kofar Mazugal

River Jakara

Dalla hill

Kofar Waika

market

Kofar Wambai

Goron Dutse

Kofar Mata

Kofar Kansakali

Kofar Nassarawa

Kofar Kabuga

Kofar Na Isa

Kofar Dan Agundi

Kofar Gadon Kaya

Kofar Duka Wuyal

	twelfth century
	fifteenth century
	seventeenth century
	age doubtful

0   1   2 km

176

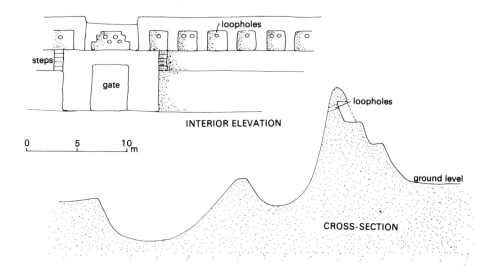

281 *Elevation and cross-section of Hausa town walls, Kano, northern Nigeria, about 1903.*

282 *Hausa palace, Kano, northern Nigeria, about 1950.* The photograph shows a courtyard within the emir of Kano's palace. The fine incised lines on the walls were typical of the decoration on several of the rooms in the palace.

283 *Interior of Hausa palace, Kano, northern Nigeria, about 1960.* This photograph shows painted decoration on a vaulted ceiling of the emir's palace. Inset into the intersection of the ribs were imported porcelain bowls. Earlier photographs of roofs within the palace (taken in 1903 and 1945) show how this type of decoration is not static and merely copied with repainting but changes considerably over time. The earliest photograph shows several non-geometric motifs.

284 *Hausa house, Kafin Madaki, northern Nigeria, about 1960*. Kafin Madaki was one of the series of new towns established in the wake of the Sokoto Jihad as a means of increasing political and religious influence. It is situated 45 km north of Bauchi and was built in about 1850 by the Madaki of Bauchi emirate in answer to specific attacks by the Ningi. This house is reputed to have been built at that time.

285 *Hausa council house, Bauchi, northern Nigeria, about 1960*. This building was also built about 1850. It was for meetings of the emir's cabinet and for courts. It has been extensively renovated in recent times and the walls are now rendered with cement.

286 *Hausa bricks, northern Nigeria, 1969.* A distinctive feature of Hausa building technology is the use of these sun-dried pear-shaped bricks. Mud for these bricks is carefully selected and mixed with water and chopped straw. The mortar is prepared in rather the same way but has to be mixed several times over a period of about two weeks. (The holes from which the mud is gained can be seen in no. 292.) The bricks are laid in courses, with points uppermost. Finishing plaster is described in Chapter 6.

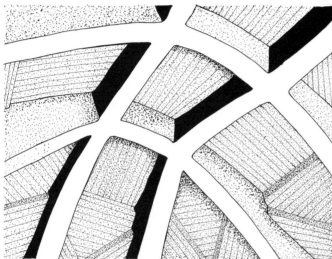

287 *Drawing of interior of roof of Hausa house, Zaria, northern Nigeria, 1969.* In northern Hausaland most of the roofs are flat and built in the same way as Djenne roofs (see no. 262). In the more southerly towns, however, where the annual rainfall is higher (Zaira, 1150 mm; Abuja, 1280 mm, as against Daura's 530 mm) the roofs are vaulted. In the very wettest areas of Hausaland the vaults are thatched. This drawing shows the interior of a vaulted roof.

288 *Drawings showing construction of Hausa roofs, northern Nigeria.* On vaulted roofs the basic framework was mud arches reinforced with palm fronds, while on flat roofs it was horizontal palm-frond beams. These frameworks were spanned by split, palm-frond pieces arranged in a herringbone fashion and plastered on both sides with mud.

DOMED ROOF

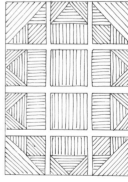

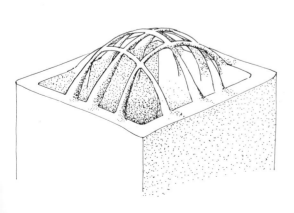

DOMED ROOF   FLAT ROOF

DOMED ROOF

289 *Hausa house, Zaria, northern Nigeria, 1969.* This photograph shows part of the exterior walls of an urban Hausa compound in Zaria old city. The crackled finish to the walls was the result of weathering; it would have been remedied by re-plastering. The domed roofs are typical of Zaria. The gutters can be seen projecting through the parapet.

290 *Hausa zaure (entrance building), Zaria, northern Nigeria, about 1969.* For many centuries Zaria was the interface between Hausaland and the peoples of the 'middle belt' (between the forest and Sudan zones), who mostly built round houses. In Abuja (the southern limit of Hausaland since 1828), as shown in no. 299, the buildings were round and thatched. In Zaria city (though not in rural Zaria) round buildings were comparatively rare, as can be seen in no. 292.

291 *Plan of Hausa homestead near Zaria, northern Nigeria, about 1950.* This was the homestead of a village farmer. Notice the matting walls round the compound. Most rural Hausa homesteads had matting rather than mud walls. To build a mud wall was a privilege the head of the household had to obtain from the Hausa kings (and later the Fulani emirs).[49] Mud walls could of course be used as a defence against an emir or king. The round plan buildings would have had thatched roofs.

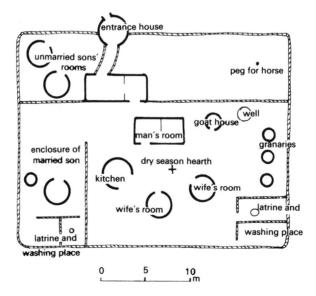

entrance house

unmarried sons' rooms

peg for horse

goat house

well

man's room

granaries

enclosure of married son

dry season hearth

kitchen

wife's room

wife's room

latrine and washing place

latrine and washing place

0   5   10 m

292 *Aerial view of the Hausa town of Zaria, northern Nigeria, about 1955.* This photograph shows an aerial view of parts of the old city of Zaria. The vaulted and often multi-vaulted roofs, and the intensity of cultivation can be seen.

293 *Hausa mosque, Zaria, northern Nigeria, about 1950.* This mosque was built in 1862 of mud reinforced with palm fronds.

294 *Hausa house, Zaria, northern Nigeria, about 1960.* This photograph shows relief decoration on an exterior wall. This type of decoration was formerly confined to the lintels and jambs of doors on entrance buildings and was unpainted. Latterly it has become common to have whole house fronts decorated and painted in this way.

295 *Hausa house, Zaria, northern Nigeria, about 1960.*

296 *Hausa house, Turunku, northern Nigeria, 1970.* Turunku was the precursor of Zaria city. Local tradition has it that the building shown was part of the house of Bakwa who was ruler in the mid-sixteenth century at the time the capital was moved to Zaria. (Notice the stone foundations.) There are several reasons why the capital may have been moved in this way, but perhaps the most obvious is the inadequate water supply at Turunku.

297 *Hausa town gate, Zaria, northern Nigeria, about 1960.* This is not an original town gate. It was rebuilt during this century, but traditional techniques have been used.

298 *Hausa town wall, Turunku, northern Nigeria, 1970.* This wall appears to have survived without repair since the town was abandoned in the sixteenth century. The stone of its construction is especially significant because it does not appear to have been used in any other Hausa town walls. (see page 162).

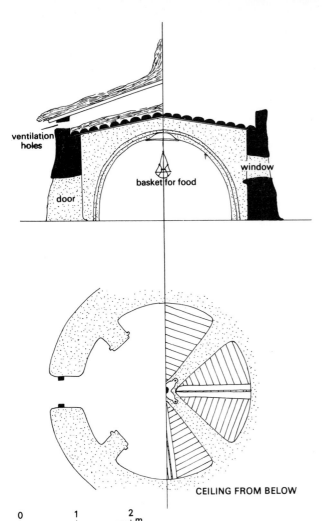

ventilation holes

window

door

basket for food

CEILING FROM BELOW

0 1 2 m

299 *Cross-section of roof of Hausa house, Abuja, northern Nigeria, about 1960.* Abuja is in the south of Hausaland where the rainfall is higher. Here the mud vaults were covered with thatch (see no. 287).

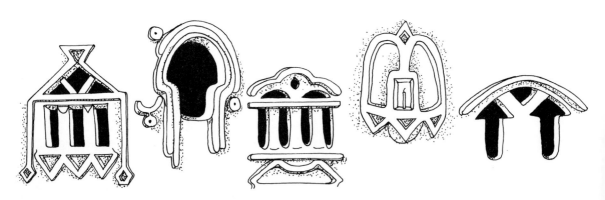

300 *Details of Hausa house, Abuja, northern Nigeria, about 1960.*

301 *Drawing of Bornu town, Kukawa, northern Nigeria, about 1850.* Following the destruction of Ngazagarmo by the Fulani in 1808, a new capital of Bornu was built in 1814 by Al Kanemi at Kukawa about 25 km from Lake Chad. (Unlike Hausaland, in the Chad Basin the Fulani only destroyed and never succeeded in consolidating the destruction of the capital.) Barth[50] described the buildings in Kukawa as a 'most interesting medley of large clay buildings and small thatched huts, of massive clay walls surrounding immense yards and light fences of reeds in a more or less advanced state of decay and with a variety of colour according to their age from the brightest yellow down to the deepest black'. Here as in all Bornu towns there was a main avenue or Dendal which led up to the ruler's house and where the market was held. In Kukawa the Dendal was in the main town which was walled and separated from a secondary town by about half a mile. By the time Kukawa was founded, the technique of burnt-brick manufacture had been abandoned in this area (see page 162). The mud buildings were of sun-dried bricks. They were rectangular in plan and of one or two storeys. The walls and pillars in some of the interiors of the houses were ornamented with frescoes in three colours, like the murals at Zinder.

302 *Lobi house, Ghana, about 1965.* Recent linguistic research casts doubt on the existence of a cohesive group called the Lobi, but certainly the peoples who inhabit the banks of the Black Volta near the conjunction of Ghana, Ivory Coast and Upper Volta are so called by their neighbours. Within this territory there are many ruins of stone houses. The houses in this photograph were, however, built of swish-puddled mud. The chameleon on the granary may have been a protection symbol, as was the case on Nankanse houses (where the chameleon concealed a piece of iron). The chevron decoration around the top of the buildings in this photograph was a type usually reserved for chiefs' wives' houses. It was sometimes painted and sometimes incised.

303 *Lobi house, Ghana, about 1965.*

304 *Bobo village, Koro, near Bobo Dioulasso, Upper Volta, about 1950.* The Bobo live in semi-arid country where population densities often exceed 40 persons per km². Bobo Dioulasso was an interface between the Muslim kingdoms to the north and west and the forest zones to the south. It was also a centre for the Diola merchants who traded between the two. Many Bobo houses were previously built underground. The reasons for this are explored in Chapter 5.

305 *Ssola house, northern Togo, about 1923.* These 'tower' houses occurred in several small areas of the Volta Basin. It seems that in the nineteenth century they were, locally, more common. It is interesting that they were in most cases found in the same areas as underground houses which were basically constructed in a similar way.

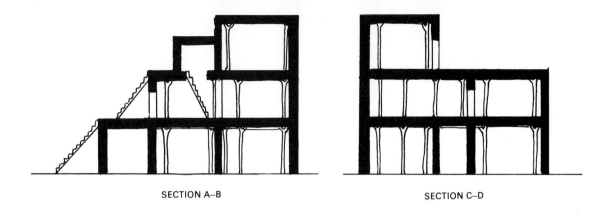

SECTION A–B   SECTION C–D

0 ⊢——————⊣ 5 m

306 *Plan and cross-section of Somolo house,
Upper Volta, about 1908.*

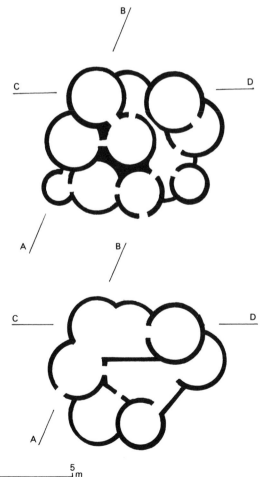

307 *Tambernu house, Upper Volta, about
1923.*

0 ⊢——————⊣ 5 m

187

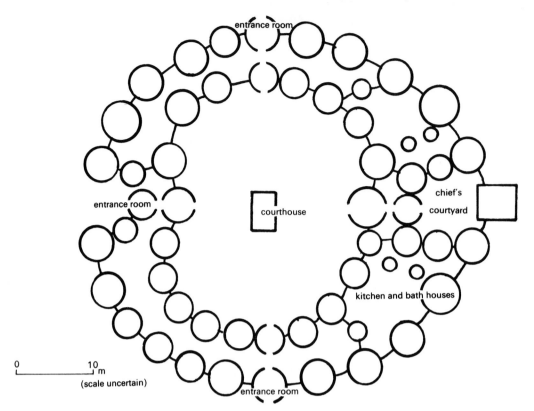

308 *Plan of Mandinka fort, Bisandugu, Guinea, about 1880.* The collapse of the Mali empire in the thirteenth century did not extinguish the pride or unity of its people. They developed their function as middlemen and by the mid-nineteenth century many towns had expanded into sizable states. By 1870 they had become united under 'Almamy' Samory who ruthlessly set about reviving their greatness by increasing their power through trade and unifying them through Islam. This plan shows Bisandugu, his capital. Bisandugu is in the high mountains and commands the magnificent pass between the Niger Basin and the forest lands of Liberia. A contemporary account of the fort says the buildings inside were thatched; this would be consistent with the high rainfall.

309 *Mandinka fort, Tiongi, Mali, about 1890.* This fort was in a drier area north of Bisandugu (no. 308). The buildings would probably all have had flat roofs.

10 The Impact of Modernization

All over tropical Africa sweeping changes over the last century have inevitably disturbed traditional life and culture and much of what has been discussed in preceding chapters has disappeared. Even where building styles have largely been preserved, changing economic, political and social conditions have altered peoples' basic architectural requirements. It may be as well to begin this chapter by examining some of the ways in which so-called 'modernization' has affected aspects of the social system relevant to architecture.

Colonial governments often stated that their policy was not to intervene directly in matters of indigenous culture; and in terms of numbers probably not all that many people were actually forced to change their settlement patterns. There were, however, two major circumstances in which such compulsion did occur. The first and most conspicuous was the alienation of land to accommodate expatriate settlers or miners or government schemes. This has been well documented for Kenya, Rhodesia and Zaïre; but in every colonial territory a certain amount of alienation took place. In a few countries, like Nigeria and Ghana, only a very small proportion of the land was taken, mainly for new towns, agricultural experimental stations, dams and a few commercial plantations. In others, however, the displacement was on a much bigger scale and the need for new building was therefore greater. Independent governments have naturally been chary of pursuing similar policies, but in the interests of 'development' many have been driven to doing so.

The second major way in which colonial governments interfered in habitation arrangements (and many independent governments have followed them) was fairly widespread and consisted of trying to persuade people to live in settlements suitable for local development policies. They were mostly encouraged to group together in large villages and abandon their family homesteads or small scattered hamlets. Sometimes government persuasion and the attraction of modern services and utilities was sufficient; but for the more obdurate coercion was by no means unknown. For example, over-zealous British colonial government officers are reported to have burnt the houses of hill people in mid-western Nigeria, Ghana and the Sudan after they had resisted movement to the plains.[1] The eastern Ekoi now live in villages composed of two single rows of houses bordering a long straight street, into which they were forced by the Germans. They explained their dislike for this new arrangement by saying that epidemics spread more quickly and witches were able to contact more people and thereby cause more deaths.[2] In other places governments tried to get people to spread out more. The Germans in East Africa persuaded the Sukuma to leave the hills, where they were previously confined, and move to the plains.

Most of the forces of disequilibrium were, however, indirect. The mere imposition of government on a large scale gave rise to the need for revenue collection, and often property was used as a determinant of tax liability. Even when other determinants were used, the more or less gradual change from a subsistence to a cash economy was inevitable. This not only affected patterns of employment and agricultural production but also family size.

The governments also set up new towns and expanded old ones, attracting people by providing not only paid employment but also educational and medical facilities. Colonial administrative centres were often deliberately placed in a traditional void, somewhere which did not come under the hegemony of any traditional ruler. From the outset the new town populations were therefore heterogenous and impersonal and this usually meant that social life was freer than in the villages, a factor which in turn attracted further settlers. New roads cut across traditional settlement patterns linking administrative centres, and villages therefore had to move to the roads to take advantage of the transport facilities, particularly where cash crops were grown. In the Central African Republic the attraction of the new administrative centres was peculiarly marked. Most of the population now seems to be housed in village clusters around these new towns; and farms are only visited during the growing season. One of the main motivating forces for this wholesale movement was, it has been suggested, the desire to escape being coerced by the French colonial government into growing cotton as a cash crop.[3] All over the continent, however, there has been an increasingly rapid drift towards the towns, for a variety of reasons which it is not suitable to analyse here.

Modernization has also brought with it a drastic change in the pattern of communications. The introduction of large cargo boats and air services between Europe and Africa meant that the trans-Saharan trade lost most of its impetus. Some of the towns which had been staging points or terminals of the caravans dwindled in size and some completely disappeared. Several deserted towns in Mauritania are fast becoming completely engulfed by sand. Other trade routes have also been overtaken by the growth of road and rail transportation systems. Riverain and maritime communities have suffered especially from this, but in a less obvious way so have countless little villages which previously would have been visited by horsemen or head porters but which now are remote from roads or railways. It has recently been suggested that much of the trans-Saharan trade was village-based.[4]

Colonial rule in most parts brought with it stability and peaceful conditions. People were able to abandon defences, so that walls, palisades and cactus hedges were left to decay. In many cases this relaxing of defences brought with it a certain fragmentation of the community, and young men would move away to farm more productive land away from the town or village. In both Hausaland and Yorubaland, for example, farms miles away from the major defensive systems are now permanently occupied, whereas before they would only have been visited occasionally. People who had fled to the hills in the nineteenth century began to move down to the plains. So did other longer established hill-dwellers, many of whom had to be persuaded or coerced, like the Sukuma, who have already been mentioned in this connection. Their move, although in the long run quite definitely to their economic advantage (their agricultural progress has been quite remarkable), was struck by disaster in the early stages when they were virtually decimated by sleeping sickness. Experiences like this frighten other peoples from taking undue risks in movement, and in East Africa there are many examples today of people from highland areas (for example the Chagga and the Nyakusa) who are convinced (and with good reason) that diseases like malaria will strike down families who move to the lower plateaux or coastal plains. In Nigeria, the Gwari have been reluctant to move down from their inselbergs because of the quality of the water on the hills. They have mostly moved down now, but the Gwari villages which were initially established at the bases of the inselbergs have been, for the most part, deserted by the younger folk, who have established farmsteads at some distance away. The villages are still occupied by the very old people and they still have strong emotional, religious and political significance.

Governments evidently thought that hill-dwellers would be easier to administer on the plains. What they did not anticipate was the breaking up of communities which took place nor the changes in agricultural practice. Many of the hill peoples had exceedingly efficient and highly intensive systems of agriculture using manuring, terracing, irrigation, crop rotation, and so on. When they moved to the plains these were mostly abandoned for an extensive system, with profound consequences in matters as diverse as family structure and soil structure, all of which in turn influence architectural considerations.

In other areas a directly opposite effect can be seen, and previously dispersed migrant communities have become nucleated and settled. For example, the growing of cash crops and the introduction of irrigation schemes and artificial fertilizers (among other things) has tended to encourage peripatetic farmers to become sedentary and cultivate land all the year round. In some areas this has had serious repercussions for pastoralists, hampering their free movement in the dry season. In other areas, money acquired by farmers from cash crops has been invested in cattle and so they no longer need the pastoralists' cattle, which used to manure the land as they grazed the remains of harvested crops. This again has limited the pastoralists' domains and as a result many are settling and starting to practise some agriculture as well.

The pastoralists' environmental adaptation has been upset in other ways. Government policies of immunization of herds and haphazard provision of water supplies have sometimes produced much larger herds which in turn have meant over-grazed land, especially near the water supplies. All this has led to enforced extensive migrations, especially in some parts of Sudan[5] and the West African Sahel.

The examples could be multiplied. The main theme that emerges is that the movement or change in livelihood of one group of people inevitably has repercussions on other peoples. And even those who wish to remain living in their villages and following their traditional way of life cannot escape the disruptive forces. Either their freedom of movement has been curtailed or enough members of the family have left to make the old economic unit no longer viable. In pastoral societies which also practise some agriculture there have been several cases of suicide amongst old men whose children have gone away to school and left no one to look after the cattle.

In new settlements houses are often sited with complete disregard for the family ties which regulated the old village patterns even though traditional shapes and materials might still be used. Even in traditional urban centres which have become swollen by rising birth rates and continued immigration, the old compound plans are fast disappearing. They are first divided up and then infilled with new buildings as the large traditional families split up. This loosening of family ties must be related to a diminution in status of the head of the household, as his dependants find new status in paid employment, together with the pull of the new religions such as Christianity which express a preference for nuclear families.

What has changed the physical appearance of settlements more than anything else was the introduction of new building materials from Europe. Corrugated iron sheeting and cement have had perhaps the greatest effect. The main attraction of corrugated iron (or 'bati' or tin) roofs is that they are fireproof, and they were therefore quickly adopted in the residential areas which grew up around the new towns. In Uganda, for example, feuds were traditionally often ended by setting fire to neighbours' houses. Here, obviously, tin roofs quickly became very popular. However, it is almost impossible to roof a circular house with corrugated sheeting; so its introduction in some areas changed not only the roofing material but also the basic shape of the house to a rectangular one. It was in this way that traditional patterns tended to persist longer where the basic shape of the house was rectangular rather than circular.

In the new communities the more prosperous businessmen often tried to distinguish themselves from the traditional extended family and build houses to reflect their status. In southern Nigeria the so-called 'Brazilian' style, introduced by freed slaves returning to West Africa, has fulfilled this purpose, with flamboyant 'storey' houses built in cement and embellished with heavy ornamental pillars, balustrades, and so on. In the more northern Hausa towns, merchants have begun to adorn the outside walls of their otherwise fairly traditional houses with elaborate moulded designs executed in cement. Elsewhere, in villages and small towns, traditional moulded decoration on clay walls has given way to painted decoration executed in bought paint and sometimes in figurative patterns in complete contrast to the old non-figurative ones.

African societies were by no means static in the past. But the changes in the twentieth century may be more cataclysmic and irreversible than any before. Will traditional architecture completely vanish under a plethora of cement and 'bati' roofs or will it somehow adapt itself to the twentieth-century way of life? Bureaucratic forces are difficult to counter. For instance, edicts (such as the one made in Sokoto in 1969 by the North-West State Government) may prevent any traditional buildings being erected in the city centre; resettlement schemes rehouse people made homeless by dams, plantations, and so on; municipal houses are erected for quickness and cheapness and small, expensive plots of land in cities make 'compound' houses prohibitively expensive. Under all these conditions the individual has no choice but to accept what is offered or possible.

Some government departments and developers have tried to emulate traditional shapes in modern materials or to use traditional materials in modern shapes. For instance at the Kainji dam resettlement scheme in Nigeria, some of the houses are round with concrete domes. A 'concrete hut' has also been developed, which is a reinforced concrete skin formed over an inflated plastic shape. On a Tanzanian village settlement scheme settlers were provided with steel frames for their houses which they then had to infill with traditional materials. (This idea came to a rather sad end when it was found that the only suitable material was burnt bricks which of course did not need a steel frame.) Schools and other community buildings have been built with thatched roofs. But all these essays seem essentially to be trying to preserve the shapes and materials of traditional buildings rather than their spirit.

As has been stressed earlier, one of the advantages of these buildings was their flexibility because of their relatively short life and the fact that they were essentially geared to the contemporary family requirements. To fossilize a traditional pattern in concrete and give it to a family which probably no longer has the same requirements as its predecessors seems to be preserving the wrong aspect of traditional architecture. Similarly, trying to use traditional materials in modern shapes also runs into difficulties, as many people have found. A good thatch roof in many houses often lasted ten years and sometimes as many as sixty,[6] but usually only because a fire was kept alight inside which deposited a layer of soot on the underside of the roof which discouraged insects. A thatch roof on a school or dairy where no fire is kept burning will last a much shorter time.

Should the traditional styles be allowed merely to decay? This is of course a question which can only be answered by each community of people concerned. It is certainly not for outsiders to dictate policies which may be said to spring from sentimental European notions of conservation or a hankering for a return to pre-industrial harmony. What is important, though, is that those making the decisions—including ordinary citizens as well as administrators and planners—should not still be inhibited by the feeling that everything about traditional architecture is wrong. In many cases the old materials may be unsuitable for modern living, though many people find that a mud floor and a thatched or mud roof is far more comfortable than a concrete floor and a tin roof. But surely the spirit of making buildings sufficiently flexible so that they can be adapted to meet the needs of each generation of inhabitants can never be wrong at any time or in any place?

REFERENCES

1. Fortes, M., *The Web of Kinship among the Tallensi* (Oxford, 1957); Gleave, M. B., 'Hill Settlements and Their Abandonment in Tropical Africa', *Transactions of the Institute of British Geographers*, 40 (1966); Riefenstahl, L., *The Last of the Nuba* (London, 1976)
2. Talbot, P. A., *The Peoples of Southern Nigeria* (Oxford, 1926)
3. Groves, A. T., *Africa South of the Sahara* (Oxford, 1967)
4. Hill, P., *Rural Capitalism in West Africa* (Cambridge, 1970)
5. El Arifi, Salih A., 'Pastoral Nomadism in the Sudan', *East African Geographical Review*, 13 (1975)
6. Arderer, E. W., *Historical Notes on the Scheduled Monuments of West Cameroun* (Buea, 1965)

310 *Exterior of Swahili mosque, the Great Mosque, Kilwa, Tanzania, 1965.* This is one of many hundreds of mosques lining the East African coast built between the twelfth and nineteenth centuries. The economic history of the Swahili towns is described in Chapter 3. Most of the mosques were built of coral and mangrove poles. Dressed coral was used for the edges of mihrabs, arches and columns, while walls were of coral rubble and lime cement. The roof of the Great Mosque at Kilwa was constructed more elaborately than most. It was vaulted and domed, the domes resting on groined squinches and pointed arches springing from square capitals on octagonal columns. The Great Mosque dates from the twelfth century, although most of what is now standing is fifteenth-century work.

311 *Interior of Swahili mosque, the Great Mosque, Kilwa, Tanzania, 1965.*

312 *Detail of dome of Swahili mosque, the Great Mosque, Kilwa, Tanzania, 1965.*

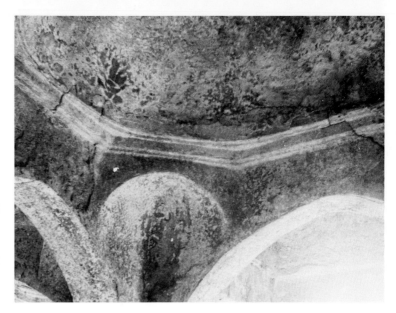

313 *Plan of Swahili mosque, the Great Mosque, Kilwa, Tanzania.* The most common plan for Swahili mosques was a single central row of columns leading to the mihrab. Two rows of columns were found infrequently; three rows were found only in large congregational mosques; and the Great Mosque of Kilwa, shown here, with its four rows of columns seems to have been unique.[51]

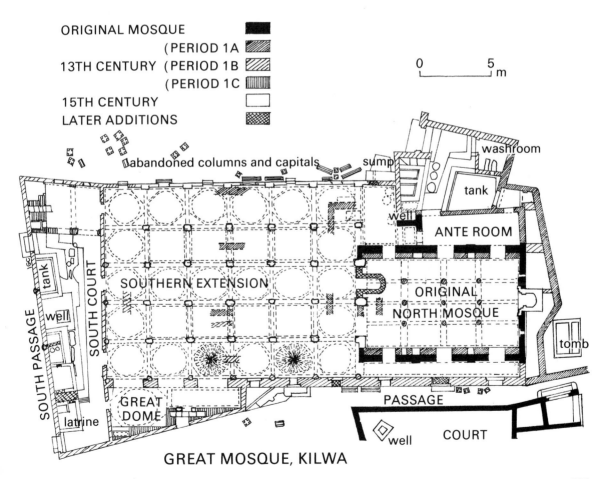

ORIGINAL MOSQUE

13TH CENTURY (PERIOD 1A
(PERIOD 1B
(PERIOD 1C

15TH CENTURY

LATER ADDITIONS

0   5 m

abandoned columns and capitals   sump

washroom

tank

well

ANTE ROOM

SOUTH PASSAGE

tank

well

SOUTH COURT

SOUTHERN EXTENSION

ORIGINAL NORTH MOSQUE

tomb

GREAT DOME

latrine

PASSAGE

well   COURT

GREAT MOSQUE, KILWA

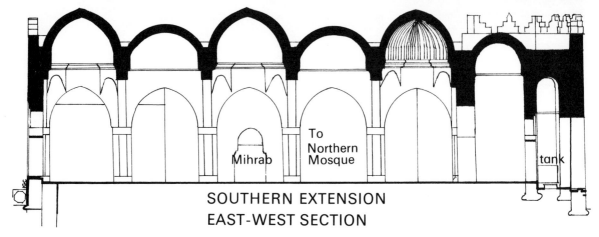

SOUTHERN EXTENSION
EAST-WEST SECTION

314 *Cross-section of Swahili mosque, the Great Mosque, Kilwa, Tanzania.*

315 *Mihrab of Swahili mosque, the Great Mosque, Kilwa, Tanzania, 1965.* This is the mihrab of the original twelfth-century mosque.

316 *Detail of roof of Swahili mosque, Tanzania, 1965.* The roofs of most mosques were flat; composite beams of mangrove poles spanned pillars and walls. Above these were further mangrove pole rafters and up to 50 cm of lime cement and coral rubble. The ceilings were sometimes decorated with square coral tiles.

317 *Fourteenth-century Swahili tomb, Kaole, near Bagamoyo, Tanzania, 1965.* Pillar tombs are a peculiarity of the East African coast. They were usually found close to mosques. Early tombs like this one were built of coral rubble. The pillar part of the tomb was decorated with inset Chinese and Persian porcelain dishes while the rest had plaster panels and dressed stone margins. It has been suggested[52] that the pillars may be a vestige of a pre-Muslim funerary practice and may be associated in some with the stone stelae at Axum, the stone pillars in the southern Ethiopian highlands, or the tall funerary urns of the Luguru Mountains.

318 *Eighteenth-century Swahili tomb, Kaole, Tanzania, 1965.* In the eighteenth century there was a revival of stone building along the East African coast associated with the revival of trade with Arabia and north-west India after the capture of Fort Jesus from the Portuguese. These later stone tombs, like the one in this photograph, had more elaborate profiles than the early ones and much shorter pillars; stepped sides, decorated finials and pyramidal roofs were characteristic features of this later phase. In this photograph notice the five recesses at the left end of the tomb; these would have held porcelain bowls.

319 *Mihrab of sixteenth-century Swahili mosque, Gedi, Kenya, 1967.* This mosque was built in the mid-fifteenth century and rebuilt a century later. The roof was flat and supported on three rows of six pillars, the middle row obscuring the view of the mihrab for most of the congregation. The spandrels of the mihrab were inset with porcelain bowls.

320 *Doorway of fifteenth-century Swahili palace, Gedi, Kenya, 1967.* Gedi is situated 6 km inland, and 3 km from a creek, and was the only Swahili town not situated right on the edge of the open sea. Most of the buildings date from the fifteenth century, in the prosperous years before the Portuguese disruption. It covered an area of about 18 ha and was surrounded by a wall with several entrance gates. In plan it was originally similar to a typical early stone Swahili house (see no. 321). Later, apartments for courtiers were added to this core.

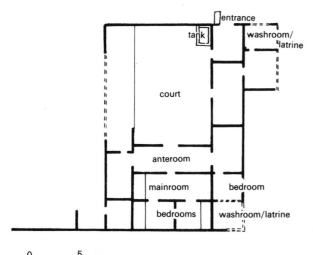

321 *Plan of fifteenth-century Swahili house, Songo Mnara, Tanzania.* Early Swahili stone house remains are rare. The best examples are at Gedi and at Songo Mnara, an island just south of Kilwa. The construction techniques were the same as in the mosques (see nos. 310 and 316). The houses were usually built around a rectangular sunken inner courtyard with all rooms opening onto it. The plans were extremely compact, consisting of a series of interconnecting rooms without corridors. Apart from two houses at Kilwa, all the early houses excavated had one storey; a second storey only became common in the eighteenth century. It should be remembered that only a small fraction of the houses in Swahili towns were built in stone. Most people lived in timber and mud buildings though recent research at Lamu has indicated that there was a good deal of movement between the two.[53]

322 *Fifteenth-century Swahili stone wall, Kilwa, Tanzania, 1965.* Each of
the courses was about 20 cm high. Originally the whole surface would
have been plastered.

323 *Swahili door, Bagamoyo, Tanzania, 1966.* Barbosa, writing about Kilwa
in about 1517, says it was a 'town with many fine houses of stone and mortar,
with many flat roofs. The doors are of wood well carved with excellent
joinery'.[54] Possibly the doors he wrote about were similar to the one above, a
type now known as a Zanzibar door. The carvings on these doors usually
contain five standard emblems: the lotus, the rosette, the chain, the fish, and
water.[55] (This calls to mind the ballad well known in Europe and parts of
Africa, 'Green Grow the Rushes-O!', where five is for 'the symbols at the
door'.) Kilwa was sacked and burned by the Portuguese early in the fifteenth
century, as were several of the Swahili towns along the coast, and later in the
century was raided by the 'Zimba'.

324 *Drawing of part of Zanzibar door, Zanzibar, Tanzania, about 1940.* This
shows the bottom half of a door jamb with the chain, water fish and lotus
motifs.

325 *Ghiorghis church, Lalibela, Ethiopia, 1940s.* The rock-hewn churches of Ethiopia date approximately from between the tenth and the fifteenth centuries. They were hewn out of solid rock, starting at the top and working downwards. Some were left attached to the rock on one or more sides, but this example is completely dug out, and is only attached at its base. Most of the church plans are basilican or cross-in-square shape. This church is unusual in its cruciform plan.

326 *Amanuel church, Lalibela, Ethiopia, 1940s.* This is a rock-hewn church, but it has been carved, both inside and outside, to imitate Axumite building technique, that is, stone reinforced with wood. It is basilican in plan with three aisles with lofts over, a barrel vault over the nave and a dome over the sanctuary.

327 *Interior of Mikael church, Lalibela, Ethiopia, 1940s.* Domes, barrel vaults and arches as well as flat coffered ceilings were all used in the rock-cut churches.

328 *Debra Labanos, near Ham, Eritrea, Ethiopia, late 1930s.* This small church was built using the Axumite techniques of stone walls reinforced with wooden beams, held in position with short cross-pieces which projected out of the walls to form 'monkey heads'. It was probably built before the sixteenth century. The Axumite building technique had been carried on since pre-Christian times in northern Ethiopia. The giant standing stelae at Axum, dated to about the fourth century, is carved to imitate a ten-storey building built in this same way.

329 *Eritrean church, Ethiopia, late 1930s.* This photograph shows a relatively recent church, but built using Axumite building techniques. The plan is quite different from the medieval churches and the sanctuary is towards the centre of the building with its roof rising a storey higher than the rest of the building.

References for Illustration Sections

1. Russell, E. R., 'Primitive Farming in Nigeria: The Mumoye Tribe', *Empire Journal of Experimental Agriculture*, VIII (1940)
2. Temple, O., *Notes on the Tribes, Provinces, Emirates and States of the Northern Provinces of Nigeria* (Cape Town, 1919)
3. Mockler, F., *Through Unknown Nigeria* (London, undated)
4. White, S., 'The Agricultural Economy of the Hill Pagans of Dikwa Emirate', *Empire Journal of Experimental Agriculture*, IX (1941)
5. *Ibid.*
6. Doresse, J., *Ethiopia* (London, 1959)
7. Willet, F., *African Art* (London, 1971)
8. Griaule, M., and Dieterlen, G., 'The Dogon of the French Sudan', in Forde, D. (ed.) *African Worlds* (London, 1963)
9. Fagan, B. M., *Southern Africa* (London, 1965)
10. Garlake, P. S., 'Rhodesian Ruins—A Preliminary Assessment of their Styles and Chronology', *Journal of African History*, XI 4 (1970)
11. Walton, J., 'Mural Art of the Bantu', *South African Panorama*, 10 (1965)
12. Wilson, M., *Rituals of Kinship among the Nyakusa* (Oxford 1956)
13. Torday, E., and Joyce, T. A., *Les Bushongo* (Brussels, 1910)
14. Durrell, G., *The Bafut Beagles* (London, 1954)
15. Fosbrooke, H. A., 'Defensive Measures of Certain Tribes in North-Eastern Tanganyika', *Tanganyika Notes and Records*, 35, 36, 37, 39 (1953–5)
16. Curtin, P. O. (ed.), *Africa Remembered, Narratives by West Africans from the Era of the Slave Trade* (London, 1967)
17. Beier, U., *African Mud Sculpture* (Cambridge, 1963)
18. Bowditch, E., *Mission from Cape Coast to Ashantee, 1817/1818* (London, 1819)
19. Dapper, O., *Description of Africa* (Amsterdam, 1668)
20. Goodwin, A. J. H., 'Recent Finds in the Old Palace at Benin', *Man*, 63 (1963)
21. Roth, L., *Great Benin* (London, 1903)
22. *Ibid.*
23. Ojo, G. J. A., *Yoruba Palaces* (London, 1966)
24. Willet, F., *Ife* (London, 1967)
25. Nicolaisen, J., *The Ecology and Culture of the Pastoral Tuareg* (Copenhagen, 1963)
26. Johnston, Sir H., *The Uganda Protectorate* (London, 1902)
27. Gebremedhin, N., 'House Types of Ethiopia', in Oliver, P. (ed), *Shelter in Africa* (London, 1971)
28. *Ibid.*
29. Burton, R. F., *The Lake Regions of Central Africa* (London, 1861)
30. Kuper, H., 'The Architecture of Swaziland', *Architectural Review*, 100 (1946)
31. Lawrence, J.C.D., *The Iteso* (Oxford, 1957)
32. *Ibid.*
33. Gray, J. R., *The Sonjo* (London, 1963)
34. Winans, E. V., *The Shambala* (London, 1962)
35. Stahl, K., *History of the Chagga, People of Kilimanjaro* (The Hague, 1964)
36. Sassoon, H., *Guide to the Kasubi Tombs* (Kampala, 1969)
37. Roscoe, J., *The Baganda* (London, 1912)
38. *Ibid.*
39. Buxton, D., *The Abyssinians* (London, 1970)
40. Stubbs, J. N., and Morrison, G. T., 'Dinka Houses', *Sudan Notes and Records*, 21 (1938)
41. Meek, C. K., *A Sudanese Kingdom* (London, 1931)
42. Kenyatta, J., *Facing Mount Kenya* (London, 1938)
43. Southall, A., 'The Peopling of Africa—the Linguistic and Sociological Evidence' in Posnansky, M. (ed.), *Prelude to East African History* (London, 1966)
44. Jaques-Meunie, D., *Cités Anciennes de Mauritanie* (Paris, 1961)
45. Quoted in Hogben, S. J., and Kirk-Greene, A. H. M., *The Emirates of Northern Nigeria* (London, 1966)
46. *Ibid.*
47. Barth, H., *Travels and Discoveries in North and Central Africa, 1849–1855* (London, 1965), centenary edition
48. Moody, H. L. B., 'Ganuwa—the Walls of Kano City', *Nigeria*, 92 (1967)
49. Davies, H. R. J., 'Rural Settlement Patterns in the Zaria Area of Northern Nigeria', *Nigerian Geographical Journal*, 17, No. 1 (1974)
50. Barth, H., *op. cit.*
51. Garlake, P. S., *The Early Islamic Architecture of the East African Coast* (Nairobi, 1966)
52. Sutton, J. E. G., *The East African Coast* (Nairobi, 1966)
53. Allen, J. de V., 'Swahili Culture Reconsidered', *Azania*, IX (1974)
54. Quoted in Freeman-Grenville, G. S. P., *The East African Coast* (Oxford, 1962)
55. Adie, J. J., 'Zanzibar Doors', *East African Annual* (1946–7)

General Bibliography

This bibliography does not include those references referred to in the chapters and illustration sections.

Alldridge, T. J., *The Sherbro and its Hinterland* (London and New York, 1901)

Ames, C. G., *Gazetteer of Plateau Province* (Jos, 1934)

Ankermann, Prof. Dr B., *Das Eingeborenenrecht-Ostafrika* (Stuttgart, 1929)

Annaerts, J., *Contribution à l'étude geographique de l'habitat et de l'habitation indigènes en milieu rural dans le province oriental et du Kivu* (Brussels, 1960)

Antubam, K., *Ghana's Cultural Heritage* (Leipzig, 1963)

Bascom, W. R., 'Urbanism as a Traditional African Pattern', *Sociological Review*, 7 (1959)

Basden, G. T., *Among the Ibos of Nigeria* (London, 1921)

Basden, G. T., *The Niger Ibos* (London, 1938)

Baumann, H., and Westermann, D., *Les peuples et civilisations de l'Afrique* (Paris, 1948)

Baumann, H., 'Die Frage der Steinbauten und Steingraber im Angola', *Paideuma*, 6 (1956)

Baumann, Dr O., *Durch Massailand zur Nilquelle* (Berlin, 1894)

Beguin, J., *et al.*, *L'habitat au Cameroun* (Paris, 1952)

Bernatzik, H., *Afrika* (Innsbruck, 1947)

Bernus, E., 'Un type d'habitat ancien en Côte d'Ivoire—La maison annularie à impluvium des Dida Mimini', *Les Cahiers d'Outre Mer*, 17 (1964)

Bertho, J., 'Habitations à impluvium dans les regions de Porto Novo et de Ketou', *Notes Africaines*, 47 (1950)

Bierman, B., 'Indlu: The Domed Dwelling of the Zulu', in Oliver, P., *Shelter in Africa* (London, 1971)

Binger, J., *Du Niger au Golfe de Guinée par le pays de Kong et le Mossi 1887–1889* (Paris, 1892)

Biobaku, S. O., *The Origins of the Yoruba* (Lagos, 1955)

Blecker, S., *The Tuareg* (New York, 1964)

Blohm, W. A., *Die Nyamwezi* (Hamburg, 1931)

Boahen, A., *Topics in West African History* (London, 1966)

Bovill, E. W., *The Golden Trade of the Moors* (London, 1958)

Brasseur, G., *Evolution de l'habitat rural au Soudan Francais*, Conférence Internationale des Africanistes de l'Ouest (Abidjan, 1954)

Buchanan, K. M., and Pugh, J. C., *Land and People in Nigeria* (London, 1955)

Buttikofer, J., *Reisbilder aus Liberia* (Leiden, 1890)

Buxton, D., *Travels in Ethiopia* (London, 1949)

Caille, R., *Journal d'un voyage à Tombocteau et à Jenne dans l'Afrique central pendant les années 1824 à 1826* (Paris, 1830)

Calame-Griaule, G., 'Notes sur l'habitation du plateau central nigerien', *Bull. I.F.A.N.*, Series B, 17 (1955)

Carson, J. B., 'The Elgeyo of the Great Rift Valley', *East African Annual* (1948–9)

Carson, J. B., 'The Colourful Suk', *East African Annual* (1959–60)

Cenival, P. de, and Monod, T., *Description de la Côte d'Afrique de Ceuta au Senegal par Valentim Fernandes (1506–1507)* (Paris, 1938)

Chittick, H. N., *A Guide to the Ruins of Kilwa* (Dar es Salaam, 1965)

Cipriani, L., *Abitazioni Indigene del'Africa Orientale Italiana* (Naples, 1931)

Clapperton, H., *Journal of a Second Expedition into the Interior of Africa* (London, 1829)

Clark, J. D., *The Prehistory of Africa* (London, 1970)

Claus, H., *Die Wagogo* (Leipzig and Berlin, 1911)

Cole, S., *The Prehistory of East Africa* (London, 1964)

Czekanowski, J., *Forschungen im Nil-Kongo-Zwischengebiet*, vols. I–VIII (1911–27)

Da Cruz, C., 'Notes sur l'habitat dans le cercle de Porto Novo', *Etudes Dahoméennes*, 11 (1954)

Daniel, W. F., 'Old Calabar', *Journal of the Ethnological Society*, 1 (1848)

Davidson, B., *The African Past* (Harmondsworth, 1966)

Davidson, B., *History of a Continent* (London, 1966)

Davidson, B., *East and Central Africa to the Late Nineteenth Century* (London, 1967)

Davies, J., *The Birom*, fol. (Kaduna, 1949)

Davies, O., *West Africa before the Europeans* (London, 1967)

Dennet, R. E., *At the Back of the Black Man's Mind* (London, 1906)

Desplagues, L., *Le Plateau Central Nigerien* (Paris, 1907)

Diop, C. A., 'Histoire Primitive de l'Humanité et l'Evolution du monde noir', *Bull. I.F.A.N.*, 24 (1962)

Duchemin, G.-J., 'A propos des décorations murales de Oualata', *Bull. I.F.A.N.*, 12 (1950)

Engestrom, T., 'The Origins of Pre-Islamic Architecture in West Africa', *Ethnos* (1959)

Fagan, B. M., *Iron Age Cultures in Zambia: Kalomo and Kangila*, vol. I (London, 1967)

Fagg, W., *Divine Kingship in Africa* (London, 1970)

Forde, D. (ed.), *African Worlds* (London, 1954)

Forde, D., *Habitat, Economy and Society* (New York, 1963)

Forde, D., *Yako Studies* (Oxford, 1964)

Fortes, M., and Evans-Pritchard, E. E. (eds.), *African Political Systems* (London, 1940)

Foyle, A. M., 'Architecture in West Africa', *Africa South*, 3 (1959)

Fraser, D., *Village Planning in the Primitive World* (London and New York, 1968)

Frobenius, L., *Erythraa* (Berlin and Zurich, 1931)

Fulleborn, F., *Das deutsche Njassa—und Ruwuma—Gebeit* (Berlin, 1906)

Gana, A. J., *Our History and Origin* (Zaria, 1965)

Gide, A., *Travels in the Congo* (Paris, 1927)

Grottarelli, V. L., 'Somali Wood Engraving', *African Arts*, 1 (1968)

Gulliver, P. H., 'A Tribal Map of Tanganyika', *Tanganyika Notes and Records*, 52 (1959)

Gunn, H. D., *Pagan Peoples of the Central Area of Northern Nigeria* (London, 1955)

Hambly, W. D., *Source Book for African Anthropology* (Chicago, 1937)

Haselberger, H., 'Wandmalerei, gravierter und modellierter Wandschmuck in den Savannen von Togo und Obervolta', *Internationale Archiv für Ethnographie*, 49 (1960)

Haselberger, H., 'Gemalter, gravierter und modellierter Bauschmuck in Dahomey', *Tribus*, 10 (1961)

Haselberger, H., 'Wandamalereien und plastischer Bauschmuck in Guinea', *Jahrbuch des Museums für Volkerkunde zu Leipzig*, 19 (Leipzig, 1962)

Haselberger, H., 'Quelques cas d'Evolution du Décor Mural en Afrique Occidentale', *Notes Africaines*, 101 (1964)

Haselberger, H., 'Les anciennes constructions dans la falaise de Niansoroni', *Notes Africaines*, 115 (1967)

Hodgson, Lady, *The Siege of Kumasi* (London, 1901)

Horton, R., *Kalabari Sculpture* (Lagos, 1965)

Huet, M., (ed.), *Afrique Africaine* (Lausanne, 1963)

Huntingford, G. W. B., 'The Azanian Civilisation of Kenya', *Antiquity*, 12 (1933)

Jesman, C., *The Ethiopian Paradox* (London, 1963)

Johnson, S., *The History of the Yorubas* (Lagos, 1921)

Johnston, Sir H., *Liberia* (London, 1906)

Kalck, P., 'En Oubangui-Chari: le village Baya traditionnel', *Tropiques*, 395 (1957)

Kirkman, J., *Gedi* (Mombasa, undated)

Kirkman, J., *Gedi: The Palace* (The Hague, 1963)

Kmunke, R., *Quer Durch Uganda* (Berlin, 1913)

Krapf, J. L., *Reisen in Ost-Afrika 1837–55* (Stuttgart, 1858)

Krige, E. J., *The Social System of the Zulus* (Pietermaritzburg, 1936)

Kruyer, Rev. Fr. J., *Notes on the Teso tribe*, fol. (c. 1920)

Labat, J.-B., *Nouvelle relation de l'Afrique occidentalle* (Paris, 1728)

Labouret, H., 'Afrique occidentale et equatoriale', in Bernard, A. (ed.), *L'habitation indigène dans les possessions françaises* (Paris, 1931)

Lebeuf, J.-P., and Masson-Detourbet, A., *La civilisation du Tchad* (Paris, 1950)

Lebeuf, J.-P., *L'habitation des Fali* (Paris, 1961)

Leiris, M., and Delange, J., *African Art* (London, 1968)

Light, R. O., *Focus on Africa* (New York, 1944)

Lindblom, G., *The Akamba of East Africa* (Uppsala, 1920)

Lopez, A., *A Habitacio Indigena na Guine Portuguesa* (Bissau, 1941)

McMaster, D. N., 'Food Storage in Uganda', *Uganda Notes and Records*, 26 (1962)

McMaster, D. N., 'Agricultural Geography', in Church, R. J. H., *Advanced Geography of Africa* (Amersham, 1975)

Madauci, I., Yahaya, I., and Daura, B., *Hausa Customs* (Zaria, 1968)

Mair, L., *Primitive Government* (Harmondsworth, 1962)

Masao, F. T., 'The Irrigation System in Uchagga', *Tanzania Notes and Records*, 75 (1974)

Mauny, R., 'Notes sur le Problème Zimbabwe', *Studia* (1958)

Mauny, R., *Tableau Géographique de l'Afrique de Ouest au Moyen Age*, Bull. *I.F.A.N.*, Mémoires, 61 (Dakar, 1961)

Merker, M., *Die Masai* (Berlin, 1904)

Meyer, H., *Der Kilimanjaro* (Berlin, 1900)

Meyorowitz, E., *The Akan of Ghana* (London, 1951)

Monod, T., 'Sur quelques détails d'architecture africaine', *Acta Tropica*, 4 (1947)

Monteil, C., *Djenne, metropole du delta central du Niger* (Paris, 1932)

Monteil, V., 'Al-Bakri', Bull. *I.F.A.N.*, Series B, 30 (1968)

Nadel, S. F., *Black Byzantium* (London, 1942)

Nadel, S. F., 'The Kede: A Riverain State in Northern Nigeria', in Fortes, M., and Evans-Pritchard, E. E. (eds.), *African Political Systems* (London, 1940)

Nai'ibi, S. and Hassan, Alhaji, *A Chronicle of Abuja* (Lagos, 1962)

Niger Government, 'Les Touaregs de l'Air', *Niger*, 3 (Niamey, 1968)

Ogot, B. A., 'Pastoralism and Agriculturalism— Interactions', in Ranger, T. O. (ed.), *Emerging Themes of African History* (Nairobi, 1968)

Oliver, P. (ed.), *Shelter and Society* (London, 1969)

Oliver, P. (ed.), *Shelter in Africa* (London, 1971)

Ozanne, P., 'Adwuku, a Fortified Hill-Top Village in Shai', *Ghana Notes and Queries* (1965-7)

Posnansky, M. (ed.), *Prelude to East African History* (London, 1966)

Prussin, L., *Architecture in Northern Ghana* (Berkeley and Los Angeles, 1969)

Puigandeau, O. du, 'L'Architecture Maure', Bull. *I.F.A.N.*, Series B, 22 (1960)

Radcliffe-Brown, A. R., and Forde, D. (eds.), *African Systems of Kinship and Marriage* (Oxford, 1950)

Raphael, P., *Through Unknown Nigeria* (London, about 1913)

Rapoport, A., *House Form and Culture* (Englewood Cliffs, N.J., 1969)

Rattray, R. S., *Tribes of the Ashanti Hinterland* (Oxford, 1932)

Richards, A., 'The Political System of the Bemba Tribe', in Fortes, M., and Evans-Pritchard, E. E., *African Political Systems* (London, 1940)

Rigby, P., *Cattle and Kinship among the Gogo* (London, 1969)

Routledge, W. S., *With a Prehistoric People— The Akikuyu of British East Africa* (London, 1910)

Rudofsky, B., *Architecture Without Architects* (New York, 1964)

Sassoon, H., *Guide to the Ruins at Kunduchi* (Dar es Salaam, 1966)

Schachtzabel, A., 'Die siedluhsverhaltnisse der Bantu Niger', *Internationale Archiv für Ethnographie* (supplement), 20 (Leiden, 1911)

Schanz, M., *Ost und Sud Afrika* (Berlin, 1902)

Sekintu, C. M., and Wachsmann, K., *Wall Patterns of Hima Huts* (Kampala, 1956)

Smith, E. W., and Dale, E. M., *The Ila-speaking Peoples of Rhodesia* (London, 1920)

Smith, M. G., *The Economy of Hausa Communities in Zaria* (London, 1955)

Smith, R. S., *Kingdoms of the Yoruba* (London, 1969)

Sousberghe, L. de, 'Cases Cheffales du Kwango', *Congo-Tervuren*, 6 (1960)

Starr, F., *Congo Natives* (Chicago, 1912)

Stuhlmann, F., *Mit Emin Pasha ins Herz von Afrika* (Berlin, 1894)

Stuhlmann, F., *Handwerk und Industrie in Ostafrika* (Hamburg, 1910)

Summers, R., *Zimbabwe* (Johannesburg, 1963)

Sutton, J. E. G., 'The Problem of the Sirikwa Holes and the So-Called Azanian Remains of the Western Highlands of Kenya', in Posnansky, M. (ed.), *Prelude to East African History* (London, 1966)

Talbot, P. A., *In the Shadow of the Bush* (London, 1912)

Thomas, L. V., 'Pour une Systématique de l'habitat Diola', Bull. *I.F.A.N.*, Series B, 26

Thomas, L. V., L'Habitat des Blis Karon et des Niomann', *Notes Africaines*, 114 (1967) (1964)

Thomas, M. C., 'The Bamenda Highlands', *Geographical Magazine*, 4 (1966)

Thorbecke, F., *Im Hochland von Mittel-Kamerun* (Hamburg, 1914)

Trowell, M., *African Design* (London, 1960)

Van den Bossche, A., 'Art Bakubu', *Brousse*, 1 (1952)

Vaughan-Richards, A., 'The New Generation', *West African Builder and Architect*, 7 (1967)

Wilks, I., *The Northern Factor in Ashanti History* (Legon, 1961)

Wilson, F., 'The Coral Dwellers of Zanzibar', *East African Annual* (1943-4)

Wilson, G. E. H., 'The Ancient Civilisation of the Rift Valley', *Man* (1932)

Wirth, L., 'Urbanism as a Way of Life', *American Journal of Sociology*, 44 (1938)

Index

The numbers in bold type are the illustration numbers.